Niger-Congo Comparative Studies

Chief Editor: Valentin Vydrin (INALCO – LLACAN, CNRS, Paris)
Editors: Larry Hyman (University of California, Berkeley), Konstantin Pozdniakov (INALCO – LLACAN, CNRS, Paris), Guillaume Segerer (LLACAN, CNRS, Paris), John Watters (SIL International, Dallas, Texas).

In this series:

1. Watters, John R. (ed.). East Benue-Congo: Nouns, pronouns, and verbs.

2. Pozdniakov, Konstantin. The numeral system of Proto-Niger-Congo: A step-by-step reconstruction.

East Benue-Congo

Nouns, pronouns, and verbs

Edited by
John R. Watters

John R. Watters (ed.). 2018. *East Benue-Congo: Nouns, pronouns, and verbs* (Niger-Congo Comparative Studies 1). Berlin: Language Science Press.

This title can be downloaded at:
http://langsci-press.org/catalog/book/190
© 2018, the authors
Published under the Creative Commons Attribution 4.0 Licence (CC BY 4.0):
http://creativecommons.org/licenses/by/4.0/
ISBN: 978-3-96110-100-9 (Digital)
    978-3-96110-101-6 (Hardcover)

DOI:10.5281/zenodo.1314306
Source code available from www.github.com/langsci/190
Collaborative reading: paperhive.org/documents/remote?type=langsci&id=190

Cover and concept of design: Ulrike Harbort
Typesetting: Sebastian Nordhoff, John R. Watters
Illustration: Sebastian Nordhoff
Proofreading: Ahmet Bilal Özdemir, Andrew Spencer, Felix Hoberg, Jeroen van de Weijer, Jean Nitzke, Kate Bellamy, Martin Haspelmath, Prisca Jerono, Richard Griscom, Steven Kaye, Sune Gregersen,
Fonts: Linux Libertine, Libertinus Math, Arimo, DejaVu Sans Mono
Typesetting software: XƎLATEX

Language Science Press
Unter den Linden 6
10099 Berlin, Germany
langsci-press.org

Storage and cataloguing done by FU Berlin

Contents

Preface   iii

1 East Benue-Congo
John R. Watters   1

2 East Benue-Congo noun classes, with a focus on morphological behavior
Jeff Good   27

3 Nominal affixing in the Kainji languages of northwestern and central Nigeria
Roger M. Blench   59

4 Nominal affixes and number marking in the Plateau languages of Central Nigeria
Roger M. Blench   107

5 Common Bantoid verb extensions
Larry M. Hyman   173

6 Third person pronouns in Grassfields Bantu
Larry M. Hyman   199

7 More reflections on the nasal classes in Bantu
Larry M. Hyman   223

Indexes   237

Preface

This volume, *East Benue-Congo: Nouns, pronouns, and verbs* is the first volume in the Niger-Congo Comparative Series of the Language Science Press (langscipress.org). The aim of the Niger-Congo Comparative Series (NCCS) is to enhance comparative-historical studies and linguistic reconstruction of proto-languages of the groups and families within Niger-Congo, and eventually, of Proto-Niger-Congo itself.

The edited volumes and monographs in this series will deal with all aspects of comparative-historical Niger-Congo studies, including both segmental and prosodic phonology, morphology and syntax, etymological dictionaries of groups and families, problems of genetic classification, application of statistical methods to the comparative-historical Niger-Congo studies, correlation of genetic relationships, contact-induced affinities, and so on. This series provides an academic forum and publishing entity for scholars to present their findings in comparative-historical studies of Niger-Congo and its subdivisions. Researchers are encouraged to join in the advancing of the frontiers of our knowledge about the historical development of Niger-Congo and its constituents.

The Niger-Congo macro-family (the biggest in the world, comprising more the 20% of all the world's languages) was postulated by Joseph Greenberg in his 1948 paper and subsequent publications. It is now widely accepted. However, most of the mid-range language families included in Niger-Congo are characterized by an insufficient level of comparative-historical study, and in certain cases, even the validity of groupings has not been adequately demonstrated.

During the 1960-80s, numerous comparative studies were carried out on different Niger-Congo subdivisions, and serious amendments to Greenberg's classification were proposed. In the 1990s, there was a lull: the potential of the first assault was more or less exhausted, and, on the other hand, an exponential growth in the amount of descriptive data available on African languages required reconsideration of the approaches that could provide reliable comparative results. A by-product of the lull was a growing skepticism about the reality of the Niger-Congo as a genetic unit, a skepticism supported by a general suspicion toward comparative linguistics — and especially, about long-range comparison - a sus-

Preface

picion which grew very popular at that time and, I dare say, remains popular among linguists, especially those who are not personally involved in comparative studies and protolanguage reconstruction.

A first attempt to curb this trend was related to the Babel Tower project headed by Sergey Starostin and Murray Gell-Mann who made a courageous attempt to survey the state of the art in protolanguage reconstruction of all the language families of the world. They organized, together with Konstantin Pozdniakov, a Niger-Congo workshop in Paris in 2004 where leading specialists in the field were invited. Among other things, the workshop discussions made it clear that Niger-Congo, which numbers more than 1500 languages, is not a family, but rather a macro-family (or phylum) whose age is at least 12 millennia — most probably, even more than that. Its major subdivisions are Benue-Congo, Kwa, Adamawa, Gur, Kru, Dogon, Ijoid, Atlantic, Mande, Kordofanian. The time depth of these subdivisions lies most often within the range of 5 to 8 millennia. They should be considered as mid-range families at the same level as Indo-European or Semitic.

In 2012, the First International Congress "Towards Proto-Niger-Congo: Comparison and Reconstruction" took place in Paris. One of the ideas of its organizers was to canalize the energy of the participants into writing a collective volume that would become a major breakthrough toward the reconstruction of the protolanguage. The volume was intended to contain chapters on mid-range families written by specialists in these families according to a template meant to cover all relevant topics.

However, the project of a "Niger-Congo volume" kept changing from its very beginning. Already at the initial stage, it became clear that the chapters would target an average size of some 30,000 words, and therefore, there should be at least two volumes, maybe even three. However, the main difficulty was not the presumable size of the volume(s), but the availability of potential authors and, on the other hand, the state of the art in the reconstructions for the mid-range families. In fact, relative to the complexity and size of Niger-Congo, there were few comparative-historical studies that could guide summaries for each major, mid-range subdivision.

Finally, it was decided that the best strategy, given the current state of affairs, was to launch a series specialized in Niger-Congo comparative studies in the Language Science Press. The authors originally invited to write chapters for the Niger-Congo volume(s) were reoriented toward producing separate books, and a more flexible approach has been taken in relation to the structure of books acceptable for the Series. The hope is that over time the accumulation of multiple studies in coming years will bring increasing clarity to our understanding of the history of Niger-Congo.

This first volume of the Series has a long history too. It was originally planned as an extended version of the East Benue-Congo (without Bantu) chapter of the Niger-Congo volume, to be published in one or two years. However, it grew clear little by little that, due to the immensity of the Benue-Congo family and the very uneven level of study of its constituent groups, it would be unrealistic to require authors to stick to the template and to cover, at the same time, all the East Benue-Congo groups. It has turned out that instead of one East Benue-Congo volume, it would be more expedient to publish three medium-size volumes, and even in this case, all the topics of the original template for the "Niger-Congo volume" will be very far from being covered. It is not an understatement to say that many more volumes will be needed to cover the topics of the original template relative to East Benue-Congo. This first volume provides comparative insights but it also serves as much as setting a foundation on various topics upon which subsequent studies can be pursued.

Publication of this book marks the end of the four-year incubation period of the series *Niger-Congo Comparative Studies*, and there are good reasons to believe that the next volume of the series will not make us wait as long as the first one. Reconstruction of Proto-Niger-Congo is an immense task, and the story of the "Niger-Congo volume project" and its sequels will serve as a vaccine against naiveté and impatience. At the same time, let it be a warning: if we want to make the Niger-Congo reconstruction commensurable with a human lifespan, we need further concentration and strenuous efforts. More scholars are needed in the project of researching and molding our knowledge of the history of Niger-Congo and its subdivisions. Such scholars are invited and encouraged to join in the process.

Valentin Vydrin

Chief Editor of the series "Niger-Congo Comparative Studies"

Chapter 1

East Benue-Congo

John R. Watters

SIL International

> Chapter one introduces this volume on East Benue-Congo (EBC) and the chapters addressing issues of nouns, pronouns, and verbs within specific branches and EBC as a whole. The chapter identifies the location of EBC and its branches as well as the external and internal classification of EBC. It situates EBC's likely original homeland and the geography of its probable expansion routes that led to the current location of its branches. It then provides a context for the chapters focused on noun classes in EBC in general and nominal affixes in Kainji and Plateau in particular, as well as the reconstruction issues they raise. It also notes certain issues related to Bantoid and to the presence of the Bantu languages within Bantoid, especially its dominance within Bantoid that has the potential of skewing historical analyses.

1 East Benue-Congo (EBC): its location

The category label 'East Benue-Congo' (or 'Eastern Benue-Congo') is a relatively recent one. It is widely known from Williamson & Blench (2000: 30-36) in their introduction to the language family 'Benue-Congo'. They report that Blench (1989) had actually proposed it a decade earlier in response to the reassignment of what had been Eastern Kwa languages into a "New" Benue-Congo, a reassignment proposed by Bennett & Sterk (1977). Blench proposed that the Eastern Kwa languages, now assigned to Benue-Congo, be given the title 'West Benue-Congo'. That left the original 'Benue-Congo' languages with the complementary title of 'East Benue-Congo'. This label represents the result of a process dating back to Greenberg (1963) and even earlier to Westermann (1927) and Johnston (1919/22). Westermann had given a set of West African languages the title 'Benue-Cross'. Greenberg (1963) then added the Bantu languages to Westermann's Benue-Cross,

John R. Watters. East Benue-Congo. In John R. Watters (ed.), *East Benue-Congo: Nouns, pronouns, and verbs*, 1–25. Berlin: Language Science Press.

expanding the set of related languages and assigning it the new name 'Benue-Congo'. These details and more on the historical process of categorization from Greenberg's proposed Benue-Congo to today's Benue-Congo are provided in Williamson (1989: 247-274) and Williamson & Blench (2000: 30-36).

A few points are worth highlighting and reiterating from this history about Benue-Congo and its relationship to the EBC of this volume. First, the content of the category 'East Benue-Congo' has not changed since Greenberg (1963) proposed it as 'Benue-Congo'. In fact, the category label referred to in much of the literature from Greenberg in 1963 until Williamson & Blench in 2000 was simply 'Benue-Congo' or 'Eastern South-Central Niger-Congo' from Bennett & Sterk (1977). For example, de Wolf's (1971) study *The noun class system of Proto-Benue-Congo* concerned the languages that are now being referred to as 'East Benue-Congo', a subset of the new, current Benue-Congo family.

Second, Greenberg made the decision, a radical one for its time, yet a reasonable one, that all the Narrow Bantu languages formed a subgroup within a subgroup of Benue-Congo. Greenberg's proposal is now generally accepted. This inclusion of the Bantu languages has not changed with the adoption of the label 'East Benue-Congo'. All Bantu languages are a subgroup of the Bantoid branch within EBC.

Third, Greenberg identified four branches within his Benue-Congo, namely, Plateau, Jukunoid, Cross River, and Bantoid (Greenberg 1966[1970]: 8-9). Plateau is sometimes referred to as Platoid (Gerhardt 1989). However, more recently Williamson & Blench (2000: 31) identified the Kainji languages as forming a fifth branch. The Kainji languages in Greenberg's and previous classifications was positioned as a Plateau subgroup, specifically formerly Plateau 1a, b. It now forms a fifth branch of the new EBC.

Fourth, Williamson & Blench (2000: 31-32) note that Shimizu (1975) and Gerhardt (1989) proposed that Jukunoid be included within Platoid. Another way to state their proposal is that Jukunoid is more closely related to Platoid than it is to Cross River or Bantoid. Williamson and Blench indicate this conclusion in their figure Figure 2.11 Williamson & Blench (2000: 31) by including Jukunoid as a branch of a larger genetic unit that includes the parallel branches of Kainji, three Platoid groupings, Beromic, and Tarok. This proposed grouping provides some internal structure to EBC, namely, a two-way division of the five EBC branches into what Williamson & Blench label 'Central Nigerian' (i.e. Kainji, Plateau with further elaboration, and Jukunoid) and 'Bantoid-Cross' (i.e. Cross River and Bantoid).

1 East Benue-Congo

The simplified map in Figure 1 identifies the current general location of each branch of EBC. Two branches, Kainji (1) and Platoid (2) are found entirely within Nigeria. The other three branches, Jukunoid (3), Cross River (4), and Bantoid (5) are represented in both Nigeria and Cameroon, but the representation of Jukunoid (3) and Cross River (4) in Cameroon is minimal. Bantoid (5) in Nige-

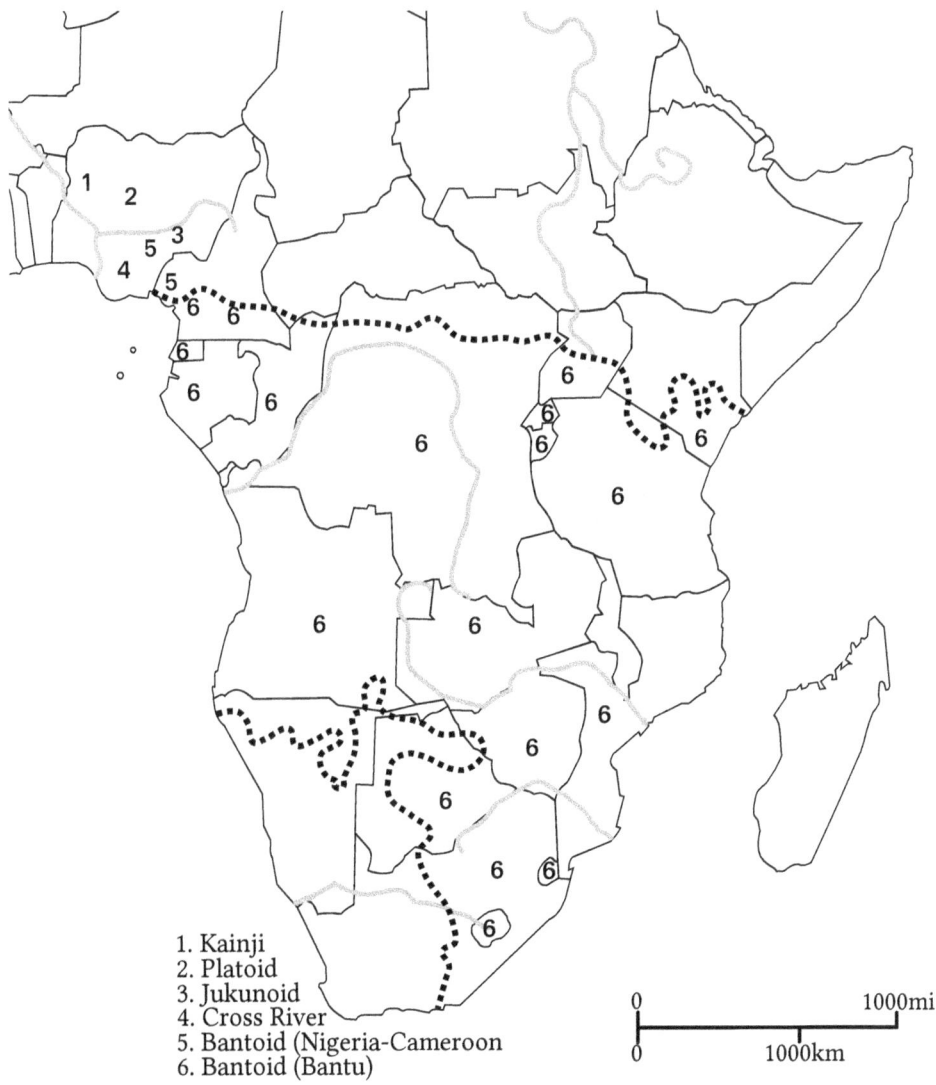

Figure 1: The locations of the five branches of EBC

ria and Cameroon, however, includes the following groups in both countries: Jarawan[1], Dakoid[2], Mambiloid, Tivoid, Beboid, Grassfields[3], and Ekoid. Nyang and Tikar are only found in Cameroon. Meanwhile, the Bantu group (6) within Bantoid is not found in Nigeria, but is found in Cameroon and multiple countries across central, eastern, and southern Africa, as the map shows. The Bantu languages are found between the dotted lines in Figure 1 that run across this central, eastern, and southern region of Africa. The Bantu group is the dominant group within Bantoid and even within EBC in terms of its geographic spread, the number of languages included, and the number of speakers involved. However, the map provides a helpful reminder that the size of a branch or a group or subgroup is not determinant in the process of comparison and reconstruction. The smaller branches must also be considered as being as potentially significant as a dominant group like the Bantu subgroup in reconstructing proto-Bantoid, proto-Bantoid-Cross, and proto-EBC.

The distribution of EBC branches strongly suggests that EBC originated in Nigeria. (See §3 for more details and references.) This conclusion derives from the assumption that where a language family is more fragmented and shows greater diversity, that is where the given language family likely originated. Diversification develops over time and so greater linguistic diversity in one region generally represents greater historical time depth than a more homogeneous region. Henrici (1973) and Heine (1973) demonstrated that the most diverse region in Bantu is its northwest region that borders on the other Bantoid groups in Cameroon. Building on that observation, the other EBC branches outside Bantoid represent even greater diversity, with Kainji and Platoid indicating significant time depth. This is seen in the modifications and reconfigurations of their noun class systems as shown by Blench (Chapter 3 & Chapter 4) in this volume.

---

[1] Simons & Fennig (2018) report two Jarawan languages in Cameroon: Mboa is listed with 1,490 speakers in 2000, and Nagumi is listed as extinct.

[2] Boyd (1989: 182-183) was not convinced that Daka (Dakoid) was closer to Bantoid (represented by Vute, Mambiloid, Bantoid) than it was to some Gur languages. However, eleven years later Williamson & Blench (2000: 27) state that the inclusion of Dakoid within Benue-Congo "is now widely accepted". The most recent consideration of Dakoid being Bantoid is found in Blench (2012) in which the use of nominal suffixes is pointed out as a trait that Dakoid shares with Mambiloid.

[3] Of the 67 Wide Grassfields languages only two or three are also spoken in Nigeria.

2 EBC: its classification

Turning from the geographic location of the EBC branches and their possible relative time depths, Figure 2 summarizes the current understanding of the external and internal classification of EBC. Externally, EBC is a sister subfamily of the subfamily West Benue-Congo within the larger family of Benue-Congo languages. Internally, the five branches of EBC divide into two major units: Central Nigerian (Kainji, Plateau, and Jukunoid) and Bantoid-Cross (Cross River and Bantoid).

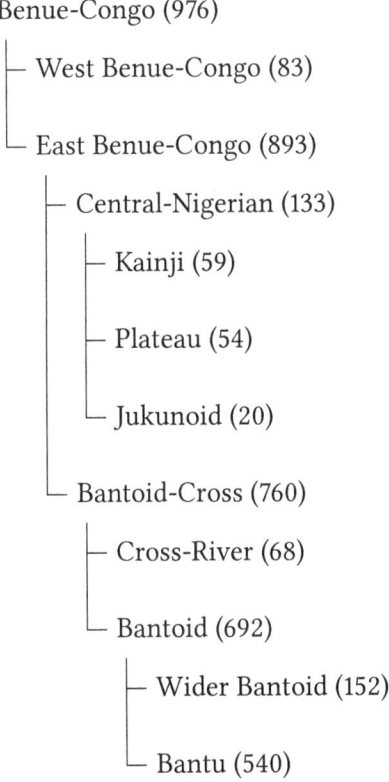

Figure 2: The external and internal classification of East Benue-Congo

To gain a sense of the number of languages involved in EBC, a proposed number of languages associated with the given unit in Figure 2 is provided from Simons & Fennig (2018). The Niger-Congo macrofamily is listed as the largest language family in the world in that it has the greatest number of listed living languages: 1,539. Benue-Congo is the largest family within Niger-Congo, listed with 978 languages or 63% of all Niger-Congo languages. Of those 978 Benue-Congo languages, EBC is listed with 893, or 58% of all Niger-Congo languages and 91% of all Benue-Congo languages. Within EBC, Bantoid has 692 languages or 45% of all Niger-Congo and 71% of all Benue-Congo languages and is clearly the dominant grouping. Within Bantoid, the Bantu languages account for 78% of all Bantoid languages and more than one-third of all Niger-Congo languages. That leaves 153 Bantoid languages in the nine other Bantoid groups.

The EBC languages are distributed over an extraordinary land mass. They cover much of Nigeria from the northwest and north to the center and the east and southeast; all of southern Cameroon; and multiple nations of central, eastern, and southern Africa, as shown in Figure 1. The speakers of these languages number in the hundreds of millions.

It should be noted at this point that the classification within EBC, at the level of its branches and their internal groups, is still not fully settled. This is also true at the macro level of Niger-Congo. Various proposed groups have indeterminate boundaries with those that are considered most closely related to them. Both Blench (2006: 109-122) and Good (to appear) make this point emphatically. Many groups have a certain coherency, but it is still a matter of further research as to where the actual boundaries between groups lie and what linguistic features identify those boundaries. This includes the boundary between Bantu and the other Bantoid groups along the northwest boundary of Bantu Zone A. The use of trees and references to groups by name does not mean that the status of the group relative to other groups is well defined. What defines the boundaries is often unclear in part due to a lack of reconstructions of phonologies, morphologies, and lexicons. Given this uncertainty in classification, it may be more helpful in some cases to identify a core set (or sets) of languages within a given group that appear to bear a close genetic relationship to one another. Reconstruction of the phonology, morphology, and lexicon of such core sets could then be compared to other core sets, hopefully assisting in the comparative process and reconstruction of larger groupings and potentially identifying relevant boundary markers. However, for now, the impact of the imprecise nature of boundaries is that it will not always be easy to identify what is an innovation or what is a shared inheritance. Also, it may have to be accepted that the imprecise nature of classification of these languages will remain with us due to incomplete data sets, the methods used, and ultimately the linguistic histories of these languages.

1 East Benue-Congo

3 EBC: likely origins and expansion

Williamson (1989: 269-272) and Blench (2006: 134) follow Armstrong (1981). They propose that the ancestral center of the Benue-Congo languages is likely located in the region of the confluence of the Niger and Benue Rivers. This location is indicated in Figure 3 as the "Benue-Congo Homeland." The subsequent expansion from that location is mapped out in Figure 3.

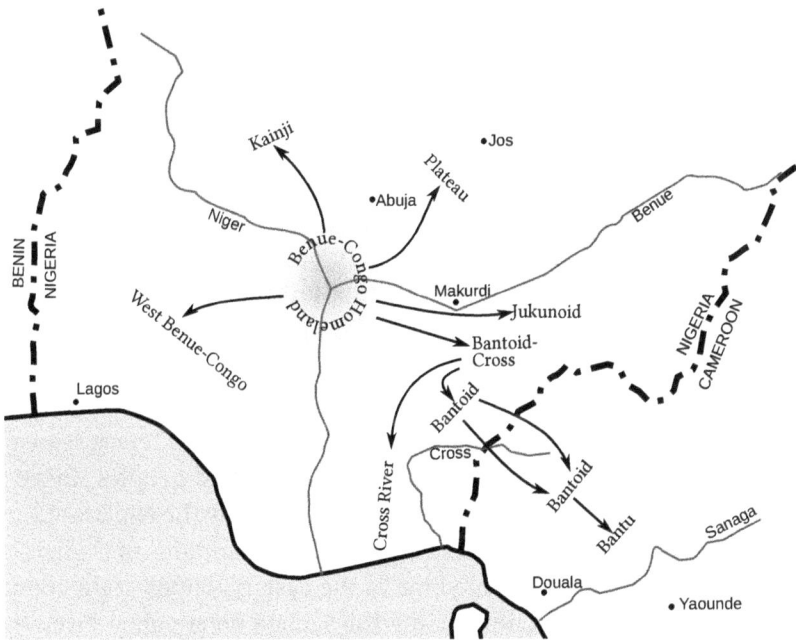

Figure 3: Benue-Congo expansion from homeland to current locations

The proposal that the confluence of the Niger and Benue rivers was the likely point of origin of East Benue-Congo is the most reasonable one despite the extraordinary current geographical distribution of the Benue-Congo languages (Figure 1). It is reasonable based on two assumptions.

First, it is the location that most easily allows for a shared origin of both the West Benue-Congo and EBC languages, providing a plausible point of origin. Whether there is a clear linguistic demarcation between the West and East sectors of Benue-Congo or not, the region around the Niger-Benue confluence provides the simpler explanation of their distribution in the absence of evidence to the contrary.

Second, the greatest linguistic diversity is found in the western region of EBC, that is, in Nigeria and Cameroon, whereas the Bantu languages further east do not display anything close to the same linguistic diversity even though they cover an exceptionally larger geographical expanse within Africa. Such diversity would indicate that speakers of Benue-Congo languages had been resident in the region of Nigeria and Cameroon well before the Bantu expansion began.

Figure 3 suggests the probable expansion routes of EBC people from the Niger-Benue confluence to their current locations. This multi-directional expansion was likely due to agricultural, ecological, economic, and social factors. It recognizes the two-way division of Benue-Congo into western and eastern areas. The ancestors of the West Benue-Congo largely migrated southwest of the confluence except for the Igboid, who crossed to the eastern side of the Niger, while the ancestors of the East Benue-Congo languages migrated northwest, north, and east of the confluence. The Kainji are distributed primarily northwest of the Niger-Benue confluence; the Plateau are essentially north of the confluence; and the Jukunoid are to the east, up the Benue River basin. The Bantoid-Cross likely also migrated east up the Benue River basin, but probably south of the river and the Jukunoid, settling in a region marked out by modern-day Makurdi, Wukari, and Gboko. Later the Cross River peoples migrated south into to the Cross River basin and expanded along its western banks to the Atlantic coast, later crossing over to the eastern banks of the Cross River. Some of the Bantoid peoples stayed in the Bantoid-Cross homeland or spread out along what is now the Nigeria-Cameroon border. Others migrated further to the east into the mountains of Cameroon and then across the Cameroon Volcanic Line to the eastern slopes of the mountains of western Cameroon and eventually into the Sanaga River valley. From this last region Bantu began its expansion into central, eastern and southern Africa.

For some temporal perspective, Blench (2006: 126-138) discusses models of the Niger-Congo expansion. He proposes the beginning of Benue-Congo to be around 5500 BP, Bantoid to be around 4500 BP, and the Proto-Bantu period to 4000 BP. Ehret (2016: 106-116) dates Proto-Bantu to 3000 BCE, and provides further elaboration of the Proto-Bantu communities and their continuing expansion.

4 EBC: nouns, pronouns, verbs

This volume is the first in what will hopefully be a growing set of edited volumes and monographs concerning Niger-Congo comparative studies. This first volume addresses matters that are relevant to the entire EBC family as well as the particular branches of Kainji, Plateau, and Bantoid. The Jukunoid and Cross River branches are not the subject of these chapters, but they will be addressed in the next volume concerning EBC. In the case of Bantoid, the particular focus is on Grassfields and Bantu though other Bantoid subgroups are referenced. The potential topics for comparative studies among these languages are numerous, but this volume is dedicated to the specific issues of nominal affixes, third person pronouns, and verbal extensions.

In terms of comparative studies, these chapters fall under various topics. Three chapters concern the wider issue of comparative morphology. In particular, they concern the morphology of noun class systems and the possibility of reconstructing the nominal affixes and concord elements of the proto-classes. Good's chapter addresses the issue of identifying the systemic attributes that make up Niger-Congo and EBC noun class systems. Blench's chapters on nominal affixes in Kainji and Plateau demonstrate the significant challenges that exist in reconstructing the nominal systems of these two EBC branches.

Three other chapters concern wider issues of reconstructing Bantoid. One of these issues involves the dominance of Bantu in relation to the nine other identified Bantoid subgroups. It is generally assumed that Bantu is the most conservative group within Bantoid as well as EBC. Yet, at the same time, Bantu certainly has innovated. So, to what extent can one assume that Proto-Bantu equals Proto-EBC, Proto-Bantoid-Cross, let alone Proto-Bantoid that most narrowly includes Bantu within its grouping? This is a tempting assumption to make, but it is a process of attribution that can be suspect. The relationships within Bantoid probably involve layering of units which involve both historical processes of retention and innovation as well as language contact and areal processes. The challenge is to know if a given phenomenon reconstructed at one level can automatically be attributed to the higher level available. This issue presents itself in Hyman's chapters on verbal extensions and nasal nominal prefixes. Finally, Hyman's other chapter on third person pronouns in Grassfields provides an excellent example of internal reconstruction within a subgroup in which the divergences are identified and validated as historical retentions in one case and innovations in the other.

5 Reconstructing nominal affixes of Proto-EBC: Kainji and Plateau

Noun classes, with their system of nominal affixes and associated concord markers, are perhaps the major distinguishing feature of the Niger-Congo macrofamily as well as its branches like the EBC family. In order to reconstruct the noun class system of Proto-EBC and each of its branches, reconstruction will need to start at the lowest levels within each branch, using the comparative method. As Campbell & Poser (2008: 162) write: "The comparative method has always been the primary tool for establishing these relationships." It has served Indo-European studies well over the past century. As Hall (1950) notes for studying Proto-Romance, referencing Trager[4] for support, the comparative method is the best method in reconstructing Proto-Romance. Research began at the dialect levels of the Romance languages and was built up into larger and larger units until the forms of Proto-Romance were determined. Relative to the languages of EBC outside of Bantu, however, this method has been difficult to use in the past because of the lack of data. Access to each dialect level of most of these languages is simply not available, so using mass comparisons has been the common method. Yet, more language data is available today than forty years ago when de Wolf (1971) proposed a reconstruction of the noun classes of Proto-EBC ("Proto-Benue-Congo" at that time).

In this context, Blench provides valuable overviews of noun class systems in the Kainji languages in Chapter 3 and the Plateau languages in Chapter 4 of this volume. These branches are further away from Proto-Bantu and Bantoid, where our understanding of what may have been included in the Proto-EBC noun class system is clearer. They demonstrate how opaque a noun class system can become over time relative to more conservative contexts such as the Bantu and Bantoid ones. Along with the overview of noun class systems Blench provides an updated proposal for the comprehensive classification of these major subgroups. He also provides with each chapter a significant set of references, important material for future researchers.

In the case of Kainji (Chapter 3), a challenge to a straightforward comparative reconstruction of the Proto-Kainji noun class system presents itself. Blench points out that the Kainji languages and its subgroups are marked by significant diversity in noun class systems. This diversity suggests systems that have undergone various cycles involving analogical change, mergers, loss, and affix renewal. This means that it is highly unlikely that the full system for Proto-Kainji can be reconstructed. On the other hand, subunits of Kainji might lend themselves to

---

[4]Trager (1946: 463) wrote concerning the change of emphasis in the study of historical linguistics: "It seems to me that historical linguists must now restate their tasks much more precisely. When we have really good descriptive grammars of all existing French dialects, we can reconstruct Proto-Francian, Proto-Burgundian, Proto-Norman-Picard, etc. Then we can reconstruct Proto-French; then, with a similarly acquired statement of Proto-Provencal, we can formulate Proto-Gallo-Romaic; next, with similar accurately developed reconstructions of Proto-Ibero-Romaic, Proto-Italian, etc., we can work out Proto-Romaic as a whole."

some reconstruction and so provide possible insights when these are compared to the larger set of EBC languages. It would be important to do as much reconstruction as possible at the lower levels in order to provide as much comparative data as possible from Kainji.

Encouragingly, Blench notes that there is sufficient evidence for Proto-Kainji having classes 1/2 for persons, class 6a for liquids and some mass nouns, and a diminutive affix *kV-. The class pair 1/ 2 *u-/*ba- is cognate with the Proto-Bantu *mu-/*ba-. The class 6a prefix *mV- is cognate with a class prefix *ma- found throughout Niger-Congo. The diminutive prefix *kV- is likely cognate with the diminutive prefix ke- that is attested in Plateau languages (Blench p.c.) and with kɛ- in the Bantoid, Ekoid language Mbe (personal notes), suggesting it is likely a Proto-EBC diminutive prefix.

On the other hand, Blench is uncertain about the possibility of reconstructing a homorganic nasal prefix for Proto-Kainji. Such a prefix shows up in Bantoid languages as the prefix for noun classes 9 and 10.

He also notes that the vowels of CV- prefixes are often underspecified. A similar process is found elsewhere in EBC where the phonological or even phonetic quality of the prefix vowel harmonizes with the quality of the first vowel of the root.

An unusual proposal for Proto-Kainji is that it might have had class trios rather than class pairs. The three-way distinction would involve distinguishing singular, countable plural, and non-countable plural.

The major conclusion is that Kainji must have inherited a significant noun class system from Proto-EBC. At the same time, the Kainji languages appear to have experimented with that inheritance more vigorously than other major EBC subgroups and perhaps had more time to do so if they were the first group to separate from EBC. This diversity makes the reconstruction of the exponents of these classes, i.e. their nominal affixes and concord affixes, for the Proto-Kainji noun class system a challenge and will likely result in a limited, partial view.

In the case of Plateau (Chapter 4), the situation may be even bleaker for reconstructing Proto-Plateau noun class exponents than in Kainji. Blench notes in his concluding notes that "the connection with Niger-Congo noun classes remains tenuous."

He does note evidence for a possible class pair referring to persons, the prefixes being *V-/*bV-, as well as a nasal class used with "liquids, mass nouns, and abstracts". Both of these are relevant to Proto-EBC and the larger Niger-Congo macrofamily. The form of this nasal prefix in Proto-Plateau is uncertain, though *ma- may be a possibility even if it is not common synchronically. Proto-Plateau may also have had homorganic nasal prefixes, but their possible relationship to Proto-EBC is not clear because their likely semantic relationship is unknown.

The conclusion in the case of the Plateau languages is that noun classes were a definite feature of Proto-Plateau. However, what can be reconstructed as exponents of those classes is limited. As with Kainji, detailed reconstruction of some subunits of Plateau may be productive and serve as a substitute for identifying the exponents of Proto-Plateau.

Therefore, it appears likely that the results from further research on these two major subgroups of EBC will not make a determinative contribution to the reconstruction of Proto-EBC noun classes, but could play an important supportive role in confirming hypotheses about Proto-EBC as they develop. This challenge to detailed reconstruction of EBC noun class exponents raises the question as to whether there might be another way to gain insight into the EBC noun class system. This other way would be to look at the noun class system from a systemic perspective as opposed to the micro level of morphemes. Blench (p.c.) reminds me that the data available to de Wolf (1971) could not justify his reconstruction of the exponents of the noun classes of EBC but instead he was influenced by knowledge of Bantu. I will return to the influence of Bantu studies below in §7.

6 Noun class systemic topics in EBC

Good (Chapter 2) offers a perspective of EBC noun class systems that focuses on their morphological properties. These properties will be noted two paragraphs below. Some might contest this perspective, contending that it is merely typological, with no relevance to the reconstruction of the Proto-EBC noun class exponents. However, I would suggest that a careful consideration of the points Good makes offers insights into reconstructing various features of the Proto-EBC noun class system. They can provide frames for understanding the architecture of the subsystems that may have been operating in the larger system.

Good notes that in the reconstruction of EBC noun classes, the focus is on discrete exponents of the noun classes that form pairings to mark number on nouns. However, these exponents are elements in a larger system involving the classification of nouns that is associated with a variety of morphosyntactic properties. The identification of these properties (see below) as they obtain to Proto-EBC is a valid and crucial research area in expanding our knowledge of Proto-EBC noun classes and their systems. The research on the properties of the Proto-EBC noun class system is not in opposition to detailed reconstruction, but is complementary. Given the less than sanguine conclusion about reconstructing exponents in Proto-Kainji and Proto-Plateau above (see §3), system-based analysis could be helpful in expanding our understanding of Proto-EBC noun classes.

So what are some of these properties? In the case of Proto-EBC and its subgroups, the reduction of noun classes in individual languages or subgroups must consider areal influence and not simply language-internal structural processes. Context matters.

Within that context, there is the issue of kinds of affixes. Nominal prefixes are predominant, but there are EBC languages that have suffixes as exponents of a noun class as well. Even circumfixal elements are found. The possibility of prefixing, suffixing, and even circumfixal affixation needs to be accounted for in any full history of EBC noun classes. This includes the interplay of prefixes and suffixes according to the morphosyntactic context of the noun as seen in the language C'lela in Kainji. A given noun will have a prefix in one grammatical context but a suffix in another.

In terms of concord markers, several questions must be resolved. What are the domains of concord that are relevant to reconstructing Proto-EBC noun classes? What is the minimal set of domains within the concord system for Proto-EBC? How is concord with a given noun class indicated within the noun phrase, sentence, and discourse? Furthermore, how many series of noun class concord markers might there have been? Two seems to be the minimum, but there could have been more.

Finally, there is also the need to determine noun class identity and class pairing. Humans in classes 1/2 seems stable for many languages, but many of the other pairings are not so stable. To what extent did the Proto-EBC noun class systems have a non-canonical pairing structure for some classes? So while the past is viewed through the lens of the synchronic realities of current EBC languages, how much can be accounted for by the reconstruction of the Proto-EBC noun class system and how much can be accounted for by losses and innovations through time, remembering all the while that the Proto-EBC system is unlikely to have been a fully elegant, symmetrical, transparent system?

7 The long shadow of Bantu on Bantoid and potentially EBC

7.1 Brief historical review

Comparative and historical studies in EBC benefit from and are challenged by the coherence of the Bantu languages. They form one subgroup within Bantoid, but it must be remembered that means they are also part of the larger EBC family. When Greenberg (1963) proposed that Bantu was actually a subgroup of Bantoid, he stepped into an existing division among scholars as to the relationship between the Bantu languages and the languages of West Africa. Some viewed the similarities between the two groups of languages as the result of accident while others viewed them as the result of a genealogical relationship, a shared origin.

Guthrie (1962) attempted to explain the "Bantuisms" of the West Sudanic languages by claiming that speakers of a language or languages related to Proto-Bantu had been absorbed into certain communities of West Sudanic speakers. This absorption (i.e. "contamination" or "mixed language") theory supposedly gave a sufficient account for the Bantuisms found in these languages. Guthrie specifically claimed that languages such as the Ekoid languages had only false reflexes of the Proto-Bantu forms of the noun class prefixes and concord elements (cf. Guthrie 1962.20 footnote 3). These languages were like Bantu but not Bantu, so he called them "Bantoid".

However, by 1971 Guthrie had slightly modified his position concerning the Bantoid subgroups such as Ekoid. His modification, however, was put in the most tentative, non-committal terms possible:

> It may therefore be tentatively inferred that the Ekoid languages may to some extent share an origin with some of the Zone A languages [namely, Bobe and Yambassa], but that they seem to have undergone considerable perturbations. (Guthrie 1967-1971/1971.v.2.15 – brackets are mine)

This statement indicates that Guthrie was never able to shake himself free from his Bantu-centric point of view and see that the likely relationship between other Bantoid subgroups and Narrow Bantu involved a shared origin. In fact, he does not clarify for us how the genetic relationship could ever be "to some extent". In what way can one have a partial genetic relationship between two languages? This possibility would imply that the Bantoid subgroups had multiple genetic origins, an implausible state of affairs until demonstrated.

A different position was taken by Johnston (1919/22) and Westermann (1927) and Westermann & Bryan (1952), who viewed the shared "Bantuisms" as deriving from a common origin. To make his point, Johnston referred to them as "Semi-Bantu" languages. So when Greenberg (1963) classified Bantu languages with a multitude of other subgroups within the Benue-Congo family, he was motivated by genetic considerations and, as noted by Winston (1966), this limitation to genetic considerations was Greenberg's major contribution to the debate in African language classification. Guthrie's classification by contrast was as dependent on typological considerations as on genetic ones (Williamson 1971.249).

7.2 Responses to Greenberg's proposal

A common response to Greenberg's proposal that the Bantu languages actually formed a subgroup within a subgroup of the EBC family was, for a number of researchers, to seek to validate this proposal. This involved research particularly in the 1960s to the 1980s.

Studies by Crabb (1965); Voorhoeve (1971); Hyman (1972; 1980a,b), and Hyman & Voorhoeve (1980), reviewed by Watters (1982), all made claims about specific language groups and their relation to Bantu. Voorhoeve and Hyman argued for a genetic relationship between the Mbam-Nkam languages of Cameroon and Bantu based on sound correspondences, cognate roots, and noun class correspondences. Crabb argued for the same relationship between the Ekoid languages and Bantu on the basis of 1) a high degree of common vocabulary with the better known Bantu languages, and 2) certain suppletive forms which appear to bear a relationship to Bantu roots and noun class prefixes which would be resistant to borrowing. Others pursued lexicostatistical studies that included at least some Bantu languages along with languages from the region to the northwest of Bantu: see Henrici (1973); Heine (1973), and Coupez et al. (1975). Their results supported the likelihood of a genetic relationship between Bantu and its northwest neighbors.

These studies were instrumental in further affirming Greenberg's proposal. In addition, many other studies and dissertations have been published that demonstrate a variety of proposed genetic relationships between a given Bantoid language or subgroup outside of Bantu and the Bantu subgroup itself, whether represented by an individual Bantu language or the Common Bantu of Guthrie or the Proto-Bantu of Meeussen (1967). Such studies continue to have their place of importance in the continuing discovery of relationships among the Bantoid subgroups and Bantu, but also the other EBC subgroups of Kainji, Plateau, Jukunoid, and Cross River and their relationships with Bantu and Bantoid.

7.3 Challenges in building an integrated view of Bantoid

The significant amount of research on Bantu languages over the past century has been an extraordinary benefit in researching the lesser known Bantoid languages. The proposed reconstructions by Guthrie (1967-1971; 1971); Meeussen (1967), and Bastin et al. (2002) of Proto-Bantu or Common Bantu forms have provided multiple suggestions as to the meaning and the role of forms in other Bantoid languages, both morphological and lexical.

In the midst of these benefits there is also a challenge. It is tempting, whether conscious or subconscious, to take a Bantu-centric view and begin conceiving Proto-Bantoid as being equivalent to Proto-Bantu, and even perhaps extending the temptation and conceiving Proto-EBC as being equivalent to Proto-Bantu. Bantu has received the attention of a multitude of linguists for more than a century and Proto-Bantu has been reconstructed in ways to which no other Bantoid subgroup can compare. Also, by comparison, Bantu languages are rich in verbal and nominal morphology in ways that are frequently minimal or non-existent in other Bantoid subgroups. They are also more numerous by far than the number of languages in other Bantoid subgroups. In fact, my impression is that the number of Bantu languages (more than 500) and the enormous amount of research done on Bantu languages over the past century set them apart from all language families of Africa.

It can be easy to treat Bantu statically and forget that Proto-Bantu and its own subgroups and individual languages have their own history of retentions, innovations and borrowings. So, in reconstructing Bantoid and EBC, caution has to be taken. Just because Bantu has a given feature does not mean it was also present in Proto-Bantoid or in Proto-EBC. It may have originated in Proto-Bantu. Within EBC and within Bantoid in particular, there likely is a layering of relationships that we still do not understand well. But let me offer a few examples of how this layering may be present and effect our claims about where a given feature was innovated. Care is needed not to attribute everything found in Proto-Bantu to Proto-Bantoid, and in Proto-Bantoid to Proto-EBC. The same holds in studying the subgroups of Bantoid and not inferring from one subgroup that a given phenomenon must be Proto-Bantoid. Here are some examples.

7.3.1 Tense in Bantu

One example involves tense in Bantu. Bantu languages are rich in tense categories. Most Bantu languages have multiple past categories and multiple future categories. Among the other Bantoid subgroups in which tense is found, the more widely publicized are the Grassfields languages. At the same time, other Bantoid languages do not mark tense as a morphological verbal category. They are aspect-prominent like most languages in West Africa. This includes Bantoid subgroups such as Ekoid, Tivoid, and Nyang (Mamfe).

Nurse recognized that tense within Bantoid was not limited to Bantu but overlapped with some of the other Bantoid subgroups when he wrote:

> [...]it would seem most likely in the present state of knowledge that tense was innovated within the community ancestral to today's Bantu languages (2.10.2(iv, vii)) (Nurse 2008: 282-283).

It was unclear whether it had been innovated within Bantoid or perhaps "at some level of Bantoid-Cross tree" (Nurse 2008: 282). A future volume in the Niger-Congo Comparative Series is in preparation to address this very topic.

However, the point I want to make here is that if Bantu as well as two or more adjacent subgroups in Bantoid also mark tense, it is easy to assume that tense was a Proto-Bantoid phenomenon. The explanation for those subgroups without tense is simply to claim that they lost their tense marking. However, one would expect to find residual forms pointing to antiquated tense markers, but these are not present.

For nearly forty years I assumed that historically the Ejagham language within Ekoid would have had marked tense categories even though there were no present-day marked tense categories (Watters 1981: 364-365). At the same time, I could not find any residual or fossilized forms to support this assumption, but the fact that Bantu marked tense and was closely related to Bantoid languages was sufficient for me to make the assumption. It was Nurse's excellent work on *Tense and Aspect in Bantu* (2008) that alerted me to the Bantu verbal realities and their contrast with the wider Niger-Congo verbal realities. It led me to reverse my assumption in 2012. This was spelled out in 2012 in what will appear as Watters (2018).

The fact is that some of the Bantu phenomena may be restricted to Bantu, some of them may be shared with some other Bantoid subgroups, and some may be inherited from Proto-Bantoid, Proto-Bantoid-Cross, or Proto-EBC. Because of the extraordinary amount of research that has been published on Bantu languages and because of their morphologically complex forms, it can be tempting to assume that Bantu has conserved what was once Proto-Bantoid and the rest of Bantoid has moved from an earlier synthetic mode to a more analytic one.

However, as is being noted and reiterated here, if what is found in Proto-Bantu traces back to Proto-Bantoid, does that mean that it also traces back to Proto-Bantoid-Cross and Proto-EBC and Proto-Niger-Congo? As we seek to better understand Bantoid, I would encourage caution in making strong claims for Proto-Bantoid, for example, until sufficient coverage on a given phenomenon has been achieved involving all or most all of the Bantoid subgroups. I would suggest we look for layering among the Bantoid subgroups as expansions proceeded from west to east and innovations were made along the way within sub-regions of Bantoid and not necessarily shared with those they left behind.

Watters (1989: 406-407) notes the contrastive hypotheses about Bantoid. Williamson (1971) and Greenberg (1974) accept a clear two-way split within Bantoid. However, Meeussen (1974) countered that it was too early to determine the internal structure of Bantoid and preferred to remain with a multibranch hypothesis since too little was still known as to the internal Bantoid relationships. Meeussen's suggestion resembles Blench (2015) noted above in §4. Up to the present, most of our judgments about the internal structure of Bantoid are based on lexicostatistics, and that will remain the case until more research on morphological and lexical reconstructions is achieved.

7.3.2 Synthetic and analytic structures: the verb

Turning to another example, Güldemann (2003: 183–187) raises the issue of Bantu word forms, morphology and their grammaticalization history." Considering the verbal word in Bantu, the most complex word form in Bantu, in Bantoid, and in even EBC, the question that could be asked is: Did Proto-Bantoid, or Proto-EBC for that matter, originally have a fully synthesized verb much like that in Bantu, so that what most Bantoid groups present today is the result of a process they went through of isolating many or all of the morphemes, thus becoming analytic in structure? Or were the earlier forms more like those in most Bantoid groups, some verbal affixes but mostly analytic with isolated morphemes or clitics that were then synthesized in early Bantu or pre-Proto-Bantu? Güldemann argues that much of the Bantu verbal morphology can be shown to have likely derived historically from a more analytic structure with isolated morphemes.

An important interaction about these matters at the levels of Bantu, Bantoid, EBC, and Niger-Congo is that between Güldemann (2011) and Hyman (2011). Güldemann proposes that Bantu synthetic forms derive from more analytic forms found elsewhere in EBC. Hyman's response is instructive in his comments about possible historical recycling of morphosyntax, and the likely areal diffusion of more recent innovations along Güldemann's proposed "Macro-Sudan belt". It is a sobering interaction that underscores the importance of *local* comparative research. Güldemann's hypothesis can provide a framework for further research, but it can also generate a healthy skepticism about macro-claims that do not have the benefit of systematic reconstructions of the given phenomenon at lower levels.

At the same time, Güldemann's proposal exemplifies the need to give the imagination freedom to look beyond Bantu and the related Bantoid groups to EBC and all its branches and even Benue-Congo at an even higher level, and ask questions such as: Where do the morphologically complex verb forms of Bantu best fit, as a Bantu innovation or as Bantu retention, but if a retention, a retention of what historical level?

7.3.3 Verbal extensions in Bantoid

Another example involves verbal extensions. Hyman (Chapter 5) provides a valuable, detailed overview of verbal extensions in Grassfields and Bantoid. There are challenges in relating Proto-Bantu Zone A verbal extensions to verbal extensions in the other Bantoid subgroups. In Bantu, extensions such as causative, applicative, passive etc. mark the valency of the given verb. By contrast, in Bantoid languages they may mark either valence values or aspectual values. Hyman provides an excellent panorama comparing particular verbal extensions found in Grassfields with those in Bantu Zone A. He notes the semantic innovation of the Grassfields in reassigning extensions more aspectual values than the valence ones while next door valence values are commonly found in the Bantu Zone A languages. This overview serves as an excellent foundation for future comparative studies of verbal extensions in all Bantoid subgroups as well as languages of Cross River, Jukunoid, Plateau, and Kainji, in order to better understand how they may have been present at the level of Proto-EBC and each of its major subgroups. It also points to the difficulty of defining a clear boundary between Bantu and its Bantoid neighbors.

The questions I have raised above about the layering of evidence for innovation and retention relate to Hyman's article as follows: Just as it can be tempting to project Proto-Bantu onto Proto-Bantoid, it might be tempting to project Proto-Bantu plus Proto-Grassfields and other eastern Bantoid subgroups (e.g. Beboid, Mambiloid, Tikar) onto Proto-Bantoid. The region within Grassfields where the largest number of contrastive verbal extensions are found outside of Bantu could be a region of innovation rather than retention, and those Bantoid groups to the west of Grassfields may instead better represent Proto-Bantoid with their reduced number of extensions and their –CV shape. However, Hyman notes that the direction of change for extensions is to begin as valency marking morphemes. They then change to primarily marking aspect with some residual valence functions that become lexicalized. Finally, they change to having only aspectual values. This suggests that these verbal extensions are Proto-Bantoid extensions and likely much older, having undergone this transition from valency to aspect marking. So the extensions are not a case of inappropriate projections of Proto-Bantu categories onto Proto-Bantoid. But this line of questioning may need to be used with each Bantu extension individually.

Turning to another topic raised by verbal extensions, Hyman's study provides a possible answer to the boundary issue between Bantu and the other Bantoid groups. His chart of extensions for Bantu Zone A languages and selected Bantoid languages gives evidence to support the claim that the presence and absence of the passive is a likely boundary marker (see Watters 1989: 416). The Sanaga River valley (or Bantu Zone A) serves as a boundary between those languages with a passive extension (i.e. Narrow Bantu languages) and those without a passive extension (i.e. the remainder of the Bantoid languages). These other Bantoid languages commonly use the third person plural verbal prefix but with non-specific reference to mark the passive notion. Another possible boundary may be the applicative, being present in Narrow Bantu but absent in the remainder of Bantoid. Hyman (p.c.) also notes the possible role of the applicative in this matter. For the passive and applicative in Bantoid other than Bantu, see Watters (1981: 360) for Ejagham in the Ekoid group and Watters (2003: 252) for the multiple languages in the Grassfields group.

7.3.4 Nasal nominal prefixes in Bantoid & EBC

To continue the topic of how Bantu can be an influence in analyzing other Bantoid subgroups and Bantoid as a whole, Hyman (Chapter 6) presents the matters of Bantu nasal nominal prefixes. He provides an important overview of the questions revolving around the presence and absence of nasal prefixes in Bantu noun classes 1, 3, 4, 6a, 9, 10, and their cognates. Class 6a generally occurs throughout Niger-Congo displaying a form cognate with *ma- as the prefix, so this class is not the major focus. Hyman (1980a) covers similar details but using data that was available more than thirty years ago. More is known today, as demonstrated in Hyman (Chapter 6 of this volume) and Blench (2015).

The questions Hyman raises are numerous and complex. He provides the possible answers and their competing assumptions to these questions. In terms of research on Bantoid and, more widely, all EBC, it appears likely that Proto-EBC used oral vowels for these prefixes while Proto-Bantu used nasal consonants in a CV- structure: *mʊ-, *mɪ-, *ma- (classes 1, 3, 4); or a homorganic nasal *N- (classes 9, 10). Whatever may have existed in Proto-Niger-Congo or whatever may have happened across the Niger-Congo macrofamily in terms of having a full set of nasal nominal prefixes for cognates to Proto-Bantu noun classes 1, 3, 4, 6a, 9, and 10, it might advance our understanding if we could unravel the layers within Bantoid first, reconstructing the noun classes for each Bantoid subgroup, and then for Cross River and Jukunoid, and possibly then from possible insights from reconstructions of various subunits within Kainji and Plateau. A place to start would be to reconstruct the nominal prefixes and concord affixes for each Bantoid subgroup. Even at this level it is not always straightforward. Good & Lovegren (2017) demonstrate that reconstructing nasal classes can be complicated even within what is clearly a dialect cluster.

Indeed, within Bantoid, subgroups vary relative to the presence of nasal and oral prefixes. For example, Grassfields is divided in this matter (Stallcup 1980: 55). Western Grassfields has oral prefixes in classes 1 or 3, and nasal prefixes on only some nouns in classes 9 and 10. This contrasts with Eastern Grassfields which has nasal prefixes in classes 1 and 3, and homorganic nasal prefixes on all nouns in classes 9 and 10. Leaving the Grassfields and going farther west, Hyman points to Tiv that does not have nasal prefixes in classes 1, 3, 4, 9, or 10 (Voorhoeve & de Wolf 1969: 52). Contrastively, also to the west, Proto-Ekoid likely had nasal prefixes in classes 1, 3, 4, 9, and 10 (Watters 1981; 1980; 2016). This uneven distribution of nasal prefixes in Bantoid subgroups does not clearly point to Proto-Bantoid having a full set of nasal prefixes. The layering of their presence suggests the possibility that the innovation started with some subgroups but not in others, and in the case of Grassfields, with its two-way division, it may involve different waves of migrations into the Grassfields. A first wave that became Eastern Grassfields possessed (or innovated?) the set of nasal prefixes while a later wave (or waves) that became Momo and Ring languages did not arrive with nasal prefixes. Only over the centuries of contact with Eastern Grassfields language they have begun marking some nouns in classes 9 and 10 with homorganic nasal prefixes.

One hypothesis put forward some forty years ago was that Bantoid could be divided into two groups, the Bane group and the Bantu group. In testing this hypothesis, Voorhoeve (1980, see also Watters 1982: 89) found that grammatical criteria and lexical criteria gave contradictory conclusions. He also discussed nasal prefixes in noun classes 1, 3, and 6, raising significant questions for any kind of definitive criteria for distinguishing Bantu and the other subgroups of Bantoid. Areal spreading of various features seems to have been involved.

7.3.5 Third person pronouns in Grassfields

Finally, Hyman (Chapter 7) provides a fascinating presentation of third person pronouns in Eastern Grassfields, Momo, and Ring (the two together form Western Grassfields), and their relation to Proto-Bantu forms. It is clear that Momo and Ring have innovated new forms for third person pronouns by using demonstratives and the noun 'body' as the sources for the innovations. In contrast, Eastern Grassfields maintains the original pronominal forms and these are closely related to Proto-Bantu forms.

This is the kind of comparative study needed for each subgroup or closely related subgroups on various topics. The goals in each case would be to determine the earliest forms and identify any innovations and what the sources of those innovations might be. Such studies would provide an excellent database for comparing Bantoid subgroups and assist in reconstructing the history of Bantoid.

Our understanding of the relationships between the groups of languages beyond the Bantu boundary is still at a rudimentary level. It is hoped that these six chapters will alert others to the challenges and motivate them to join the process of clarifying their history.

Acknowledgements

I am grateful to Roger Blench, Jeff Good, Larry Hyman, and Valentin Vydrin for fruitful comments on earlier drafts of this chapter.

References

Armstrong, Robert G. 1981. The Idomoid language sub-family of the Eastern Kwa borderland. In Herrmann Jungraithmayr (ed.), *Berliner afrikanistische Vorträge, XXI*, 7–23. Berlin: Dietrich Reimer.

Bastin, Yvonne, André Coupez, Evariste Mumba & Thilo C. Schadeberg (eds.). 2002. *Bantu lexical reconstructions 3 / reconstructions lexicales bantoues 3*. Tervuren: Royal Museum for Central Africa. http://linguistics.africamuseum.be/BLR3.html. Online database.

Bennett, Patrick R. & Jan P. Sterk. 1977. South Central Niger-Congo: A reclassification. *Studies in African Linguistics* 8. 241–73.

Blench, Roger M. 1989. New Benue-Congo: A definition and proposed classification. *Afrikanistische Arbeitspapiere* 17. 115–147.

Blench, Roger M. 2006. *Archaeology, language, and the African past*. Lanham, MD: AltaMira Press.

Blench, Roger M. 2012. *The North Bantoid hypothesis*. Cambridge: Kay Williamson Educational Foundation. Electronic ms.

Blench, Roger M. 2015. *The Bantoid languages* (Oxford Handbooks Online). Oxford: Oxford University Press. http://www.oxfordhandbooks.com/view/10.1093/oxfordhb/9780199935345.001.0001/oxfordhb-9780199935345-e-17?rskey=MiYuUo&result=1.

Boyd. 1989. Adamawa-Ubangi. In John Bendor-Samuel (ed.), *The Niger-Congo languages*, 178–215. Lanham, MD: University Press of America.

Campbell, Lyle & William J. Poser. 2008. *Language classification: History and method.* Cambridge: Cambridge University Press.

Coupez, André, E. Evrard & Jan Vansina. 1975. Classification d'un échantillon de langues bantoues d'après la lexicostatistique. *Africana Linguistica* 6. 133–158. , Tervuren: Musée Royal de l'Afrique Centrale.

Crabb, David W. 1965. *Ekoid Bantu languages of Ogoja, Eastern Nigeria* (West African Languages Monographs 4). Cambridge: Cambridge University Press.

de Wolf, Paul P. 1971. *The noun class system of Proto-Benue-Congo.* The Hague: Mouton.

Ehret, Christopher. 2016. *The civilizations of Africa: A history to 1800.* 2nd edn. Charlottesville: University of Virginia Press.

Gerhardt, Ludwig. 1989. Kainji and Platoid. In John Bendor-Samuel (ed.), *Niger-Congo*, 359–376. Lanham, MD: University Press of America.

Good, Jeff & Jesse Lovegren. 2017. Remarks on the nasal classes in Mungbam and Naki. In Raija Kramer & Roland Kießling (eds.), *Mechthildian approaches to Afrikanistik: Advances in language based research on Africa: Festschrift für Mechthild Reh*, 83–99. Köppe: Köln.

Greenberg, Joseph H. 1963. The languages of Africa. *IJAL* Part II, No. 1(29).

Greenberg, Joseph H. 1966[1970]. *The languages of Africa.* 3rd edn. Bloomington: Indiana University.

Greenberg, Joseph H. 1974. Bantu and its closest relatives. *Studies in African Linguistics sup* 5. 115–119. 122–134.

Güldemann, Tom. 2003. Grammaticalization. In Derek Nurse & Gérard Philippson (eds.), *The Bantu languages*, 182–194. London: Routledge.

Güldemann, Tom. 2011. Proto-Bantu and Proto-Niger-Congo: Macro-areal typology and linguistic resconstruction. In Osama Hieda, Christa König & Hiroshi Nakagawa (eds.), *Geographical typology and linguistic areas: With special reference to Africa* (Studies in Linguistics 2 2), 109–141. Amsterdam: Benjamins.

Guthrie, Malcolm. 1962. Bantu origins: A tentative new hypothesis. *Journal of African Languages* 1. 9–21.

Guthrie, Malcolm. 1967-1971. *Comparative Bantu. 4 vols.* Farnborough: Gregg.

Guthrie, Malcolm. 1971. *Comparative Bantu: An introduction to the comparative linguistics and prehistory of the Bantu languages.* Vol. 2. Farnborough: Gregg.

Hall, Robert A. 1950. The reconstruction of Proto-Romance. *Language* 26. 6–27.

Heine, Bernd. 1973. Zur genetishen Gliederung der Bantu-Sprachen. *Afrika und Übersee* 56. 164–185.

Henrici, Alick. 1973. Numerical classification of Bantu languages. *African Language Studies* 14. 81–104.

Hyman, Larry M. 1972. *A phonological study of Fe?fe?-Bamileke*. UCLA dissertation.

Hyman, Larry M. (ed.). 1980a. *Noun classes in the Grassfields Bantu borderland* (Southern California Occasional Papers in Linguistics 8). Los Angeles: Department of Linguistics, University of Southern California. http://gsil.sc-ling.org/pubs/SCOPILS_6_7_8_9/Noun_classes_in_the_grassfields_bantu_borderland.pdf.

Hyman, Larry M. 1980b. Reflections on the nasal classes in Bantu. In Larry M. Hyman (ed.), *Noun classes in the Grassfields Bantu borderland* (Southern California Occasional Papers in Linguistics 8), 179–210. Los Angeles: Department of Linguistics, University of Southern California.

Hyman, Larry M. 2011. The Macro-Sudan belt and Niger-Congo reconstruction. *Language Dynamics and Change* 1. 3–49.

Stallcup, Kenneth L. 1980. La géographie linguistique des Grassfields. In Larry M. Hyman & Jan Voorhoeve (eds.), *L'expansion bantoue: Actes du colloque international du CNRS, Viviers (France) 4–16 avril 1977. Volume I: Les classes nominales dans le bantou des Grassfields*, 43–57. Paris: SELAF.

Hyman, Larry M. & Jan Voorhoeve (eds.). 1980. *L'expansion bantoue: Actes du colloque international du CNRS, Viviers (France) 4–16 avril 1977. Volume I: Les classes nominales dans le bantou des Grassfields*. Paris: SELAF.

Johnston, Harry H. 1919/22. *A comparative study of the Bantu and Semi-Bantu languages*. Oxford: Clarendon Press.

Meeussen, A. E. 1967. Bantu grammatical reconstructions. *Africana Linguistica* 3. 79–121.

Meeussen, A. E. 1974. Reply to Prof. Greenberg. *Studies in African Linguistics sup* 5. 119–121.

Nurse, Derek. 2008. *Tense and aspect in Bantu*. Oxford: University Press.

Shimizu, Kiyoshi. 1975. A lexicostatistical study of Plateau languages and Jukun. *Anthropological Linguistics* 17. 413–418.

Simons, Gary F. & Charles D. Fennig (eds.). 2018. *Ethnologue: Languages of the world*. 20th edn. Dallas, TX: SIL International. http://www.ethnologue.com.

Trager, George L. 1946. Changes in the emphasis in linguistics: A comment. *Studies in Philology* 43. 461–464.

Voorhoeve, Jan. 1971. The linguistic unit Mbam-Nkam (Bamileke, Bamun and related languages). *Journal of African Languages and Linguistics* 10. 1–12.

Voorhoeve, Jan. 1980. Bantu et Bane. In Larry M. Hyman & Jan Voorhoeve (eds.), *L'expansion bantoue, 1. Les classes nominales dans le bantou des Grassfields: Col-*

loques internationaux du Centre National de la Recherche Scientifique, Viviers (France), 4-16 avril 1977, 59–77. Paris: SELAF.

Voorhoeve, Jan & Paul P. de Wolf (eds.). 1969. *Benue-Congo noun class systems*. Leiden: Afrika Studiecentrum.

Watters, John R. 1980. The Ejagham noun class system: Ekoid Bantu revisited. In Larry M. Hyman (ed.), *Noun classes in the Grassfields Bantu borderland* (Southern California Occasional Papers in Linguistics 8), 99–137. Los Angeles: Department of Linguistics, University of Southern California.

Watters, John R. 1981. *A phonology and morphology of Ejagham – with notes on dialect variation*. Los Angeles: University of California at Los Angeles Doctoral dissertation.

Watters, John R. 1982. Review of hyman and voorhoeve (1980) les classes nominales dans le bantou des Grassfields. L'Expansion bantoue, vol. 1. *Journal of African Languages and Linguistics* 4. 87–92. .f.

Watters, John R. 1989. Bantoid overview. In John Bendor-Samuel (ed.), *The Niger-Congo languages*, 400–420. Lanham, MD: University Press of America.

Watters, John R. 2003. Grassfields Bantu. In Derek Nurse & Gérard Philippson (eds.), *The Bantu languages*, 225–256. London: Routledge.

Watters, John R. 2016. *An initial understanding of the Proto-Ekoid-Mbe noun class system*. Presentation at the Second Proto-Niger-Congo Conference, Paris.

Watters, John R. 2018. Ejagham without tense: Historical implications for Proto-Bantoid. In Eugene Buckley, Thera Crane & Jeff Good (eds.), *Revealing structure: Finding patterns in grammars and using grammatical patterns to elucidate language. A festschrift to honor Larry M. Hyman*, 260–272. Stanford: CSLI Publications.

Westermann, Diedrich. 1927. *Die Westlichen Sudansprachen und ihre Beziehungen zum Bantu*. Berlin: de Gruyter.

Westermann, Diedrich & Margaret A. Bryan. 1952. *Languages of West Africa: Part II*. Vol. 2. London: Oxford University Press.

Williamson, Kay. 1971. The Benue-Congo languages and Ịjọ. In Thomas Sebeok (ed.), *Current trends in linguistics*, 245–306. The Hague: Mouton.

Williamson, Kay. 1989. Niger-congo overview. In John Bendor-Samuel (ed.), *The Niger-Congo languages*, 3–45. Lanham, MD: University Press of America.

Williamson, Kay & Roger M. Blench. 2000. Niger-Congo. In Bernd Heine & Derek Nurse (eds.), *African languages: An introduction*, 11–42. Cambridge: Cambridge University Press.

Winston, F. D. D. 1966. Greenberg's classification of african languages. *African Language Studies* 7. 160–170.

Chapter 2

East Benue-Congo noun classes, with a focus on morphological behavior

Jeff Good
University at Buffalo

> Comparative studies of noun class systems in East Benue-Congo languages go back at least as far as the mid-nineteenth century work on comparative Bantu undertaken by Wilhelm Bleek. In the wider Benue-Congo context, the most significant work is de Wolf (1971), which reconstructs a noun class system for Proto-Benue-Congo and remains the most detailed study on the topic available today. This paper summarizes the results of De Wolf and also looks at various morphosyntactic aspects of Benue-Congo noun class systems en route to consideration of the possibilities for reconstruction of abstract features of the noun class system of the proto-language. These include patterns of change in the structure of these systems, the fact that both prefixing and suffixing noun class systems are attested in the family, domains of noun class concord, different series of noun class markers appearing on different morphological hosts, and the issue of how attested classes can be linked to reconstructed classes.

1 Overview of previous comparative work

Comparative studies of noun class systems in East Benue-Congo languages go back at least as far as the mid-nineteenth century work on comparative Bantu undertaken by Wilhelm Bleek (Maho 1999: 13–14). In the wider Benue-Congo context, the most significant work, by far, has been that of de Wolf (1971), who reconstructed a noun class system for Proto-Benue-Congo on the basis of an examination of representatives from languages of the Plateau, Jukunoid, Cross

River, and Bantoid subgroups (de Wolf 1971: 19–20).[1] While this work was only intended to serve as a starting point (de Wolf 1971: 21), rather than a definitive reconstruction, it remains the most detailed study on the topic available today.[2] Without intending to detract from his efforts in any way, the reason for this is not that further work was deemed superfluous but, rather, as has so often been the case with Niger-Congo studies, the limited energies of specialists have been spent on other topics.

The core comparative results of de Wolf (1971) center on the reconstruction of a number of noun class prefix forms (for nominal prefixes and some concords), typical singular/plural pairings for these noun classes, and a set of nouns belonging to each class. This reconstruction is summarized in Table 1 and draws in part on the presentation provided in Williamson (1989: 38–39), in particular with respect to the assignment of class number labels. The full treatment can be found in de Wolf (1971: 50–59), and any reader interested in the full details is advised to consult the original, where additional complications are discussed.[3] Partial results are given here since they should be sufficient for illustrating the most important points regarding the reconstructions and to allow more space to be devoted to other areas of East Benue-Congo noun class system reconstruction. The table gives (i) canonical singular/plural pairings for the various reconstructed classes or indicates if the class is one that is not associated with clear singular/plural pairings (e.g., for mass nouns), (ii) reconstructed nominal prefix and concord forms (including indication of tone in some cases), and (iii) exemplary reconstructed nouns for each of the various classes.

The class numbering conventions in Table 1 draw heavily on those associated with Proto-Bantu noun class reconstructions (see, e.g., Maho (1999: 246–255) and

---

[1] There are complications in using the term Benue-Congo that are hard to avoid in a work like this one. While the focus of this chapter is East Benue-Congo, the group of languages referred to by this term has also been labeled Benue-Congo (Williamson & Blench 2000: 30–31). Here, I will generally refer to East Benue-Congo, over Benue-Congo, in reference to the language group of primary focus here, though Benue-Congo will be used in some places where the larger group is under consideration. For the sake of brevity, Proto-Benue-Congo will be used throughout to refer to the proto-language associated with East Benue-Congo. Many points made here for East Benue-Congo will apply to larger groups, such as Benue-Congo or Niger-Congo, though this is not generally made explicit given that the focus of this volume is on the properties of East Benue-Congo rather than the similarities between East Benue-Congo and the superordinate groups that it is associated with.

[2] Williamson (1993) is a notable attempt to amend de Wolf's (1971) work. However, it appears to have received relatively little attention.

[3] For instance, de Wolf (1971: 52–53) suggests that Classes 5, 6, 8, 9, 10, 12, 14, and 15 may have also occurred as unpaired classes, alongside Class 6a which is reconstructed as only being an unpaired class, and that there may have been an additional possible Class 7/6 pairing.

2 East Benue-Congo noun classes, with a focus on morphological behavior

Table 1: Overview of de Wolf's (1971) Proto-Benue-Congo noun class system

LABEL	PFX	CONC	PFX	CONC	EXAMPLE
1/2	*ù-, *ò-	*gwu-, *à-	*bà-	*ba-	*-lume 'man'
5/6	*li-	*zí- (?)	*à-	*ga-, *a-	*-tama 'cheek'
7/8	*ki-, *ke-	*ki-	*bì-, *bè-	*bi-	*-kupe 'bone'
9/10	*e-, *i-	*zì-	*í-	*í-, *zi- (?)	*-name 'animal'
3	*ú-	*u-, *gu-	(plural 10 or 13)		*-sene 'back'
11	*lu-	*lu-	(plural 10)		*-z(w)ana 'sun'
12	*kà-	*ka-	(plural 10 or 13)		*-kama 'monkey'
13	(singular 3 or 12)		*ti-	*ti-	*-kwon 'tree'
14	*bù-	*bu-	(plural 6 or 10)		*-su 'face'; *-bogo 'fear'
15	*ku-	*ku-	(plural 6 or 10)		*-tuŋi 'ear'
6a	*mà-, *nà-	*ma-, *nà-	(unpaired)		*-luŋ 'blood'

Katamba (2003: 104)) and are not found in de Wolf (1971). They are included here due to the long-standing significance of Proto-Bantu for comparative studies of East Benue-Congo under the assumption that Bantu languages are relatively morphologically conservative (see, e.g., Williamson (1985), Jungraithmayr (1990: 29), and Hyman (2004)). I have collapsed a possible Class 4 with Class 10 in the presentation since de Wolf (1971) does not explicitly separate these, though see Williamson (1989: 38). Class 4 will be referred to here in reference to specific noun class system analyses which treat it as distinct from Class 10, even in cases where they are formally equivalent, or nearly equivalent, as is the case with Noni (Hyman 1981: 33), to be discussed below.

While Table 1 does not present the full range of the details of the reconstructions of de Wolf (1971), it should suffice to give a general impression of his proposals. Since there has not been extensive debate regarding these reconstructions since their publication, it is difficult to know which should be considered more or less secure as representing key parts of the Proto-Benue-Congo noun class system. However, to the extent that a number of these pairings have close analogs in other branches of Niger-Congo, e.g., Classes 1/2, 3/4, and 6a (see Williamson (1989: 38–39)), they seem quite likely to have been present in Proto-Benue-Congo as well.

De Wolf (1971) does not discuss semantic patterns with respect to the noun classes in detail, though his reconstructions of specific nouns as belonging to the various classes do indicate that some of the classes would have had fairly clear-cut semantics. On the whole, these class semantics are not particularly surprising from a Niger-Congo perspective (see, e.g., the semantic labels given to the various classes and pairings across Niger-Congo presented in Williamson (1989: 38–39)). The Class 1/2 pairing is associated with nouns referring to humans, and de Wolf (1971: 53) even suggests two of the Class 1/2 noun reconstructions *-tata 'father' and *-mama 'mother' were likely to have not been coded with a prefix in the singular, thereby implicitly reconstructing something along the lines of the class designated as Class 1a in the Bantuist literature (see, e.g., Maho (1999: 74) and Van de Velde (2006)). The Class 1a is used to classify nouns not showing the usual Class 1 coding but otherwise behaving like Class 1 nouns with respect to concord. The next most robust semantic associations are those of the Class 9/10 pairing with animals (though not exclusively so) and Class 6a with liquids.[4] The Class 5/6 pairing contains many body parts, as does the Class 15/6 pairing. While de Wolf (1971: 59) only gives four reconstructed nouns for unpaired Class 14 (with the meanings 'fear', 'life', 'pain/ache', and 'witchcraft'), these can all be interpreted as referring to abstract entities.

The other classes and pairings do not show such straightforward semantic categorization, and, on the whole, it appears that the results of studies of the semantics of Bantu noun classes can also be applied to the East Benue-Congo languages, which have not seen as detailed investigation in this domain (see Maho (1999: 55–88) for the most recent detailed survey of work on the semantics of Bantu noun classes). Specifically, while it is not difficult to identify semantic tendencies in the distributions of nouns into various classes and class pairings, it has proven impossible to devise a set of semantic principles that fully cover these distributions, and a degree of lexical arbitrariness in assignment seems unavoidable.[5] To the extent that domains of semantic regularity are interspersed with varying degrees of arbitrariness throughout East Benue-Congo, this seems to be the most reasonable way to reconstruct the system of the proto-language. If there ever was a time when the system was semantically regular, it would have presumably been at a more ancient time depth.

---

[4]The convention of referring to the unpaired class with a nasal consonant and associated with liquid substances as 6a is due to Welmers (1973: 163) and is connected to the fact that Classes 6 and 6a are homophonous in Bantu.

[5]Of course, we must also allow for the possibility that, in some cases, formal factors may have played a role in class assignment. This probably accounts, for instance, for the fact that loanwords from languages like English referring to non-humans can be placed in the Class 1/2 pairing in some East Benue-Congo languages (see, e.g., Lovegren (2013: 118–119) on Mungbam). Since English nouns will not begin with any sort of class prefix (unlike potential borrowings between other East Benue-Congo languages), they formally resemble Class 1a nouns, presumably accounting for such Class 1/2 assignments. Formal factors have also been implicated with respect to class assignment patterns in Bantu languages (see, e.g, Schadeberg (2009: 91)).

2 East Benue-Congo noun classes, with a focus on morphological behavior

The reconstructions seen in Table 1 were undertaken at a time when crucial data had begun to become available, but de Wolf (1971: 21) still felt the data he had access to was insufficient in various ways. By contrast, today, the problem would not seem to be a lack of data – quite a lot on the noun class systems of East Benue-Congo languages has been published in intervening decades (see, e.g., Hyman (1980a), Hyman & Voorhoeve (1980) for two collections of studies coming out in the decade following de Wolf (1971: 21), which represent merely the tip of the iceberg in this regard). Rather, the problem is that the data has, on the one hand, not been properly synthesized given the relatively low priority of comparative work in the field of linguistics in the last half century, and, on the other hand, simply fails to yield straightforward patterns. It does seem clear that progress could be quickly made within low-level subgroups if this was deemed a priority. The work of Connell (1987) on the reconstruction of the Lower Cross River noun class system is exemplary in this regard, though work of this type does not appear to be particularly common. At the same time, we must acknowledge that local patterns of language contact among multilingual populations should be expected to obscure genealogical signals in many cases throughout the East Benue-Congo area. This means that any procedure assuming a simple path for the reconstruction of Proto-Benue-Congo via a series of discrete intermediate subgrouping nodes is bound to run into difficulties (see, e.g., Di Carlo & Good (2014) for a relevant case study and contextualization). This is not to say that such work should not be undertaken. Rather, it is simply important to take into account the realities of language use and development in the East Benue-Congo area when engaging in efforts at reconstruction.

The most emblematic phenomenon seen in East Benue-Congo noun class data that has resisted straightforward analysis via subgrouping concerns the historical status of nasal consonants in some of the class markers associated with Classes 1, 3, 4, 6, 9, and 10. These classes show nasals in their nominal prefixes in Bantu languages, leading to their reconstruction with nasals for Proto-Bantu, but the distribution of these nasals in non-Bantu East Benue-Congo (and beyond) is much more complex, and there is, as yet, no consensus on their status in Proto-Benue-Congo (see Hyman (1980b) and Miehe (1991) for discussion; see also Hyman, chapter 7, this volume, for a current evaluation of these nasal classes and their possible origins).

No attempt will be made here to revise the specific reconstructions of de Wolf (1971). This is partly because the time that would be required to do so would be prohibitive and properly reporting on any such efforts would almost certainly necessitate monograph-level discussion. However, there is also a more principled reason for this. Consistent with practices of the time, the scope of de Wolf's (1971) reconstructions is relatively limited: Specific forms and pairings are proposed, but it must be recognized that, in East Benue-Congo languages, these are merely elements of a larger noun class *system* (see Good (2012)), which is associated with a range of morphosyntactic properties. Moreover, while there has not been comprehensive work specifically reconstructing the broader morphosyntactic properties of the Proto-Benue-Congo noun class system, there has, in many cases, been enough work to allow for preliminary proposals to be made – or at least for promising possible alternatives to be outlined.

The rest of the discussion here, therefore, will look at various morphosyntactic features of East Benue-Congo noun class systems where available work makes it possible to seriously consider issues of reconstruction. Specifically, §2 considers the general direction of change assumed for East Benue-Congo noun class systems, §3 examines the significance of the presence of noun class suffixes (as opposed to prefixes) in the family, §4 discusses which morphosyntactic domains were most likely to be domains of concord, §5 raises issues with respect to the presence of different form classes for concordial elements, and §6 looks at cases where a noun class's identity may be difficult to uniquely reconstruct due to complex patterns of change. A brief synthesizing conclusion is offered in §7. These topics are not chosen because they exhaust all the points of potential interest with respect to East Benue-Congo noun classes. Rather, they represent features where significant work has already been done and which seem to be especially revealing with respect to coming to a better understanding of the system as a whole.[6]

2 "Drift" in Benue-Congo noun class systems

A remarkable fact about Benue-Congo noun class systems is that languages of the family range from having some of the most elaborated such systems in the world (as evidenced by many Bantu languages) to having, in effect, no synchronic noun classes (see Good (2012) for detailed discussion in a Niger-Congo context). Languages wholly lacking in noun classes are more strongly associated with West Benue-Congo (e.g., Yoruba, Igbo, or Edo), than East Benue-Congo.[7] However,

---

[6]In choosing to focus on possibilities for system-level morphosyntactic reconstruction here, I do not mean to suggest that continued work on reconstructing the phonological shapes of specific class markers is not also an important endeavor within comparative Benue-Congo studies. I see these two lines of inquiry as complementary rather than being in opposition.

[7]Information on the (either remnant or lack of) noun classes in these West Benue-Congo languages can be found in Ogunbọwale (1970: 32–39) for Yoruba, Green & Igwe (1963: 13–20) for

2 East Benue-Congo noun classes, with a focus on morphological behavior

highly reduced systems in East Benue-Congo are present as well, as evidenced, for example, by the Bantu language Komo, which is reported to have no noun classes (Guthrie 1971: 42, Thomas 1992: 4), or the Bangangte variety of the Grassfields Bantu language Bamileke described by Voorhoeve (1968), which shows a highly reduced concord system with only five formally distinct classes that have become disconnected from the system of nominal singular/plural marking. Remarkable in this regard is the variation that one finds in closely related languages, like the small Ogoni group, where, for instance, one language of the group, Eleme, makes extensive use of class prefixes on nouns, two others, Ogoi and Khana, show traces of noun prefixes, and a final language, Gokana, shows no evidence of noun prefixes (Williamson 1985: 436–440) [8]

While the earliest work on Niger-Congo languages proposed that languages with minimal class systems represented an early "primitive" state of language development (see, e.g., Jungraithmayr (1990)), the present, quite stable, consensus treats relatively elaborated systems as closer to the historical situation. This is clearly seen in the reconstructions in Table 1. In this regard, the reconstructed Proto-Bantu noun class system can be considered relatively close to the Proto-Benue-Congo one from a broad typological perspective. However, it would be inappropriate to equate Proto-Bantu with Proto-Benue-Congo since the evidence from the group as a whole does not support Proto-Benue-Congo having as elaborated a system as Proto-Bantu. In fact, the latter group appears to have innovated a number of its noun classes, in particular with respect to less canonically nominal categories, such as those associated with locative meanings, i.e., Classes 16, 17, and 18 (see Williamson (1989: 37)).[9] Thus, Proto-Bantu is generally treated as having around twenty noun classes (Maho 1999: 51), while de Wolf's (1971) reconstruction of Proto-Benue-Congo has only fifteen.

There have been statements in the literature attributing the presence of reduced noun class systems in Niger-Congo in general, and Benue-Congo more specifically, to be the result of "drift…in the direction of the simplification of the

---

Igbo, and Dunn (1968: 207) for Edo.

[8]See Hyman et al. (1970); Faraclas (1986); Connell (1987); Gerhardt (1994) and Storch (1997) for further discussion on specific East Benue-Congo subgroups.

[9]However, one does find instances of apparently "extended" noun classes with locative meanings in East Benue-Congo outside of Bantu, such as in Mungbam (Lovegren 2013: 265) and Noni (Hyman 1981: 15–16), both non-Grassfields languages spoken at the northern edge of the Grassfields Bantu area. Watters (2003: 243–244) gives more detailed discussion on this point (see also Grégoire (1983)). This suggests that, if the development of such locative classes is treated as the result of a single innovation taking place after the breakup of Proto-Benue-Congo, this would have to be of an older time depth than Proto-Bantu (with the usual disclaimers regarding the possibility of areal diffusion applying).

nominal classification system" (Greenberg 1966: 9) (see also de Wolf (1971: 188) and Jungraithmayr (1969: 161–162)). This assessment is presumably connected to the fact that one sees reduced systems in the majority of Benue-Congo groups (to varying degrees), while it is much more difficult to find languages that evince the total number of reconstructed noun classes (see, e.g., de Wolf (1971: 188) on Benue-Congo and Maho (1999: 51) on Bantu).

However, there are reasons to doubt the validity of "drift" as an explanatory factor in the development of Benue-Congo noun class systems. First, there is no obvious general historical mechanism that can be associated with drift. So, its utility as a label for patterns of change is not clear. Second, as discussed in Good (2012: 322–324), there are a number of distinct mechanisms involved in the breakdown of noun classes that are not obviously interconnected, suggesting that their reduction is not due to some general pattern of "loss" but, rather, to independent changes which happen to co-occur in some Benue-Congo languages. Third, much of the apparent drift can be more concretely attributed to areal patterns affecting Niger-Congo languages in the Kwa-Benue-Congo subregion of the so-called Macro-Sudan Belt (see Güldemann (2008b), as well as Clements & Rialland (2008: 37)).[10] Niger-Congo languages in this region have been generally subject to processes of morphological reduction, in some cases clearly triggered by independent patterns of phonological reduction (see Hyman (2004) and Good (2012)), but these are probably relatively recent in nature when set against the broader genealogical diversification of Niger-Congo (see Hyman (2011)). This suggests that many of the observed reductions are not attributable to a gradual process of "drift" but, rather, more recent effects of contact. Finally, it is worth mentioning that one can only characterize Benue-Congo noun class systems as tending towards reduction if one ignores Bantu languages, where the pattern, if anything, goes in the opposite direction.

To these remarks, one might raise a possible methodological concern: Could it be the case that the application of the comparative method in the domain of noun class systems may accidentally tend towards the reconstruction of larger systems over smaller ones? Indeed, it is striking that both the Proto-Benue-Congo reconstructions and the Proto-Bantu ones give a relatively high number of noun classes when set against attested patterns in the daughter languages. One must wonder to what extent this reflects historical reality as opposed to being an epiphenomenon of a reconstruction methodology which might cause a proto-language to "accrete" features over the course of comparative analysis. This is not to say

---

[10] See Good (2017) for an overview of areal linguistic patterns in Niger-Congo.

that reduction of noun class systems within East Benue-Congo is not a historically real process, as evidenced by languages showing highly reduced systems or entirely lacking in functioning systems discussed above. Rather, it is to suggest that one must be cautious when assuming that a relatively robust attested noun class system is necessarily reduced because it may lack some distinctions reconstructed for some earlier historical stage.

In any event, given the extensive body of work in linguistics on language contact and linguistic areas since the time of de Wolf (1971), a fruitful direction for near-term studies of high-level patterns of change in Benue-Congo noun class systems would be to explore their development in terms of areal linguistic patterns in Africa, in particular looking for evidence of their differential development in distinctive cultural regions where Benue-Congo languages are found. Once the descriptive picture is better established in this regard, the stage would be set for an examination of genealogical patterns which takes areal insights appropriately into account.

3 Prefixal and suffixal morphology

A general puzzle for the reconstruction of noun class systems in Niger-Congo is the fact that languages of the family do not consistently show only noun class prefixes, but can also show noun class suffixes, or a complex mix of prefixes and suffixes (see, among others, Hoffmann (1967: 252–254), de Wolf (1971: 180–182), Welmers (1971: 15), Greenberg (1977; 1978), Childs (1983), Williamson (1989: 31–37), and Dimmendaal (2001: 378–381)). While this is an issue that is general to Niger-Congo rather than being specific to East Benue-Congo, East Benue-Congo is also implicated given that one finds both prefixing and suffixing patterns in the family. Prefixing patterns unquestionably dominate (even if we were to exclude the mostly exclusively prefixing systems of the Bantu languages), and this is presumably why Proto-Benue-Congo has been reconstructed as prefixing in its noun class system. However, this does not mean that the presence of suffixing patterns does not raise significant questions for the reconstruction of the properties of the noun class system on the whole nor that suffixing noun class marking, or even circumfixal class marking (as suggested by Welmers (1973: 205–210)) – whether throughout the system or only in part of it – should not be considered a possibility for Proto-Benue-Congo.[11]

---

[11]Resolving this issue would be more straightforward if East Benue-Congo subgrouping were more secure so that work could reference clear-cut instances of innovation rather than relying on a "majority-rules" approach for linguistic reconstruction.

Of particular interest are languages where the presence of nominal prefixes or suffixes is dependent on a noun's morphosyntactic context. For instance, in the Kainji language C'lela (Dakarkari), nouns in citation forms will show a prefix, as in *d-hyí* 'head', whereas this prefix is not present when the noun is followed by a concordial element, such as a demonstrative, as in *hyí də́hnà* 'this head'. (For this noun, the relevant noun class is associated with a *d*, whether on the noun itself or the demonstrative (Hoffmann 1967: 247)). While the C'lela pattern is a minority one within East Benue-Congo, it is not unique. Similar patterns are seen, for instance, in the Grassfields Bantu language Aghem (Hyman 1979: 56–58).[12] In the Cross River language Efik one sees the "reverse" of this pattern, where a limited set of nouns, when modified by adjectives, appear with a prefix that is not found in isolating forms (Faraclas (1986: 45), citing Cook (1969: 179–181)).

As pointed out at least as early as Hoffmann (1967: 253) (see Dimmendaal (2001: 380) for a recent overview), the nature of Niger-Congo noun class systems, where concordial elements such as demonstratives can frequently be found adjacent to a noun, opens up possibilities for the reanalysis of the concordant segments as coding class on the noun itself. Thus, when one considers a phrase like the C'lela expression *hyí də́hnà* 'this head', just cited above, a resegmentation of the phrase along the lines of *hyíd ə́hnà* could, in principle, result in a noun coded for its class suffixally. This sort of resegmentation would presumably be more likely in contexts where prefixes are not present on the noun since, otherwise, it would result in multiple exponence of class on nouns via a less typical circumfixal structure. Therefore, it would seem to make sense to see patterns of prefix absence and the presence class suffixes as potentially interrelated phenomena. At the same time, it must be admitted that there are cases where the distribution of prefixing and suffixing patterns does not point in any clear direction regarding their historical relationship. This is seen, for instance, in the Mambiloid language Vute, where nouns can appear with both prefixing and suffixing elements that are relatable to Proto-Benue-Congo noun class markers but which do not appear to interact with each other (Thwing 1987: 69–71) (see also Blench (1993: 111–112) for further discussion of suffixing class markers in Mambiloid).[13]

---

[12] Apparent dropping of prefixes along the lines of what is seen in languages such as C'lela and Aghem is, to the best of my knowledge, essentially unreported for Bantu languages with the exception of what is described for Sesotho in Demuth et al. (2009).

[13] For instance, while some nouns are marked with prefixes, plurals are generally formed via suffixation, and it appears from Thwing's (1987) description that the addition of a suffix to a noun to code plurality is not associated with the loss of a prefix historically associated with singular coding.

2 East Benue-Congo noun classes, with a focus on morphological behavior

In this context, it is worth revisiting a tendency in the literature to view cases such as C'lela prefix absence as involving dropping of the prefix (see, e.g., Hoffmann (1967: 246) or Hyman (1979: 27)). This is presumably based on an intuition that the citation forms of nouns are in some sense more morphologically "basic" than modified forms. However, there is no logical reason why prefixed forms could not be considered to be augmented with a prefix treated as coding a category such as "lack of modification". And, in fact, such an analysis becomes more plausible given the well-known presence of a formative commonly referred to as an *augment* (or *pre-prefix*) in many Bantu languages (see Katamba (2003: 107–108) for an overview discussion, de Blois (1970) for a detailed survey, and Williamson (1993) for consideration of the augment in the context of Benue-Congo reconstruction). This element immediately precedes the class prefix on nouns and often has a form that copies the prefix in whole or part. It is difficult to assign it a unique, general function. Its appearance can be determined by apparent referential factors (e.g., definiteness) but can also exhibit a degree of sensitivity to grammatical control (e.g., being sensitive to whether or not a verb is negated) (see, e.g., Hyman & Katamba (1993) for a detailed investigation of the functions of the augment in Ganda).[14]

The general prevalence of the marked nominative language type in Africa is also relevant here (see König 2006, 2008: 138–203). In effect, forms in languages of this type associated with more "nominative" domains (such as subjects) are morphologically more complex than forms used in more "accusative" domains, are found in a more functionally restricted range of environments, or show both classes of properties. This suggests, in general, that we should be wary of assuming that classificatory heuristics from European languages (such as "citation is the same as basic") will naturally carry over into East Benue-Congo languages. Furthermore, as discussed in Creissels (2009), while it has not yet been widely explored, one seems to find relatively frequently in Africa cases of head-marking in noun phrases where what is coded is that the head is associated with some dependent in its phrase. This indicates that we may want to view cases of apparent prefix dropping in a language like C'lela not as one noun form being derived from another but, rather, as evincing a kind of inflectional nominal paradigm of some kind, where each form of the noun is actively coding a specific morphosyntactic category with respect to its relationship to a larger syntactic construction.

---

[14]Within the East Benue-Congo area, Boum (1980: 74–75) describes a similar pattern of double prefixation in two languages of the Menchum subgroup of Grassfields Bantu where nouns in certain classes show evidence of being coded with two prefixes in citation forms, with the initial one of these not appearing in locative and possessive contexts (see also Watters (2003: 241) and Hyman (2005)).

One factor that may have obscured this as a potential analysis is the fact that the functional range of such paradigmatic oppositions does not map neatly onto categories familiar from analyses of European languages, such as definiteness or case.[15] Another reason that such an analysis has presumably not been actively proposed is that variable prefix presence has not been reported in most East Benue-Congo languages (especially if we include Narrow Bantu languages in this category), meaning that an abstract analysis of this kind would not be motivated by direct evidence in the majority of cases.[16] While these remarks pertain more directly to synchronic analysis than historical concerns, a more accurate understanding of these synchronic systems can play an important role in reconstructing a Proto-Benue-Congo noun class system that is more reflective of the actual morphosyntax of the East Benue-Congo parent language.

When we come back to consideration of these patterns in the broader Benue-Congo picture, the question arises as to whether or not we should view the Proto-Benue-Congo system, as depicted in Table 1, as relatively well-behaved, adhering to a Bantu-like canon (even if there are fewer overall classes) where noun classes are almost exclusively coded with some prefix, excluding narrow and systematic exceptions of the sort associated, for instance, with Bantu Class 1a (see §1). Alternatively, we might want to consider what features of Proto-Benue-Congo could have resulted in relatively distant languages such as C'lela and Aghem (one spoken in northwest Nigeria and the other in northwest Cameroon) to have developed in similar directions with respect to alternations between prefixed and non-prefixed nouns. There has not been any general survey on patterns of prefix absence to the best of my knowledge, and, if anything, it is probably underreported since it is not a pattern necessarily easily detected in basic elicitation, such as when collecting wordlists. It is also important in this regard to consider the relatively well attested pattern where an East Benue-Congo language may be primarily prefixing but also show some suffixal or circumfixal noun class marking (whether appearing on nouns or as concords). Such patterns were recognized

---

[15]To pick one well-described example, Schadeberg's (1986) description of tonal cases in the Bantu language Umbundu includes the category of Common Case which covers such functions as subject, second complement of ditransitive verb, object of a negative verb, and object of a progressive verb, among others (Schadeberg 1986: 433–437).

[16]I am thankful to John Watters for the latter observation. Whether the analysis of prefixes as being part of some kind of inflectional nominal paradigm of the sort just suggested should be applied to all East Benue-Congo languages with productive noun classes or just that subset showing variable prefix presence is a question of synchronic analysis that lies outside the scope of the present chapter.

2 East Benue-Congo noun classes, with a focus on morphological behavior

by de Wolf (1971: 181), and new examples have since been attested, as seen in, for example, the overview of the noun class systems of Naki (Mekaf), Mungbam (Missong), and Noni (all non-Grassfields Bantu Bantoid languages spoken in the north of the Grassfields area) as presented in Hombert (1980: 87–88).

De Wolf (1971: 182) appears to view the issue of understanding the suffixing patterns through a dichotomous lens where Proto-Benue-Congo would be viewed as either prefixing *or* suffixing. Given such a choice, it seems likely that Proto-Benue-Congo was much closer to a prefixing prototype than a suffixing one. But, we might still consider whether Proto-Benue-Congo may have allowed for prefixes on nouns to be dropped in certain contexts, thereby creating favorable conditions for the rise of suffixing class patterns in some cases. In other words, as part of the reconstruction of the noun class *system* of Proto-Benue-Congo, we should bear in mind that its properties clearly resulted in the potential for its daughter languages to develop suffixal class-marking patterns and consider what sort of system would have been likely to have promoted such developments. This remains an important open area of research on comparative East Benue-Congo noun class systems.

A final point worth raising in this regard is the possibility for reconstructing word order within the noun phrase in Proto-Benue-Congo. I am not aware of this topic having received much attention, perhaps because of the relative homogeneity of East Benue-Congo languages in key domains, such as a strong tendency towards head-initial structures, resulting in patterns such as Noun-Demonstrative order being well-attested (see, e.g., Dryer (2013)). However, there are cases reported of alternative orders being possible in specific contexts (for instance to encode emphasis). In such cases, one may find Demonstrative-Noun ordering in languages where the reverse order generally predominates. For example, Van de Velde (2005) discusses this in some Bantu languages, and Watters (1981: 254–255) and Lovegren (2013: 182) give attestations of this in Bantoid languages (see also Watters 2003: 248). This seems likely to be a relatively common pattern, though I am not aware of any systematic study of it. To the extent that noun phrases in Proto-Benue-Congo probably tended to be head-initial, grammaticalization processes could be expected to more often create innovative suffixal class-marking patterns along the lines of what was outlined for C'lela above. However, less common word order patterns where a concordial element such as a demonstrative may have preceded the noun could allow for new prefixal class marking to develop, perhaps helping us understand the rise of, for instance, the pre-

Jeff Good

prefixing augments found in Bantu languages, just discussed (see also Meeussen 1967: 99).[17]

4 Domains of concord

As discussed in §2, Bantu languages are generally taken to be conservative with respect to maintenance of the general structure of the Proto-Benue-Congo noun class system, though they may have innovated certain classes. A comparison between Bantu and the rest of East Benue-Congo is also relevant in this regard with respect to the domains where noun class concord is found. That there must have been some kind of agreement relation between head nouns and certain classes of associated elements is without question. However, what is not fully resolved is which grammatical classes those elements would have belonged to.

de Wolf (1971: 182–185) gives an overview of where concord was found in the languages he examined most carefully in his study, providing an exceptionally fine-grained list of environments where it was attested. Generalizing over his categories, throughout the family as a whole, the following domains are relevant: (i) nominal dependents, including demonstratives, adjectival elements (to the extent that they are present), numerals, possessive pronouns, and modifying interrogatives, (ii) verbs and verb-like elements (e.g., copulas), where subject concord is often found (to be discussed further below), (iii) pronouns of various kinds, and in particular anaphoric pronouns, where a prominent feature of many East Benue-Congo concord systems is a large class of third-person pronouns agreeing with the class of their referent, and (iv) associative markers and relativizers, which can agree with the noun preceding them.[18] While not a do-

---

[17] This possibility raises broader questions about the role of augmentation in accounting for the shape of noun class prefixes in East Benue-Congo languages, whether in the form of the so-called augment, just discussed above, or some other kind of morpheme which would result in something comparable to the augment in terms of form, if not necessarily function (see, e.g., Hyman (2005: 337)). Dimmendaal (2001: 381–382) discusses evidence suggesting that the presence of the augment is quite old within Niger-Congo (see also Williamson (1993)). This would open up the possibility for it to have played a role in shaping noun class prefixes throughout East Benue-Congo via parallel developments in different branches. The details of such processes, at this stage, remain somewhat speculative.

[18] The associative marker and relativizer are possibly analyzable as nominal dependents, therefore belonging to class (i) above, though in their role as connective elements between syntactic constituents, their dependency relationships are not as obvious as for elements such as demonstratives and adjectives, which is why they are given their own category here.

2 East Benue-Congo noun classes, with a focus on morphological behavior

main of concord, per se, to this we might also add another domain of marking: (v) nouns themselves, specifically when they show overt marking of their class via some sort of affixal coding. The logic for adding this final class is that, from the perspective of a formal reconstruction of the properties of the Proto-Benue-Congo noun class system, the presence/absence of class marking on nouns can vary more or less along the same lines as its presence/absence in more properly syntactic domains in the daughter languages.

No more thorough follow-up study of the domains of concord at the level of East Benue-Congo appears to have been undertaken, and this would seem to be an area where a more detailed survey would lead to worthwhile results, perhaps leading to robust generalizations regarding where concord is more likely to be maintained or lost. Still, even a cursory examination of the results in de Wolf (1971: 184) shows that absolute patterns are unlikely to be uncovered, given that a wide range of logical possibilities for combinations of class coding across domains are attested. Of particular relevance for purposes of reconstruction is work such as that of Demuth et al. (1986: 467), who propose that class coding on concordial forms is more resistant to loss as a result of language change than nominal class coding. Dimmendaal (2001: 381) further puts forth the idea that, when coding on nouns survives where agreement is lost, this can be explained as the effect of contact. Good (2012) presents a more equivocal picture about the relative historical stability of these two types of noun class marking. However, if more systematic studies revealed the robustness of concord as a significant tendency, it would suggest that future work on reconstruction of the noun class system of Proto-Benue-Congo should privilege evidence from patterns of agreement over class marking on nouns as more likely to represent archaic features. A useful step forward for further examination of this issue would be to arrive at a more detailed understanding of areal patterns of nominal class coding and class concord, including consideration of languages where only remnant patterns are found in order to clarify if any apparent typological generalizations may be better understood as contact effects.

Even if we accept that noun classes are more robustly coded via patterns of agreement than via nominal prefixes, there is still the question of which precise domains would have shown agreement in Proto-Benue-Congo. In some cases, such as demonstratives, third-person pronouns (see Hyman, Chapter 6, this volume, on third-person pronouns in Grassfields), and possessive pronouns, concord is found in a sufficiently diverse range of the family's languages (see, e.g., de

Wolf (1971: 184)) that it seems necessary to reconstruct it for the proto-language given that concord has to be reconstructed somewhere in the system.[19] Nominal prefixes are comparable in this regard, since the alternative would be to posit an improbably massive number of parallel processes of grammaticalization resulting in nominal prefixes in languages throughout the family.

At the same time, if we assume Proto-Benue-Congo had a fairly transparent noun class system in some domains of its grammar, it is also clear that processes of analogical extension and grammaticalization could have served to extend noun classes to domains where they might not have been found in the proto-language. Here, data from Bantu languages becomes useful simply by virtue of their degree of morphological elaboration and the fact that their comparative linguistics is relatively well understood. Güldemann (2008a: 386), for instance, gives a reconstruction of a grammaticalization pathway for a Proto-Bantu element *-ti, associated with quotative marking (Guthrie 1970: 105), where it began as an uninflecting manner-marking element (perhaps comparable to English *like*) but later developed verbal properties. One of these properties is an ability to appear with subject concord marking, as generally found for Bantu verbs. Another such example involves a complementizer in the Bantu language Lwena, which shows suffixal concord with the subject of its matrix clause (see Güldemann (2008a: 453), drawing on the description of Horton (1949: 181–182)). (Idiatov (2010: 832–836) offers more general discussion of this kind of agreement.) It may be possible to reconstruct some degree of subject concord for *-ti in Proto-Bantu. However, it is hard to consider the subject coding found in Lwena complementizers as representing anything other than an innovation in Bantu terms for this part of speech given its suffixing form. Thus, contrary to the implications of the drift metaphor (see §2), we must admit the possibility that Proto-Benue-Congo may have exhibited concord in more limited domains than what is found in the daughter languages, with its appearance in other domains due to later changes. That is, morphological coding of noun classes should not automatically be understood to represent the conservative situation. Working out the details, however, will have to await further, targeted study.

A comparatively controversial case of a concord domain in this regard involves subject coding on the verb by means of a prefix. Güldemann (2011: 123–129) (see

---

[19] See Kießling (2013) for discussion of attested numeral classifier systems in Niger-Congo languages, including many East Benue-Congo languages, which can potentially serve as models for the initial development of the Niger-Congo noun class system at some ancient stage of the language. By the time we can sensibly speak of Proto-Benue-Congo, however, it seems necessary to assume that a strongly grammaticalized noun class system was already present.

also Güldemann (2003: 184–185)), for instance, argues that the pattern of subject concord (as well as object concord) on the verb seen in Bantu languages should be historically interpreted not as evidence for the historical presence of such an agreement pattern in a higher-level grouping such as East Benue-Congo but, rather, as the result of a comparatively recent process of grammaticalization. Specifically, an S-Aux-O-V syntagm provided the seeds for the development of a verbal structure which is prefixally inflected for subject concord and tense-mood-aspect marking, as well as object marking.[20] (See Güldemann (2007) for general discussion of such preverbal object structures in Benue-Congo.) Hyman (2011: 21–40), by contrast, provides evidence supporting a treatment of prefixal inflection on verbs in Niger-Congo (and, by extension, East Benue-Congo as having a comparatively old time depth. While he does not propose specific reconstructions regarding subject concords, there is a clear implication that he believes that the possibility that they were present at a genealogical level well above Narrow Bantu should be seriously considered.

While Güldemann (2011) is focused on Narrow Bantu, the core of his argument could apply just as well to East Benue-Congo languages showing phonologically fused instances of subject marking that strongly suggest a prefixal analysis is appropriate, such as the Cross River language Eleme (Bond 2010). This then raises the question: Given that grammaticalization scenarios could be developed where other domains of concord (such as demonstratives or third-person pronouns, just discussed) could be viewed as arising from more analytic structures, why treat subject concord differently? In this case, significant considerations would seem to be as follows: On the one hand, concord must be reconstructed in some domains unless we set aside the idea that it is one of the defining historical features of East Benue-Congo, and the pervasiveness of concord in domains such as demonstratives and third-person pronouns makes them strong candidates for having been concord domains in East Benue-Congo as mentioned above. On the other hand, there are clear constructional sources through which subject and object concord could have developed, and these are found even in contemporary languages lacking such concord. Potential sources of other kinds of concord elements are otherwise unclear (or, at least, require more speculation).

---

[20]The coding of the class of object arguments on verbs in Bantu languages is often not clearly an example of concord since the appearance of the so-called object markers is not obligatory in all languages in cases where an overt object is present, suggesting that these markers behave more along the lines of pronominals. See Bearth (2003: 124). From a diachronic perspective, this suggests their appearance may result from a comparatively recent process of entrapment of object pronouns into a univerbating verbal complex, at least when set against subject coding on the verb, which is much more strongly associated with "true" grammatical agreement.

Nevertheless, as made clear by the discussion in Hyman (2011: 29–40), there are reasons to doubt any overly simplistic story for the presence/absence of concord in any particular domain in a group as old as East Benue-Congo, and the issue of whether or not subject concord was present must be considered unresolved, even if some plausible hypotheses can be put forward. We are, thus, left with an analytical problem: There is a reasonable diachronically shallow pathway that can be proposed for the development of subject concord in East Benue-Congo languages, but there are also patterns that suggest verbal prefixal morphology may be quite old. At this point, one can merely say that East Benue-Congo might have showed subject concord but that this is a less likely concord domain than that of, say, demonstratives or third-person pronouns.

5 Concord form classes

In addition to the issue of where concord was present in Proto-Benue-Congo, there is a further concern regarding how many different series of noun class markers there might have been. The most prominent classes where this question is relevant are almost certainly those associated with the Bantu nasal classes (see Section 1), where a nasal is found in the consonantal position of CV- nominal-marking class prefixes but not in other class-marking domains such as verbal person-coding prefixes (see, e.g, Meeussen (1967: 97–98)). In the East Benue-Congo case, the possibility of different series of class markers can be seen directly in de Wolf's (1971) reconstructions of a distinctive nominal prefix series and concordial series as presented in Table 1. It seems reasonable, therefore, to assume that there were at least two distinct series of noun class markers in Proto-Benue-Congo.[21] In many cases, the markers for specific classes would be formally identical, creating alliterative patterns of concord.[22] Nevertheless, in some classes there seems to have been partial formal divergence, with Classes 1, 3, and 6, and

---

[21]This is not to say that some variety preceding Proto-Benue-Congo necessarily had two distinct series since, at least for some cases, it would be straightforward to apply internal reconstruction to de Wolf's (1971) Proto-Benue-Congo system to propose an earlier stage with less variation. (This could, in particular, involve proposing that certain class prefixes on nouns, such as Class 6, were subject to initial consonant loss which did not affect consonants in all concordial forms.)

[22]Patterns of alliterative concord are still found in noun class systems throughout East Benue-Congo, though reconstructed alliteration for any given noun class can often be lost due to historical processes such as sound change. New patterns of alliteration can also emerge in cases where new noun classes develop analogically on the basis of existing ones, as appears to be the case, for instance, for the Bantu locative classes discussed in §2.

perhaps 9 and 10, being the most likely candidates for this, as indicated in Table 1. These are also classes associated with the historically problematic nasal classes in Bantu just discussed, and, presumably, this is not a coincidence.[23]

The possibility that more than two series of concords may need to be reconstructed for Proto-Benue-Congo does not appear to have received detailed attention. It is unambiguously the case that the noun class systems of some languages of the family can only be described by implicitly assuming more than two series of concord marking insofar as there is a need to present separate concord sets for a number of word classes, e.g., demonstratives, numerals, and adjective-like elements. This is seen in the overview of the Noni noun class system given in Hyman (1981: 33). Eight series of noun class markers are given for this language representing the following domains: (i) nominal prefixes, (ii) person pronominal elements, (iii) possessive marking for nouns (involving, among other things, an associative marker), (iv) possessive pronouns, (v) determiners, (vi) quantifier-like elements, (vii) adjective-like elements, and (viii) numerals, and even this extensive list abstracts away from various complications for elements within these series.

Often, it is straightforward in such cases to view a wealth of concord series as the result of various processes of change (especially sound change) impacting different kinds of concord-stem combinations, creating a system where concord variants need to be explicitly listed synchronically but which can be easily seen as deriving from a simpler historical system. For instance, Noni Class 4 forms all contain a palatal consonantal element, but this is realized as a modification to a stem-initial consonant in some cases rather than as a true prefix. Thus, forms for the word 'new' in Noni are based on a stem -fɛ and can appear with an unambiguous prefix as in the Class 2 form bɔfɛ or with a modified consonant in the Class 4 form as fiɛ (Hyman 1981: 26). This Class 4 form can be set against the Class 4 word for 'this' yin (based on a stem with a shape of -Vn), where a full palatal consonant is found (Hyman 1981: 23). There is, however, no reason to view this as evidence for the reconstruction of a plain and mutating series of Class 4 concords in Proto-Benue-Congo given that the overall pattern is one where a full palatal consonant is found before agreeing stems beginning with a vowel and a consonant modified with palatalization is found for stems beginning with a consonant. This simply suggests a sound change where a former segmental

---

[23] Class 4 is also such a class, not listed here, but this should be understood as an artifact of the presentation scheme where I associated Bantu class numbers with de Wolf's (1971) reconstructions in a way that collapsed a possible Class 4/Class 10 distinction on formal grounds. See also §6.

prefix with a palatal quality (presumably along the lines of *i*) before consonantal stems metathesized and fused with the following consonant, while appearing as a palatal glide before a vowel. Indeed, this change seems to be an instance of a localized areal pattern found in the part of the Cameroonian Grassfields where Noni is spoken, as discussed in Kießling (2010).

Nevertheless, the fact that we can explain some of the attested complications in series of concords as the result of straightforward processes of sound change does not mean that we should not also consider the possibility that Proto-Benue-Congo had more than two series or that, in some cases, morphophonological processes had been applied to its concord system which would have created some forms that were partly unpredictable based purely on knowledge of the general form of a concord prefix and the stem it attached to. I am not aware of specific work having been done on this question, however, and it must remain an open issue for further research.

6 Noun class identity and class pairing consistency

Implicit in much of the discussion on noun classes in Proto-Benue-Congo is the idea that a noun class is a relatively stable entity, associated with a consistent form, even if subject to different patterns of change (e.g., sound change or analogical change). Moreover, it is easy to assume that the singular-plural pairings may be more stable than they are in reality. To be sure, there are pockets of stability. For instance, while I am not aware of a study systematically verifying this, the Class 1/2 pairing seems robust both in terms of the fact that each of its component classes is well attested and the fact that the pairing itself is well-attested for certain nouns referring to humans. This is presumably explainable by reference to the semantic cohesiveness of a subclass of Class 1/2 nouns, their likely frequency of use, and the general salience of the category *human*.

However, complications to this simplified picture are not hard to find. The clearest of these is a general lack of rigidity in singular-plural pairings. This can be seen in de Wolf's (1971) reconstructions, as schematized in Table 1, where, for instance, he was unable to propose a consistent singular for Class 13, indicating it as functioning as a plural for either Class 3 or Class 12. It is important to bear in mind in this context that patterns of singular-plural pairing are seen as (at least partly) diagnostic in some descriptions of the presence of a distinct class itself. This is found, for example, in the reconstruction of distinct Classes 4 and 5 for Western Grassfields Bantu in Hyman (1980b: 183), which are formally identical but differentiated by virtue of their status as coding singular versus plural and associated patterns of pairing. It is also seen in a divergence in the schematization of de Wolf's (1971) reconstructions given in Table 1 and the summary presented in Williamson (1989: 38–39), where she gives a distinct Class 4, which is not seen here, alongside a formally identical Class 10. de Wolf (1971: 52) does not appear to make a statement on the relationship of the relevant Proto-Bantu classes associated with these numbers to his class given with form *í. These two classes are reconstructed as formally distinct in Proto-Bantu, and either could be historically connected to a class associated with *í in Proto-Benue-Congo.

In fact, de Wolf (1971) proposes pairings consistent with the presence of something like the Class 3/4 pairing in Proto-Benue-Congo, as well as the Class 9/10 pairing given in Table 1. This leaves open the question as to whether we should view this as evidence for a distinct Class 4 in Proto-Benue-Congo or whether we should treat the plurals of the relevant words as involving something like a Class 3/10 pairing, under the assumption that there is just one plural class with a form associated with *í. (Class 10 is picked over Class 4 in this case due to the fact that there is greater evidence for reconstructing a Class 9/10 pairing than a Class 3/4 one.) Obviously, the criteria one uses as diagnostic for a distinct noun class can have a significant outcome on the apparent consistency (or inconsistency) of singular/plural pairings, and the resolution of cases like these requires a less than canonical system either by proposing multiple homophonous classes with simpler pairings or less consistent patterns of pairing with fewer classes. The "ideal" analysis is probably more a matter for morphological theory than historical reconstruction. From the latter perspective, of greater interest here, the most important point to bear in mind is that the reconstructed noun class system for Proto-Benue-Congo almost certainly had non-canonical pairing structure for at least some of its classes.

It may also be the case that some of the apparent variability in class pairings could be due to the presence of "imperialistic" classes (see Gerhardt (1994: 167)) within East Benue-Congo languages, variants of which were perhaps even found in Proto-Benue-Congo itself.[24] These are classes which, for whatever reason, tend to historically "absorb" nouns from other classes. Based on de Wolf (1971), a possible candidate for such a noun class in Proto-Benue-Congo may be the *í class (here labelled Class 10), due to its ability to serve as a plural for various sin-

---

[24]In the formulation of Gerhardt (1994: 167), an imperialistic class would not only be a generally "open" class but would also be the typical class for the incorporation of loanwords and be morphophonologically "less marked". While these patterns may be generally correlated for apparently imperialistic classes, Lovegren (2013: 137) notes the existence of a plural class which appears to draw in plural nouns from other classes despite being morphophonologically "marked" by virtue of employing circumfixal class encoding on the noun.

gular classes as indicated in Table 1. To come to a better understanding of these patterns, detailed studies of noun class distribution across dialects and low-level language clusters would be useful. These would give us some measure of the rate and degree to which noun class pairings can shift within languages of the family. Watters (1981: 306–308) provides a relevant example in his description of a clinal shift in the distribution of nouns within a Class 5/8 pairing versus a Class 5/6 pairing, where the former pairing loses ground to the latter as one moves west and south within the area associated with the Bantoid language Ejagham.

Other languages suggest additional complications that would be difficult to reliably reconstruct to Proto-Benue-Congo itself but whose presence within it cannot be ruled out and which certainly raise problems when using the comparative method to reconstruct the proto-language. These problems center around the fact that the formal structure of the East Benue-Congo noun class prefixes, consisting of just CV- or V- shapes and typically making use of only a limited range of a language's available vowel contrasts, makes them relatively prone to different types of sub-morphemic reanalysis and analogical contamination, where the form of one class is influenced by that of another.

Consider, for instance, patterns of prefix reduction found in the Abar variety of the Bantoid language Mungbam as seen in Table 2 (Lovegren 2013: 136). An optional process applies to noun class prefixes in this variety wherein they lose their initial consonant. In cases where the vowel of the CV form of the prefix is ə, the reduced prefix shows the vowel a. From the standpoint of historical sound change, this pattern of consonant loss is not obviously remarkable, but, when looked at in light of the overall noun class system of the variety, it is striking that the reduced prefixes are formally identical to non-reduced prefixes associated with other classes. For instance, four non-reduced noun classes posited for this variety show a prefix with a segmental form of *i* (specifically, Classes 4, 5, and 10) and two show a prefix with a segmental form of *u* (specifically Classes 1 and 3), with additional tonal complications in some cases (Lovegren 2013: 111). As can be seen in Table 2, three of the reduced prefixes have a segmental shape of *i* as well and one shows an *u*, thus adding additional surface homophony to the system.

Patterns like those in Table 2 would clearly allow for a reanalysis of the structure of CV- prefixes as being morphologically complex, consisting of something along the lines of C-V-, and thus opening the door to various morphological developments and complications that would otherwise be unexpected. For instance, in the Munken variety of the same language, one can find apparent instances of "mixed" agreement, such as those presented in (1). The word for 'day', which most frequently is seen in the Class 14 form *būtù*, here, shows a form that would nor-

2 East Benue-Congo noun classes, with a focus on morphological behavior

Table 2: Prefix reduction in the Abar variety of Mungbam

CLASS	FULL FORM	REDUCED FORM	GLOSS
6	mɔ́-ŋkǎn	á-ŋkǎn	'hand'
6a	mɔ̄-mbǎlɔ	ā-mbǎlɔ	'oil'
13	kí-lǎm	í-lǎm	'tongue'
8	bí-ɲǔ	í-ɲǔ	'thing'
12	kə̀-jì	à-jì	'god'
14	bú-tsě	ú-tsě	'witchcraft'
19	çí-bûs	í-bûs	'cat'

mally be associated with Class 3. Moreover, this apparent Class 3 marking of the form is found not only on the noun itself but also on the following demonstrative modifier *wə́n*. However, the following word *bū*, the object of a postposition, shows the expected Class 14 form, resulting in an inconsistent class coding pattern. The most straightforward interpretation of this pattern is to see it as resulting from a kind of "confusion" of classes triggered by their formal similarities and facilitated by processes of sound change, such as initial consonant loss, that would result in surface homophony of the sort just dicussed above for the Abar variety of this language.

(1) À humiliation ūtù wə́n bū   ŋɔ̄n.
    DS humiliation 3.day 3.DEM 14.OBJ LOC
    "There is humility on this day."

While this sort of class confusion and contamination was not likely to have been a feature of Proto-Benue-Congo itself, its noun class system clearly provided the seeds for it. This means, when attempting to reconstruct the system from attested data, one must consider the possibility that the daughter languages may have been impacted not only by comparatively regular processes, such as sound change or typical kinds of analogical extension, but also by more complex forms of analogical change, such as those triggered by sub-morphemic analysis.

Jeff Good

7 Towards a reconstruction of the noun class *system*

An important theme of this chapter has been that we should consider the problem of reconstruction of the Proto-Benue-Congo noun classes not simply as an exercise in arriving at a set of forms which can be associated with various class markers but, rather, in terms of the reconstruction of an entire noun class system, paying attention, in particular, to the morphosyntactic properties of the system, such as whether class marking on nouns may have ever been optional in Proto-Benue-Congo (see Section 3) or how many distinct series of concords may have been present (see Section 5), among other questions. The reason for doing this is, on the one hand, the fact that even in the absence of a resolution on the shapes of specific forms, progress might still be made with respect to the reconstruction of these more abstract properties of the proto-system. On the other hand, a better understanding of these properties is ultimately likely to yield significant insight into why attested East Benue-Congo noun class systems are the way they are, even at the formal level.

Moreover, if there is a general consideration that emerges from this overview, it is that we should probably not assume the Proto-Benue-Congo noun class behaved as regularly as tabular presentations such as the one in Table 1 might be taken to imply. We can expect there to have been opacity in the principles of class assignment, variability in singular/plural pairings, differences in concord realization across various morphosyntactic constructions, and so on. Whether some of these "irregularities" should be modeled as variability in the usage of particular speakers or representative of dialect diversity among whatever community we can identify with Proto-Benue-Congo may not prove completely reconstructible, though reconstructing significant dialect diversity would be completely reasonable given that, within the East Benue-Congo area, salient dialect diversity within speaker communities seems to be the norm. Furthermore, while de Wolf (1971) does not appear to make an explicit statement about this, it is worth bearing in mind that an examination of the specific historical scenarios relating his Proto-Benue-Congo reconstructions to the noun class systems of his sample languages shows that they are not reducible to simple statements of sound change or clear-cut analogical changes. Rather, one has the impression of systems often being generally maintained while combinations of regular, semi-regular, and apparently irregular changes impact them.

I would like to close by briefly considering how we might move forward in our efforts to understand the nature of the Proto-Benue-Congo noun class system. As mentioned in §1, if the goal is to improve on the efforts begun by de

Wolf (1971), then the most natural step would involve reconstructing the noun class systems of low-level subgroups and working upwards in systematic fashion.[25] Our dataset has improved to a point where quick progress could be made for many such groups, even if reconstructing higher-level positions in the tree might still be somewhat elusive. If the goal is more generally historical in nature, namely using language as a means to understand Niger-Congo prehistory, then this approach is probably too limited, and increased knowledge of the structural and typological characteristics of the system is likely to be more worthwhile, especially since these are likely better windows into patterns of language contact and areal influence than purely formal reconstructions. This survey has emphasized the latter approach over the former. On the one hand, this should be viewed as reflecting changing priorities in the field since de Wolf (1971), especially given the explosion of work on language contact phenomena since the publication of Thomason & Kaufman (1988). On the other hand, it also follows a general expository goal here of laying out a "bigger picture" view of possible directions for future work on East Benue-Congo noun class systems, rather than presupposing that one way forward is to be inherently preferred over another.

Acknowledgements

I would like to thank Larry Hyman, John Watters, and an anonymous reviewer for feedback on a draft of this paper. Portions of the research underlying this proposal were supported by U.S. National Science Foundation award number BCS-1360763.

References

Bearth, Thomas. 2003. Syntax. In Derek Nurse & Gérard Philippson (eds.), *The Bantu languages*, 121–142. London: Routledge.

Blench, Roger M. 1993. An outline classification of the Mambiloid languages. *Journal of West African Languages* 23. 105–118.

Bond, Oliver. 2010. Intra-paradigmatic variation in Eleme verbal agreement. *Studies in Language* 34. 1–35.

---

[25]Bruce Connell (personal communication) suggests that the available data on Upper Cross, for example, should now make it quite feasible to reconstruct its noun class system. (See Dimmendaal (1978: 190–195) for initial work in this direction.)

Boum, Marie Anne. 1980. Le groupe menchum: Morphologie nominale. In Larry M. Hyman (ed.), *Noun classes in the Grassfields Bantu borderland* (Southern California Occasional Papers in Linguistics 8), 73–82. Los Angeles: Department of Linguistics, University of Southern California. http://gsil.sc-ling.org/pubs/SCOPILS_6_7_8_9/Noun_classes_in_the_grassfields_bantu_borderland.pdf.

Childs, G. Tucker. 1983. Noun class affix renewal in Southern West Atlantic. In Jonathan D. Kaye, Hilda J. Koopman, Dominique Sportiche & André Dugas (eds.), *Current approaches to African linguistics*, vol. 2, 17–29. Dordrecht: Foris.

Clements, George N. & Annie Rialland. 2008. Africa as a phonological area. In Bernd Heine & Derek Nurse (eds.), *A linguistic geography of Africa*, 36–85. Cambridge: CUP.

Connell, Bruce. 1987. Noun classification in Lower Cross. *Journal of West African Languages* 17. 110–125.

Cook, Thomas L. 1969. *The pronunciation of Efik for speakers of English*. Bloomington, IN: African Studies Program & Intensive Language Training Center, Indiana University.

Creissels, Denis. 2009. The construct form of nouns in African languages. In Peter K. Austin, Oliver Bond, Monik Charette, David Nathan & Peter Sells (eds.), *Proceedings of Conference on Language Documentation and Linguistic Theory 2*, 73–82. London: SOAS.

de Blois, Kees F. 1970. The augment in the Bantu languages. *Africana Linguistica* 4. 85–165.

de Wolf, Paul P. 1971. *The noun class system of Proto-Benue-Congo*. The Hague: Mouton.

Demuth, Katherine, Nicholas G. Faraclas & Lynell Marchese. 1986. Niger-Congo noun class and agreement systems in language acquisition and historical change. In Colette G. Craig (ed.), *Noun classes and categorization*, 453–471. Amsterdam: Benjamins.

Demuth, Katherine, 'Malillo Machobane & Francina Moloi. 2009. Learning how to license null noun-class prefixes in Sesotho. *Language* 85. 865–883.

Di Carlo, Pierpaolo & Jeff Good. 2014. What are we trying to preserve? Diversity, change, and ideology at the edge of the Cameroonian Grassfields. In Peter K. Austin & Julia Sallabank (eds.), *Endangered languages: Beliefs and ideologies in language documentation and revitalization*, 229–262. Oxford: OUP.

Dimmendaal, Gerrit J. 1978. *The consonants of Proto-Upper Cross and their implications for the classification of Upper Cross languages*. Leiden: Leiden University Doctoral dissertation.

Dimmendaal, Gerrit J. 2001. Areal diffusion versus genetic inheritance: An African perspective. In Alexandra Y. Aikhenvald & R. M. W. Dixon (eds.), *Areal diffusion and genetic inheritance: Problems in comparative linguistics*, 359–392. Oxford: OUP.

Dryer, Matthew S. 2013. Order of demonstrative and noun. In Matthew S. Dryer & Martin Haspelmath (eds.), *The World Atlas of Language Structures online*. Leipzig: Max Planck Institute for Evolutionary Anthropology. http://wals.info/chapter/88.

Dunn, Ernest F. 1968. *An introduction to Bini*. East Lansing, MI: African Studies Center, Michigan State University.

Faraclas, Nicholas G. 1986. Cross River as a model for the evolution of Benue-Congo nominal class/concord systems. *Studies in African Linguistics* 17. 39–54.

Gerhardt, Ludwig. 1994. Western Plateau as a model for the development of Benue-Congo noun-class system. *Afrika und Übersee* 77. 161–176.

Good, Jeff. 2012. How to become a "Kwa" noun. *Morphology* 22. 294–335.

Good, Jeff. 2017. Niger-Congo languages. In Raymond Hickey (ed.), *The Cambridge handbook of areal linguistics*, 471–499. Cambridge: CUP.

Green, M. M. & Rev. G. E. Igwe. 1963. *A descriptive grammar of Igbo*. Berlin: Akademie-Verlag.

Greenberg, Joseph H. 1966. *The languages of Africa*. The Hague: Mouton (also *International Journal of American Linguistics* 29(1) part 2).

Greenberg, Joseph H. 1977. Niger-Congo noun class markers: Prefixes, suffixes, both or neither. *Studies in African Linguistics* Supplement 7. 97–106.

Greenberg, Joseph H. 1978. How does a language acquire gender markers? In Joseph H. Greenberg (ed.), *Universals of human language*, vol. 3: Word structure, 47–82. Stanford: Stanford University Press.

Grégoire, Claire. 1983. Quelques hypothèses comparatives sur les locatifs dans les langues bantoues du Cameroun. *Journal of West African Languages* 13. 139–164.

Güldemann, Tom. 2003. Grammaticalization. In Derek Nurse & Gérard Philippson (eds.), *The Bantu languages*, 182–194. London: Routledge.

Güldemann, Tom. 2007. Preverbal objects and information structure in Benue-Congo. In Enoch O. Aboh, Katharina Harmann & Malte Zimmermann (eds.), *Focus strategies in African languages: The interaction of focus and grammar in Niger-Congo and Afro-Asiatic*, 83–112. Berlin: Mouton de Gruyter.

Güldemann, Tom. 2008a. *Quotative indices in African languages: A synchronic and diachronic survey*. Berlin: Mouton de Gruyter.

Güldemann, Tom. 2008b. The Macro-Sudan belt: Towards identifying a linguistic area in northern Sub-Saharan Africa. In Bernd Heine & Derek Nurse (eds.), *A linguistic geography of Africa*, 151–185. Cambridge: CUP.

Güldemann, Tom. 2011. Proto-Bantu and Proto-Niger-Congo: Macro-areal typology and linguistic reconstruction. In Osamu Hieda, Christa König & Hirosi Nakagawa (eds.), *Geographical typology and linguistic areas: With special reference to Africa*, 109–141. Amsterdam: Benjamins.

Guthrie, Malcolm. 1970. *Comparative Bantu: An introduction to the comparative linguistics and prehistory of the Bantu languages*. Vol. 3. Farnborough: Gregg.

Guthrie, Malcolm. 1971. *Comparative Bantu: An introduction to the comparative linguistics and prehistory of the Bantu languages*. Vol. 2. Farnborough: Gregg.

Hoffmann, Carl. 1967. An outline of the Dakarkari noun class system and the relation between prefix and suffix noun class systems. In M. Gabriel Manessy (ed.), *La classification nominale dans les langues négro-africaines, Aix-en-Provence, 3–7 juillet 1967*, 237–254. Paris: CNRS.

Hombert, Jean-Marie. 1980. Noun classes of the Beboid languages. In Larry M. Hyman (ed.), *Noun classes in the Grassfields Bantu borderland* (Southern California Occasional Papers in Linguistics 8), 83–98. Los Angeles: Department of Linguistics, University of Southern California. http://gsil.sc-ling.org/pubs/SCOPILS_6_7_8_9/Noun_classes_in_the_grassfields_bantu_borderland.pdf.

Horton, A. E. 1949. *A grammar of Luvale* (Bantu grammatical archives). Johannesburg: Witwatersand Press.

Hyman, Larry M. 1979. Phonology and noun structure. In Larry M. Hyman (ed.), *Aghem grammatical structure: With special reference to noun classes, tense-aspect and focus marking* (Southern California Occasional Papers in Linguistics 7), 1–72. Los Angeles: University of Southern California Department of Linguistics. http://gsil.sc-ling.org/pubs/SCOPILS_6_7_8_9/Aghem_grammatical_structure.pdf.

Hyman, Larry M. (ed.). 1980a. *Noun classes in the Grassfields Bantu borderland* (Southern California Occasional Papers in Linguistics 8). Los Angeles: Department of Linguistics, University of Southern California. http://gsil.sc-ling.org/pubs/SCOPILS_6_7_8_9/Noun_classes_in_the_grassfields_bantu_borderland.pdf.

Hyman, Larry M. 1980b. Reflections on the nasal classes in Bantu. In Larry M. Hyman (ed.), *Noun classes in the Grassfields Bantu borderland* (Southern California Occasional Papers in Linguistics 8), 179–210. Los Angeles: Department of Linguistics, University of Southern California. http://gsil.sc-ling.org/pubs/SCOPILS_6_7_8_9/Noun_classes_in_the_grassfields_bantu_borderland.pdf.

Hyman, Larry M. 1981. *Noni grammatical structure: With special reference to verb morphology* (Southern California Occasional Papers in Linguistics 9). Los Angeles: University of Southern California Department of Linguistics. http://gsil.sc-ling.org/pubs/SCOPILS_6_7_8_9/Noni_grammatical_structure.pdf.

Hyman, Larry M. 2004. How to become a "Kwa" verb. *Journal of West African Languages* 30. 69–88.

Hyman, Larry M. 2005. Initial vowel and prefix tone in Kom: Related to the Bantu augment? In Koen Bostoen & Jacky Maniacky (eds.), *Studies in African comparative linguistics with special focus on Bantu and Mande: Essays in honour of Y. Bastin and C. Grégoire*, 313–341. Köln: Rüdiger Köppe Verlag.

Hyman, Larry M. 2011. The Macro-Sudan belt and Niger-Congo reconstruction. *Language Dynamics and Change* 1. 3–49.

Hyman, Larry M. & Francis X. Katamba. 1993. The augment in Luganda: Syntax or pragmatics? In Sam A. Mchombo (ed.), *Theoretical aspects of Bantu grammar*, 209–256. Stanford: CSLI.

Hyman, Larry M., Erhard F. K. Voeltz & Georges Tchokokam. 1970. Noun class levelling in Bamileke. *Studies in African Linguistics* 1. 185–209.

Hyman, Larry M. & Jan Voorhoeve (eds.). 1980. *L'expansion bantoue: Actes du colloque international du CNRS, Viviers (France) 4–16 avril 1977. Volume I: Les classes nominales dans le bantou des Grassfields*. Paris: SELAF.

Idiatov, Dmitry. 2010. Person–number agreement on clause linking markers in Mande. *Studies in Language* 34. 832–868.

Jungraithmayr, Herrmann. 1969. Class languages of the Tangale-Waja District (Bauchi Province, northern Nigeria). *Afrika und Übersee* 52. 161–206.

Jungraithmayr, Herrmann. 1990. Evolution or reduction? On the history of research into the development of African languages. *Aiōn: Annali del Seminario di studi del mondo classico, Sezione linguistica* 12. 19–33.

Katamba, Francis X. 2003. Bantu nominal morphology. In Derek Nurse & Gérard Philippson (eds.), *The Bantu languages*, 103–120. London: Routledge.

Kießling, Roland. 2010. Infix genesis and incipient initial consonant mutations in some lesser known Benue-Congo languages. In Armin R. Bachmann, Christliebe El Mogharbel & Katja Himstedt (eds.), *Form und Struktur in der Sprache: Festschrift für Elmar Ternes*, 188–220. Tübingen: Narr.

Kießling, Roland. 2013. On the origin of Niger-Congo nominal classification. In Ritsuko Kikusawa & Lawrence A. Reid (eds.), *Historical Linguistics 2011: Selected papers from the twentieth International Conference on Historical Linguistics, Osaka, 25–30 July 2011*, 43–65. Amsterdam: John Benjamins.

König, Christa. 2006. Marked nominative in Africa. *Studies in Language* 30. 655–732.

König, Christa. 2008. *Case in Africa*. Oxford: OUP.

Lovegren, Jesse. 2013. *Mungbam grammar*. Buffalo, NY: University at Buffalo dissertation.

Maho, Jouni Filip. 1999. *A comparative study of Bantu noun classes*. Gothenburg: Acta Universitatis Gothoburgensis.

Meeussen, A. E. 1967. Bantu grammatical reconstructions. *Africana Linguistica* 3. 79–121.

Miehe, Gudrun. 1991. *Die Präfixnasale im Benue-Congo und im Kwa: Versuch einer Widerlegung der Hypothese von der Nasalinnovation des Bantu*. Berlin: Reimer.

Ogunbọwale, P. O. 1970. *The essentials of the Yoruba language*. London: University of London Press.

Schadeberg, Thilo C. 1986. Tone cases in Umbundu. *Africana Linguistica* 10. 423–447.

Schadeberg, Thilo C. 2009. Loanwords in Swahili. In Martin Haspelmath & Uri Tadmor (eds.), *Loanwords in the world's languages: A comparative handbook*, 76–102. Berlin: De Gruyter Mouton.

Storch, Anne. 1997. Where have all the noun classes gone? A case study of Jukun. *Journal of African Languages and Linguistics* 18. 157–170.

Thomas, John Paul. 1992. *A morphophonology of Komo: Non-tonal phenomena*. Grand Forks: University of North Dakota MA thesis.

Thomason, Sarah G. & Terrence Kaufman. 1988. *Language contact, creolization, and genetic linguistics*. Berkeley: UC Press.

Thwing, Rhonda Ann. 1987. *The Vute noun phrase and the relationship between Vute and Bantu*. Arlington, TX: University of Texas at Arlington. (M.A. thesis).

Van de Velde, Mark L. O. 2005. The order of noun and demonstrative in Bantu. In Koen Bostoen & Jacky Maniacky (eds.), *Studies in African comparative linguistics with special focus on Bantu and Mande*, 425–442. Tervuren: Royal Museum for Central Africa.

Van de Velde, Mark L. O. 2006. Multifunctional agreement patterns in Bantu and the possibility of genderless nouns. *Linguistic Typology* 10. 183–221.

Voorhoeve, Jan. 1968. Noun classes in Bamileke. *Lingua* 21. 584–593.

Watters, John R. 1981. *A phonology and morphology of Ejagham – with notes on dialect variation*. Los Angeles: University of California at Los Angeles Doctoral dissertation.

Watters, John R. 2003. Grassfields Bantu. In Derek Nurse & Gérard Philippson (eds.), *The Bantu languages*, 225–256. London: Routledge.

Welmers, William E. 1971. The typology of the Proto-Niger-Kordofanian noun class system. In Chin-Wu Kim & Herbert Stahlke (eds.), *Papers in African linguistics*, 1–16. Carbondale, IL & Edmonton, AB: Linguistic Research Inc.

Welmers, William E. 1973. *African language structures*. Berkeley: University of California Press.

Williamson, Kay. 1985. How to become a Kwa language. In Adam Makkai & Alan K. Melby (eds.), *Linguistics and philosophy: Essays in honor of Rulon S. Wells*, 427–443. Amsterdam: Benjamins.

Williamson, Kay. 1989. Niger-Congo overview. In John Bendor-Samuel (ed.), *The Niger-Congo languages*, 3–45. Lanham, MD: University Press of America.

Williamson, Kay. 1993. The noun prefixes of Benue-Congo. *Journal of African Languages & Linguistics* 14. 29–45.

Williamson, Kay & Roger M. Blench. 2000. Niger-Congo. In Bernd Heine & Derek Nurse (eds.), *African languages: An introduction*, 11–42. Cambridge: CUP.

Chapter 3

Nominal affixing in the Kainji languages of northwestern and central Nigeria

Roger M. Blench
McDonald Institute for Archaeological Research, University of Cambridge

> The Kainji languages of northwest and central Nigeria remain little-researched and sparsely described. Their nominal morphology strongly resembles Bantu typologically, but finding segmental cognates remains problematic. They show systems of alternating prefixes and alliterative concord, as well as diminutive and augmentative prefixes and CV- prefixes with underspecified vowels, where the -V of the prefix harmonises with the stem vowel. The limited segmental cognates point to radical restructuring through affix loss and renewal. Indeed one language, Shen, has lost all nominal morphology and it is severely reduced in some branches. Reshe is typologically similar to other Kainji languages, but the affixes seem to have been completely restructured. The paper presents an overview of the literature on Kainji and then describes the nominal affixing in individual branches. It concludes by suggesting what hypotheses can be made about the Kainji system as a whole.

1 Introduction: the Kainji languages

Kainji (formerly Plateau 1a,b) is a family of some eighty languages or lects spoken in northwestern and central Nigeria. A large subset of these, the East Kainji languages, are spoken north and west of the Jos Plateau and are geographically separate from the other branches. Rowlands (1962); Greenberg (1963); Gerhardt (1989) and Crozier & Blench (1992) treat 'East Kainji' and 'West Kainji' as a primary division of the family, but there is no linguistic evidence to support this. Kainji languages are characterised by an extremely diverse morphology and relatively low percentages of common lexical items. It is only comparatively recently that their unity and distinctiveness have been recognised. They form one branch

Roger M. Blench. Nominal affixing in the Kainji languages of northwestern and central Nigeria. In John R. Watters (ed.), *East Benue-Congo: Nouns, pronouns, and verbs*, 59–106. Berlin: Language Science Press.
DOI:10.5281/zenodo.1314337

of the East Benue-Congo family,[1] itself a major division of Niger-Congo, and their nearest relatives are Plateau and Jukunoid (Williamson 1971; 1989; Williamson & Blench 2000).

Typologically, Kainji languages are difficult to characterise, but the more conservative branches have both nominal and verbal morphology highly reminiscent of Bantu (as indeed the *-tu* root for 'person'). The nominal systems are characterised by alternating affixes and concord on adjectives and some numerals. In some branches these affixes have either collapsed or been heavily restructured, resulting in contrastive consonant length as well as alternating C- prefixes, and rare systems of double-affixing. At least one language, Shen, has lost all trace of nominal affixes and has compensated by evolving a complex tonal inventory. The alternating affixes of one language, Reshe, show almost no segmental cognates with the remainder of the group and an innovative system must somehow have developed. Some branches have complex verbal morphology highly reminiscent of Bantu, with verbs taking long strings of suffixes. Word order is typically S (AUX) V O. Kainji languages are grossly under-represented in standard typological sources such as WALS and the summaries of existing material are quite inaccurate.

Most of the West Kainji languages are still commonly spoken, which is surprising, given that some are encapsulated by Hausa (McGill & Blench 2012). However, East Kainji languages, with few exceptions, are severely threatened and some have disappeared in recent decades. A few Kainji languages have significant numbers of speakers, but most populations are under 10,000. Western Kainji languages have been the subject of numerous literacy projects and these community initiatives appear to be sustainable, but Kainji languages otherwise have a very low profile in the media.

The human geography of Kainji-speaking peoples is very striking. As Figure 1 shows, there are outliers of Kainji spoken near Makurdi, far from the likely homeland area in the northwest. It is likely that the dispersal of the Basa peoples is a consequence of the destructive effects of the nineteenth century slave-raiding era, although this is not confirmed by recorded oral traditions. However, the twentieth century has also seen important migrations. The Hun-Saare peoples

---

[1] This term has a tortuous history. Originally 'Benue-Congo' included Plateau, Kainji, Jukunoid, Cross River and Bantoid. Later 'Benue-Congo' was expanded to include 'Eastern Kwa', i.e. Yoruboid, Edoid, etc. Williamson & Blench (2000) subsequently divided Benue-Congo into two branches: West and East. The West branch consisted of the previous 'Eastern Kwa' while the East branch consisted of the previous 'Benue-Congo' languages. Thus, 'East Benue-Congo' used here is equivalent to the original 'Benue-Congo' used in the literature from the 1960s to the 1990s.

3 Nominal affixing in the Kainji languages

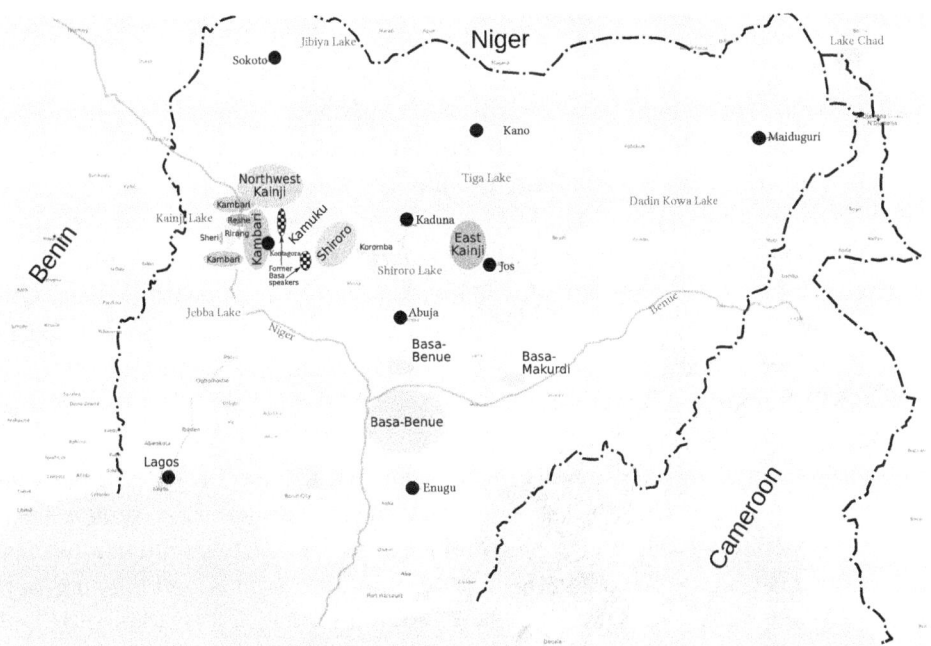

Figure 1: : The Kainji languages. Background map © OpenStreetMap contributors.

have formed a number of colonies outside their home area to take advantage of more fertile farmland.

Kainji languages are spoken in quite inaccessible areas, and even today, the home areas of many languages can be reached only through arduous motorbike trails. This explains why a comprehensive list of these languages is still to be established. The first attempt to compile a comparative Kainji wordlist was the work of Clark Regnier, a young SIL linguist who began surveys in the late 1980s. Clark was unfortunately the victim of a fatal motor accident in 1992. From the dry season of 2010, a joint programme to physically visit and record the speech of as many Kainji communities as possible has been undertaken by Roger Blench and Stuart McGill. Much of the data used in this paper was collected by the author and Stuart McGill in 2010-2012 and remains unpublished, although an extensive comparative wordlist is available online. At the same time, there has been considerable progress in the development of literacy in individual languages, strongly associated with literacy and bible translation projects (McGill & Blench 2012).

Roger M. Blench

The first lexical material on a Kainji language appears to be the *Kambali* lists in Koelle (1854). Johnston (1919-22, I:732-746) noted that the noun-class systems of the 'Semi-Bantu' languages of northwestern Nigeria showed marked resemblances to those of the Bantu languages and published comparative wordlists linking Kamuku, Gurmana and Basa. Thomas (in Meek 1925, II:137) put the known West Kainji languages into 'Nigerian Semi-Bantu' but joined Lopa and Laru with Bariba in 'Volta' i.e. Gur. In the 1950s, Westermann & Bryan (1952: 70) largely followed Thomas, although recognising that Kambari, Hun-Saare [Duka], and possibly Kamuku and Lela [Dakarkari] were grouped together. These languages were then listed in a catch-all category 'class languages' under the general heading of 'isolated units'. The recognition that the group now known as West Kainji forms a genetic unit is due to Bertho (1952: 264-6) who asserted its coherence on the basis of unpublished wordlists. Bertho rejected the Gur affiliations of Lopa and Laru proposed by Thomas and stated that the affiliations of the '*groupe Kamberi*' were with central Nigerian Plateau languages. A nearly simultaneous classification was proposed by Greenberg (1955) who created a large Plateau group encompassing what would now be called East and West Kainji (as Plateau 1a and b) as well as Tarokoid and Jukunoid. The term Kainji was informally introduced in the 1980s but was established in an article on Plateau in the reference volume on Niger-Congo published at the end of the decade (Gerhardt 1989). No evidence was put forward to support the classification published. Since that date there has been a significant expansion of field data, most of it still in manuscript. The major unpublished sources are listed in Table 30 in the Appendix A.

As our knowledge of the Kainji languages has improved, we can better characterise their internal structure and relationships. The main points are:

1. The distinction established in Rowlands (1962) and Greenberg (1963) between 'East and West Kainji' (1a and 1b in Greenberg) has never been demonstrated and seems unlikely to be valid.

2. Kainji divides into a number of distinct subgroups, each with highly marked but extremely diverse morphological characteristics.

3. Although Proto-Kainji has structural properties similar to Proto-Bantu, segmental cognates of morphology are difficult to establish.

Figure 2 shows an abbreviated high-level subclassification of the Kainji languages, which proposes names for nodes at different classificatory levels. If further work confirms the tree outlined here then these names can either be adopted or replaced by something more culturally appropriate. More detailed subclassifications of each major branch are given in the relevant numbered sections of §3 below.

Figure 2 arranges the subgroups of Kainji roughly west to east, except for East Kainji, and the arrangement of §3 follows the same ordering. For reasons of space, information about other aspects of these languages is very reduced and the material is strictly confined to the data available for actual languages and what can be reasonably reconstructed.

This chapter provides an overview of Kainji nominal affixes and associated concord systems. These are very similar to those described for Bantu and consist of (usually) a prefix on a noun root which marks number and which changes in the plural. Typically there is alliterative concord, where the corresponding affix on a qualifier (adjectives, demonstratives, quantifiers, lower numerals) shows agreement with the prefix. A couple of examples illustrate how this operates. The first example is from the Ut-Ma'in [Fakai] languages, described in Smith (2007). A typical alternating prefix would be

(1) Ut-Ma'in: alternating prefix
    ār-tāʔār 'stone'   āt-tāʔār 'stones'

The class prefix is C4 (i.e. noun class 4) and both the quantifier and the demonstrative show alliterative concord with 'shea tree' using C4 concord markers.

(2) Ut-Ma'in: alliterative concord
    ās-fàr   ās-bɛ̄:t sɛ̄   hɛ̄:g
    C4-shea.tree C4-all C4.DEM fall.PST
    'all the shea trees fell'

Cicipu, a language in the Kambari cluster, has an extremely transparent agreement system (McGill 2007).

(3) Cicipu agreement system
    màdíyá mè-pénâu 'big hare'
    ìndíyá ìm-pénàu 'big hares'

Various publications and theses have described the noun class systems for individual languages (e.g. Crozier (1984), McGill (2009); Paterson (2012)) but little has been written concerning the overall pattern they form. The chapter begins with a summary table of nominal affixing systems and then goes through what is known about each branch. A tentative model of the situation that can be attributed to Proto-Kainji is given in a final section together with a summary of the evidence for nasal affixes in Kainji. The numbers assigned to noun classes are those in the source materials. Analysis is far from the point where a standard system of numbers can be established for Kainji languages.

It cannot be emphasised too strongly that the quality of data for different branches is very uneven and that as the great majority is unpublished it should be treated as preliminary. It is unfortunate that a lack of pressure to publish means that preliminary language analyses circulate in manuscript and are made available by the authors on an informal basis. In particular, individual authors use affix numbering devised for a specific language and thus comparison across languages is more difficult. Tone-marking in particular is somewhat impressionistic. In general, in three-tone languages such as Reshe, mid-tone is unmarked. Where the data is too poor to mark tone with certainty, this is flagged in the text.

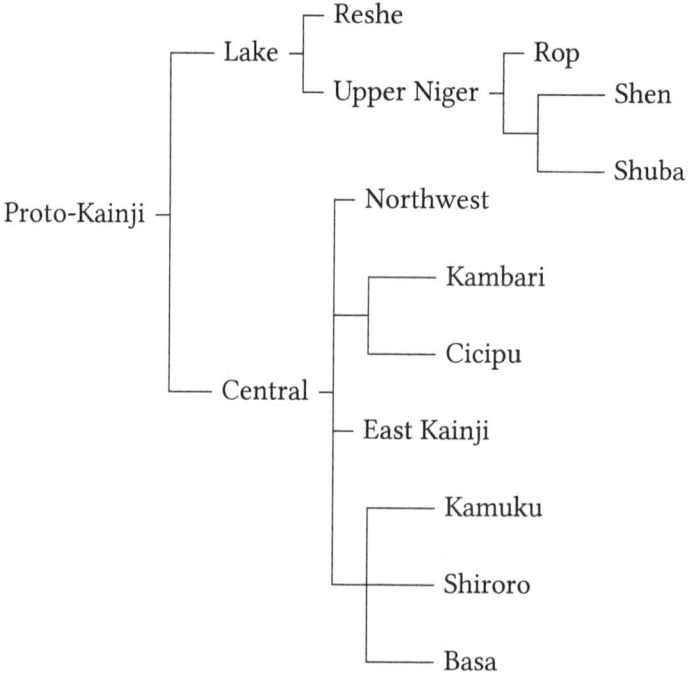

Figure 2: Subclassification of Kainji languages

2 Nominal affixes: overview

Given the prevalence of alternating affixes and concord in some Kainji languages, it is reasonable to suppose that a system of this type was present in Proto-Kainji. Nonetheless, the synchronic diversity within the family is such that these systems are lost or severely reduced in many languages. Table 1 & 2 summarise the situation in various Kainji subgroups.

3 Nominal affixes by subgroup

3.1 Reshe

Tsureshe, the language of the Reshe people, is spoken at the northern end of Lake Kainji (Dettweiler & Dettweiler 2002).[2] Reshe has a characteristic Niger-Congo noun class system, reminiscent of Bantu in several ways, although the class pairings are much reduced.[3] The noun stem is preceded by a class marker, either V- or CV-, which alternates between singular and plural and shows concord with adjectives and other parts of speech. There are six paired classes, four of which clearly have semantic motivation: those containing human beings, animals, body parts and mass nouns, although the class including body parts is more weakly defined than the others (Table 3). Class 6, which is invariant, includes mass nouns such as liquids, powders and similar items. Membership of the other two noun classes appears to be arbitrary. Table 3 summarises Reshe noun-class pairings. The tones of the prefixes are highly variable, so it is difficult to determine the underlying tone of the prefix. There is no evidence for tonal changes in the stem between singular and plural and the tone of the plural prefix is always the same as the singular.

Reshe has a complete set of object pronouns which correspond to the nominal affixes. However, where the pronoun refers to something unknown or despised, *là*, a generic pronoun not marked for number is used. This is an allomorph of the subject pronoun for inanimates, *lə*.

---

[2]Throughout this chapter, class prefixes are deleted in language and ethnic group names to create a uniform reference term.

[3]Work on Reshe was conducted jointly between the author and Appollos Agamalafiya in 2010 and 2011. See also the unpublished Boettger & Boettger (1967).

Table 1: Nominal affixing in Kainji Languages

Branch	Subgroup	Language	Comment
Reshe		Reshe	Alternating affixes and concord
Upper Niger	Rerang	Rop	Alternating affixes and concord
	Laru	Shuba	Affix system very reduced
		Shen	Affix system absent
Northwest	Lela	cLela	Reduced affix system with C-prefixes and concord
	Hun	tHun/sSaare	Reduced affix system with C-prefixes and concord
	Gwamhi	Gwamhyə, Wurə, Mba	Reduced affix system with C-prefixes and concord
	ut-Ma'in	All	Alternating affixes and concord
	?	Damakawa	Moribund
		CiShingini	Alternating affixes and concord
		Tsivadi	Alternating affixes and concord
		Baangi	Alternating affixes and concord
		Tsikimba	Alternating affixes and concord
		Agwara	Alternating affixes and concord
		Cicipu	Alternating affixes and concord
East		All	Alternating affixes and concord
		Shama	Alternating affixes and concord

3 Nominal affixing in the Kainji languages

Table 2: Nominal affixing in Kainji Languages (continuation of Table 1)

Branch	Subgroup	Language	Comment
Kamuku		Rogo-Shyabe	Alternating affixes and concord
		Səgəmuk	Alternating affixes and concord
		Cinda	Alternating affixes and concord
		Regi	Alternating affixes and concord
		Kuki	Alternating affixes and concord
		Zubazuba	Alternating affixes and concord
		Hungwəryə	Complex alternating affixes and concord
Shiroro		Fungwa	Alternating affixes and concord
		Rin	Alternating affixes and concord
		Wəgə	Unclear since moribund
		Gurmana	Alternating affixes and concord
	Baushi	All	Affix system in partial breakdown
Basa Basa			Extinct
		Basa-Gumna	Extinct
		Kɔrɔmba	Affix system functional
		Basa-Gurara	No information
		Basa-Benue	Three-term alternating affixes and concord
		Basa-Makurdi	Affix system in breakdown

67

Table 3: Reshe noun-class affix pairings

No.	sg.	No	pl.	Semantic content
1	u~w	2	bV-	human
3	hi~hy-	4	i~y-	animals and borrowed words
6	mV-		invariant	mass nouns
7	ú-	8	á-	body parts
9	ú~w-	10	tʃ~ts(u)~Ø-	miscellaneous
11	ri~ry-	12	a-	miscellaneous

(4) Reshe: generic pronoun *là*
 ù sárì là
 s/he cut it/them
 's/he cut it/them'

There are a small number of unusual items, shown in Table 4, that do not form part of the noun class pairings given above. These are invariant nouns, either mass nouns or inherently plural.

Table 4: Extra-systemic Reshe nouns

Tsureshe	Gloss
ḕhɛ̃	'tears'
èena	'waves'
ɔ́-ʃìmà	'fat'
ɔ́-rira	'river'

Surprisingly, if they are replaced by a pronoun in a sentence, the pronoun is *ɔ́bɔ̀* usually associated with humans.

Reshe, like many languages in this region, has distinctive incorporated possessives for kin terms and related nouns for persons. The affixes appear on the surface to have class-pair alternation, but the associated concord is that of the underlying noun. So, for example, in the word for 'age-mate', the *mu-/ba-* alternation strongly recalls Bantu prefixes, but in Reshe these probably originate with possessives (Table 5).

3 Nominal affixing in the Kainji languages

Table 5: Reshe: *mu-/ba-* alternation recalls Bantu prefixes

Sg.	Pl.	Gloss	Literal
mú-banɛ	bà-	'age-mate, colleague'	lit. 'my another'

The singular first person possessive is *mú*, which has been paired with the usual class 1/2 plural prefix *bà-*.

(5) Reshe
   mú úló
   'my friend'

3.2 Upper Niger (Shen and Rerang)

Like the Reshe, the Laru (Shen) and Lopa (Rerang) are fishing peoples who live around the edge of Lake Kainji. Research in 2011 and 2012 showed that 'Lopa' is in fact two distinct languages. Even more surprisingly, despite the ethnic label Rerang and the assertion of a common culture between the Rop and the Shuba, Shuba is clearly a conservative type of Shen, but which still retains at least some nominal morphology. The correct terminology for the Upper Niger languages is shown in Table 6.

Table 6: Ethnonyms and reference names of the Upper Niger Group

Usual name	Group name	One person	People	Language	Reference name
Laru		shen		shen gwe	Shen
Lopa	Rerang	dɔ̀rìrã́ŋ	ò:rìrã́ŋ	òl:èrã́ŋ	
	Rop	dɔ̀róp	ò:róp	òl:óp	Rop
	Shuba				Shuba

Shen exhibits a virtually complete loss of the nominal morphology system. All nouns either have no plural, or a plural suffix *bà(u)*. Shen has come under heavy influence from the Busa language, which is Mande and thus also has similar characteristics. Despite their different morphology, Shuba and Shen clearly share a significant amount of common lexicon.

By contrast, Shuba has not only a relatively rich system of nominal affixation, but demonstrates reprefixing, with unproductive prefixes now incorporated into the stem. Shuba, like many other Kainji languages, has underspecified vowels in CV- prefixes which frequently show harmony with the stem vowels. The following examples[4] show typical singular//plural pairs.

(6) Shuba prefixation

    a. ø-/SV-

	'tree' (generic)	ʃə	ʃi-ʃə
	'leaf'	fwã	sə-fwã

    b. ø-/a-

	'moon/month'	'yuuru	a-'yuuru
	'sun'	gwi	a-gwi

    c. rV/a-

	'field'	ra-hãi	a-hãi
	'seed/stone/pip'	re-kero	a-kero
	'mountain'	ri-yam	a-yam
	'nose'	ro-hɔ̃ro	a-hɔ̃ro

The word for 'nose' is an interesting example of double affixing, which probably arises through the copying of demonstratives (see Hoffmann 1967 for examples from cLela). Shuba is cognate with tHun *r-ho* for 'nose' and the prefix has been copied as a suffix.

    d. fV/a-

	'rubbish-heap'	fɔ-kũhũ	a-kũhũ
	'tooth'	fo-yefə	a-yefə
	'farm'	fu-tuma	a-tuma

    e. sV/a-

	'dew'	sə-myem	a-myem
	'room'	su-rukwə	a-rukwə

    f. N/a-

	'water'	m-mi	a-mi
	'sorghum-beer'	ŋ-kwa	a-kwa

    g. do-/bV-

	'person/people'	do-hũmwa	bo-hũmwa
	'man'	do-rumburu	bu-rumburu

    h. ø-/bV-

	'child'	bi	bu-bi
	'chief/ruler'	tɔ̃ĩʃa	bə-tɔ̃ĩʃa

---

[4] Unfortunately, when the data was collected, tones were not marked

3 Nominal affixing in the Kainji languages

But:

i. ø-/-bə-

Gloss	Sg.	Pl.
'father'	metõ	mebətõ
'friend'	medo	mebədo

The infixing of a -bə- sequence is probably a special case of ø-/bV-. The *me-* is probably a fused possessive, cognate with Reshe *mú-* (see above).

As an example of how reprefixing works, the word for 'vulture' is almost certainly a borrowing from Nupe *gùlŭ*. When first borrowed, it seems to have been attributed an *sV-* prefix, rather like 'tree' above. However, it was then re-analysed as part of the sV/a- class, hence the current synchronic form. Similarly with 'pot' which has an old rV- prefix, fused with the stem and also copied as a final syllable.

(7) Shuba reprefixing

Gloss	Sg.	Pl.
'hooded vulture'	saguru	a-saguru
'pot'	ruburu	a-ruburu

This diversity suggests that many of the prefixes are innovative. The nasal in mass nouns recalls the Class 6 prefix and the plural of *do-/bV-* Class 2, the plural of 'persons'. Figure 3 summarises the Shuba singular/plural affix alternations: The merger of many plural affixes to *a-* resembles the universal plural prefix *a-* in the Gbari languages (Hyman & Magaji 1970).

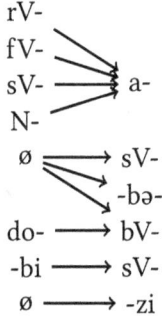

Figure 3: Shuba noun-class affix pairings

Roger M. Blench

3.3 Northwest Kainji

Lela (as Dakarkari) is often used as a cover-term for the peoples of the region between Rijau and Donko in reference books such as Gunn & Conant (1960). This name is now generally rejected, and it is here proposed to adopt the term 'Northwest Kainji' to cover this branch, which consists of the cLela, Hun-Saare, Kag clusters and the Wurə-Gwamhyə-Mba languages. The group is unified by a striking morphological feature, the reduction of nominal prefixes to single consonants. A consequence of this is the loss of harmony between prefix and stem vowels. Nominal affixing in the Northwest Kainji languages is relatively well-described, with analyses for cLela (Dettweiler 2015), Hun-Saare (Bendor-Samuel et al. 1973) and Ut-Ma'in (Paterson 2012). A particular feature of this group is affix copying (first noted in Hoffmann 1967) which results in suffixes in animate classes (cf. an example in §3.3.1 below).

Figure 4 shows a subclassification of the Northwest Kainji languages, based on lexical innovations. Damakawa is a moribund language recorded by McGill (pers. comm.) for which the data is too fragmentary to classify it with certainty.

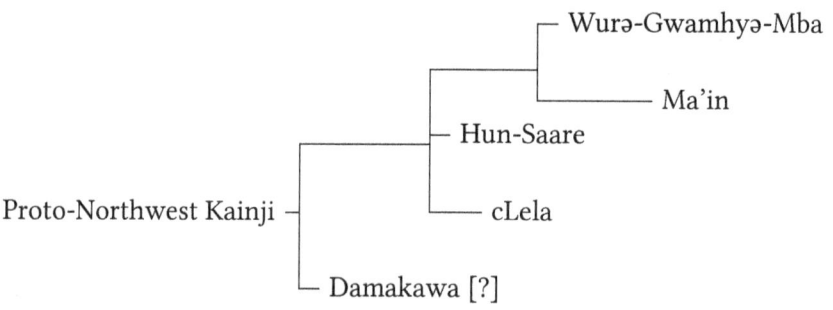

Figure 4: Subclassification of the Northwest Kainji languages

3.3.1 cLela (Dakarkari)

cLela has ten noun classes marked by six consonant prefixes: *c-*, *d-*, *k-*, *m-*, *s-*, *v-*; three vowel prefixes: *a-*, *i-*, *u-*; and a common noun *-n* suffix (Hoffmann 1967; Dettweiler 2015). Number is marked on inanimate nouns with prefixes; while in animates plurality is indicated by an -nV suffix. Classes 1-9 are all inanimates, while animates are all grouped in a single class.

3 Nominal affixing in the Kainji languages

Table 7 summarises the noun class affixes of cLela in Dettweiler (2015).

Table 7: cLela noun class affixes

| | Singular | | Plural | |
No.	Prefix	No.	Prefix (Inanimate)	Suffix (Animate)
1	a-	2	c-	–
3	u-	2	c-	–
4	d-	2	c-	–
5	k-	2	c-	–
6	v-	7	s-	–
8	i-	9	m-	–
9	m-			–
10	ø-	10	–	-nV-

A published dictionary of cLela provides a broad variety of examples of noun-class pairings (Rikoto et al. 2001). The singular and plural affixes are exemplified below in Table 8.

Table 8: Examples of cLela noun class affix pairings

Class	Singular	Gloss	Class	Plural	Gloss
1	a-cù	'face'	2	c-cù	'faces'
3	u-bèlà	'farm'	2	c-bela	'farms'
4	d-isá	'eye'	2	c-isá	'eyes'
5	k-wècé	'cloud'	2	c-wècé	'clouds'
6	v-hwèn	'rope'	7	s-hwèn	'ropes'
8	i-hònò	'calabash'	9	m-hònò	'calabashes'
9	m-hò	'water'			
10	nàamá	'cow'	10	nàam.ná	'cows'
10	nètà	'woman'	10	nètà.ná	'women'

The animates class ø-/-nV is related to the forms in the neighbouring tHun language but is innovative within Kainji. Only the mass noun prefix m- (here class 9) corresponds to Niger-Congo 6, but has merged with the plural of Class 8 above.

Like Shuba and Reshe, cLela has *mV-* for inalienable possession of kin (Dettweiler 2015). Thus:

(8) cLela: inalienable possession
    hə̀n-mí   'sibling-my'   hə̀n-mí-nì   'sibling-my-PL'
    ʧèt-mé   'father-my'   ʧèt-mé-nè   'fathers-my-PL'

where *-nV* is the Class 2 plural for persons.

A striking feature of Northwest Kainji is double-affixing in compounds, first noted in Hoffmann (1967). This arises when the prefix of the head noun is displaced to the associated noun and precedes its own prefix. Thus:

(9) cLela: double-affixing in compounds
    Gloss   cLela   Components
    'spine'   tèl k-ə̂dcìnə̀   k-tèlè 'bone' + d-cìnə̀ 'back'

This displacement also occurs on demonstratives:

(10) cLela: displacement of nominal prefix to demonstratives
    c-gyàŋ   'eggs'   gyàn cə́hnà   'these eggs'

3.3.2 Hun-Saare (Duka)

The Hun-Saare people live directly south of the Lela, straddling the border of Niger and Kebbi States. They are conventionally divided into two groups, the Hun and the Saare, but are commonly known in Hausa as Duka and their language as Dukanci (Dettweiler & Dettweiler 2003b). They are first mentioned by Temple (1922: 96-100). The noun-phrase is described in Bendor-Samuel et al. (1973). An electronic dictionary and grammar of tHun (Dukawa) is available, associated with the translation and literacy project (Heath p.c. a,b).

The presentation of Hun-Saare nominal affixing is far from transparent and is moreover, given in orthographic representations. The class marker can move from before to after the noun root. When the marker is before the noun it is the object of the verb and when it follows, the noun is the subject. Table 9 shows the system of tHun nominal affixes and concord, based on Heath (p.c.). Note that Bendor-Samuel et al. (1973) give a somewhat different presentation.

An example of the movement of affixes in relation to intraclausal position is the following (Heath n.d.):

3 Nominal affixing in the Kainji languages

Table 9: tHun nominal affixes and concord

	Singular			Plural		
No.	Affix	Pronoun	No.	Affix	Pronoun	Semantics
1	o-	wə	6	-nɛ	ɛ	persons
2	-ər-	ɔ	7	-ɛgɛ-, -ɛ-	yo	miscellaneous
3	-m-	yo	8	-ət-	sɛ	miscellaneous
4	ø-	de	9	-ər-	rɔ	miscellaneous
5	-m-	mɔ	10	-m-	mɔ	mass, uncountable

(11) tHun: nominal affix on subjects and objects
hɔ.m ʃo'ostɛ o.wak
water.CM filled CM.swamp
'water filled the swamp'

As with cLela, a class pair marking persons and a mass noun affix can be discerned, but otherwise, tHun shows few cognates with other systems.

3.3.3 The Kag (Ut-Ma'in or Fakai) cluster

The first mention of the languages of the Kag cluster is Temple (1922: 89) who refers to 'Kelinchi' [? = Kelanci, i.e. Ker-ni]. Rowlands (1962) gives short lists of nouns in 'Fakawa', Kelawa and Zusu. Regnier (2003) conducted a sociolinguistic survey among five of the eight named Fakai cluster members in 1991-1992. Paterson (2012) represents new in-depth fieldwork on the Ror language, now named Ut-Ma'in by its speakers. Table 10 shows the peoples and languages of this cluster.

Table 10: Peoples and languages of the Kag cluster

Hausa name	People	Language
Fakkawa	Kag-ne	ət-Kag
Fakkawa	əs-Us	ət-Us
Gelawa	a-Jiir	ət-Jiir
Zuksun	a-Zuksun	ət-Zuksun
Kukumawa	əs-Fer	ət-Fer
Kelawa	Kər-ni	ət-Kər
Tuduwa	aor	ət-maor
Kuluwa	a-Koor	ət-ma-Koor

Table 11: Ut-Ma'in noun classes (Paterson (2012))

Class	Prefix	Object Pronoun	Ut-Ma'in	Gloss
1a	ū-	ú/wá	ū-mákt	'barren woman'
			ū-rāg	'stupid person'
1b	ø-	wá	ø-hámət	'visitor'
			ø-zʷàr	'young man'
2a	ø-	ɛ	ø-ná	'oxen, bovines'
			ø-hʲə	'guinea corn (pl)'
			ø-rɛgɛr	'stars'
2b	ø-	-nɛ	ø-nɛtnɛ	'people'
3a	ū-	ɔ	ū-bù	'house'
			ū-kʰóm	'arm'
			ū-sɛp	'song'
3b	ø-	ɔ	ø-bòʔ	'dream'
			ø-ʤāb	'heart'
			ø-sʷás	'fish trap'
4	əs-	sɛ	əs-bòʔ	'dreams'
			əs-rā	'muscle'
			əs-bà:t	'medicine'
5	ər-	dɛ	ər-kɔk	'calabash'
			ər-ʤāb	'liver'
			ər-hí	'head'
6a	ət-	tɔ	ət-kɔk	'calabashes'
			ət-ís	'eyes'
			ət-rīn	'charcoal'
6b	əm-	mɔ	əm-nɔːg	'oil'
			əm-hʲə	'blood'
			əm-hʲərəg	'sand'
7a	ū-	já	ū-ná	'bovine'
			ū-ʧān	'feather'
			ū-nín	'tooth'
7b	ø-	já	ø-ʧámpá	'man'
			ø-mārímárí	'the dead'
			ø-rʲâm	'cripple (n)'
AUG	ā-	á	ā-kɔk	'huge calabashes'
			ā-bà	'big lake'
DIM	ī-	ɛ	ī-kɔk	'tiny calabash'
			ī-gʷá	'tiny (piece of) grass'
			ī-ràndí	'thread'

Table 11 shows the thirteen noun classes in Ut-Ma'in, following Paterson (2012). Three classes share the same *ū-* prefix, but their distinct concords suggest class merger. Four classes have a null ø- prefix, but with similarly diverse agreement morphemes. I have added Class 2b, which is the *-nɛ* plural suffix marking some persons, cognate with similar *nV-* suffixes in cLela and tHun. The first column gives a class affix number, corresponding to Bantu where possible. For the diminutive and augmentative classes of ut-Ma'in the labels DIM and AUG are used. The second column shows the nominal prefix and the third column represents the agreement targets, indicated by the object pronoun. The last two columns give sample lexemes from each class.

As elsewhere in the group, the 1/2 class pairing marks persons and the *əm-* prefix marks uncountable nouns. A common feature of Northwest Kainji is the suffix *-nV* marking the plural of nouns for 'persons'. In Kainji languages and elsewhere in Benue-Congo (cf. the Benue-Congo Comparative Wordlist) *-net* is a common word for person and it is possible the suffix is an old compound which has been generalised across the group. If so this creates a certain amount of redundancy. For example:

(12)   Ut-Ma'in: suffix *-nV* for plural of nouns for 'persons'
       'persons' *nɛtnɛ*

No other clear source for this suffix has been identified.

3.4 Kambari

3.4.1 Introduction

The Kambari are perhaps the largest of the Kainji subgroups, numerically. Their languages have been studied more extensively than others in the group although much research has never been completely published. Kambari (Kamberi, Cumbri etc.) is an outsiders' name, but since there is no overall name for the group it is retained here.

Present studies suggest that Kambari has two major divisions, usually referred to as Kambari I and II. These crudely correspond to east and west, but in some regions the two are territorially intertwined (Blench 1982). Table 12 shows the common names of the various Kambari sub-groups and the correct names of the people and language. The initial consonant of the root is marked with upper case.

Table 12: The Kambari languages

Usual Name	Other Names	One person	People	Language
Kambari I				
Agadi	Kakihum		aGadi	tsiGadi
Abadi, Evadi	Ibeto		aVadi	tsiVadi
Bangawa		vuBaangi	aBaangi	ciBaangi
	Salka	sShíngíní or məShíngíní	əShingini	ciShingini
Kambari II				
Agaushi	Auna, Wara		aGaushi	tsiGaushi
Kimba			aKimba	tsɨkimba
Ngwunci	Agwara	maWunci	ŋWənci	tsuWənci
Cicipu	Acipawa	Cípù pl.	Àcípù	Cìcípù

3.4.2 Cicipu

Cicipu, the Western Acipa language, was formerly considered part of the Kamuku cluster, along with eastern Acipa.

Table 13 lists the Cicipu noun classes and corresponding prefixes.

Class 1, 3b, 4, 6, 7 and 9 prefixes occur with singular nouns.

Class 2, 3a and 5 prefixes occur with plural nouns.

Class 8 prefixes can occur with either singular or plural nouns.

Dettweiler & Dettweiler (2003b) present a comparative wordlist for three lects spoken in the towns Kumbashi, Kakihum and Karisen. In this report they point out that 'Western Acipa' is so different from all the other languages in the group that it would be better to assign it to a separate branch. Stuart McGill (2007; 2009; 2010) proposed that this language has been misclassified and is in fact part of the Kambari group. Alternatively, it could have come under extremely strong influence from Kambari (not impossible since the two languages are neighbours in Kakihum). However, now that a more in-depth description of the grammar and morphology of Cicipu is available, this seems less likely.

The Cicipu noun class system is similar to the Kambari languages, and so the numbering system used by Hoffmann (1963) and Crozier (1984) for Central Kam-

3 Nominal affixing in the Kainji languages

Table 13: Cicipu noun class prefixes (Adapted from McGill (2009)

Class	Noun prefix	Agreement prefix	Example	Gloss
1	kA-	kA-	kà-bárá	'elder'
			kɔ̀-kɔ́	'egg'
			kò-jóo	'lizard'
			kè-téré	'bone'
			kɔ́-ɔɓí	'he-goat'
2	A-	A-	à-bárá	'elders'
			ɔ̀-kɔ́ɔ	'eggs'
			ò-jóo	'lizards'
			è-téré	'bones'
3a	i-/y-	i-/y-	ì-námà	'meat'
			yɔ́-ɔmɔ́	'monkeys'
3b	ri-		rì-hyá'ằ	'arrow'
			rú-usì	'rainy season'
4	mA-	mA-	mà-díyá	'hare'
			mɔ̀-tɔ́ɔ	'chick'
			mò-kóotó	'kitchen hut'
			mè-pésé	'twin'
5	N-, mi-	N-, mi-	ǹ-díyá	'hares'
			ǹ-tɔ́ɔ	'chicks'
			m-pésé	'twins'
			mì-nnú	'birds'
6	ti-, tu-, ci-, cu-	ti-, tu-	tì-sí'ì̃	'hair'
			tù-mócì	'friendship'
			cì-lúu	'leopard'
			cù-kúlú	'tortoise'
7	u-/w-	u-/w-	ù-pépí	'wind'
			wɔ́-ɔvɔ́ɔ	'fear'
8	Ø-, C-, v-	Ø-, C-, v-	Ø-cìccérè	'star'
			c-cɔ́'ɔ	'sheep'
			d-dɔ̂ɔ	'horse'
			z-zá	'person'
			vɔ́-ɔmɔ̀	'monkey'
9	ku-/kw-	ku-/kw-	kù-cígà	'cockerel'
			kwé-etú	'medicine'

bari is followed. Cicipu has a very coherent system of underspecified vowels in noun prefixes, usually copying V_1 of the root. Where C_1 is palatalised, the vowel of the prefix is -i.

Figure 5 shows Cicipu noun-class affix pairings. The dotted lines indicate pairings only rarely attested.

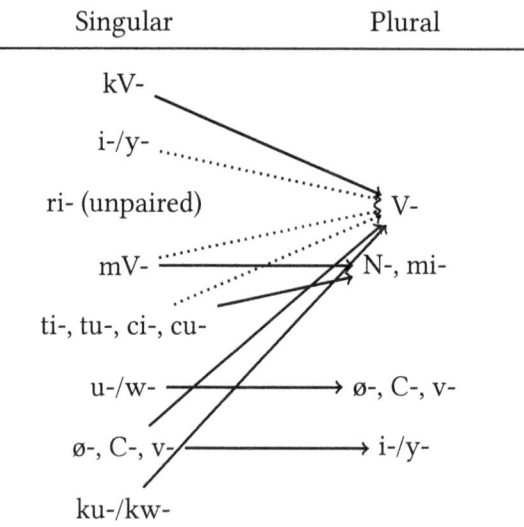

Figure 5: Cicipu noun-class affix pairings (Adapted from McGill (2009))

There appears to be no semantic unity in the noun classes and that even common Niger-Congo classes such as Class 6 for mass nouns[5] and 1/2 for persons are absent. If we count the number of noun classes by the prefix on the noun there are ten morphological classes. However, two of these (3a and 3b) share the same agreement markers and should possibly be merged.

3.4.3 Cishingini (Salka Kambari)

The nominal affixing of Cishingini, the Kambari of Salka is described in Hoffmann (1963) and Crozier (1984). Table 14 shows the noun class and concordial prefixes in Cishingini as summarised in Crozier (1984). Figure 6 illustrates the pattern of Cishingini noun-class affix pairings.

The classes have not been renumbered, but the unpaired *ma-* and *tsɨ-* classes, containing mass nouns, language names and nouns of manner and style, correspond to Proto-Bantu classes 6 **ma-* and 7 **ki-*. Unlike Bantu, Cishingini classes 3

---

[5]Or else the Class 4 *mV-* prefix has been re-assigned.

3 Nominal affixing in the Kainji languages

Table 14: Noun class and concordial prefixes in Cishingini (Adapted from Crozier (1984)

Class	Number	Prefix	1. Polar Tone	2. Low Tone 2	3. Low Tone 2
1	sg.	a:-	a:-	à:-	`- à:-´
2a		a-	a-	à-	`- à-´
2b	pl.	naN-			
3	sg. +/- pl.	i:-	i:-	ì:-	`- ì:-´
4	sg.	mV-	ma-	mà-	`- mà-´
5	pl.	N-	N-	ǹ-	`- ǹ-´
6	sg. +/- pl.	tsi-	tsi-	tsì-	`- tsì-´
7	sg.	u:- C-	u:-	ù:-	`- ù:-´
8a	sg. +/- pl.	vi- li-	C- vi-	`C- vi-	`- `C-´ `- vi-´
8b	sg.	0-			

Class	Singular	Class	Plural
1	a:-	2a,b	a- naN-
3	sg+/- pl.		i:-
4	mV-	5	N-
6	tsi-		
7	u:- C-		
8a	vi- li-		
8b	0-		

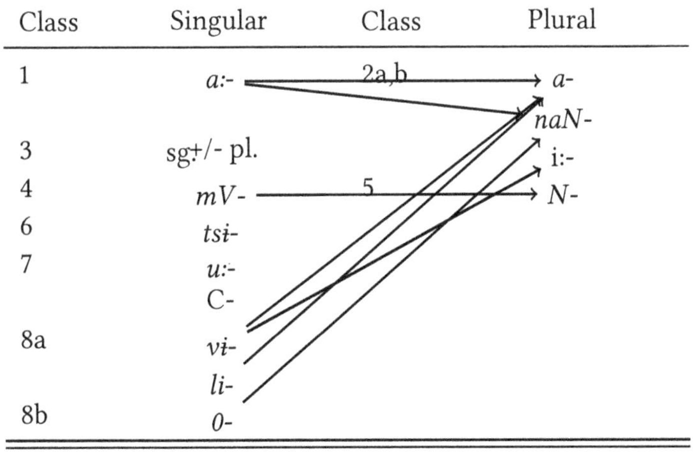

Figure 6: Cishingini noun-class affix pairings (Adapted from Crozier 1984)

and 8a occur as both singular and plural when paired with other classes. The class pair 1/2a includes the majority of nouns. In contrast to Bantu, Cishingini has only three sets of concordial prefixes. Crozier (1984) analysed noun semantics and showed that the majority of humans are associated with the affix pairs 8/2, while other animates fall into 4/5 and 8a/3. Inanimates are common in 1/2a. The *mV-* prefix Class 4 shows harmony between the prefix and stem vowel and corresponds to a syllabic nasal prefix, class 5. The majority of words in this class pair seem to be animals and plants.

3.5 East Kainji

3.5.1 General

The East Kainji languages are a poorly studied group of some 35 languages spoken north and west of the Jos Plateau in Central Nigeria. Compared with the branches of West Kainji, which have undergone a wide variety of morphological changes, the East Kainji languages for which data exist are comparatively similar to one another. Shimizu (1979; 1982a; 1982) collected numerous short wordlists of East Kainji languages and sketched the noun-class prefix pairs that could be extracted from this material. The two languages for which detailed information on nominal prefixing exist are Map (Di Luzio 1972; Anderson 1980) and Boze [=Buji] (Blench & Boze Literacy Committee (BLC) n.d.). Shimizu (1968) is a sketch of the noun-class system of iBunu. Data for many languages consists of fragmentary wordlists, often orthographic with no tones or plurals. Figure 7 show the languages and internal structure of East Kainji as far as can be gauged from existing data.

Some of the names are new, representing languages first recorded in 2016. Former names are given in square brackets, but languages such as Ngmgbang will not be found in standard references.

The threat to East Kainji languages cannot be emphasised too strongly; many have only a few speakers and are rapdily switching to Hausa. Others are only now remembered and can be recovered by urgent fieldwork. Figure 8 shows Sarkin Yakubu, the last rememberer of Ziriya, interviewed in 2003. No more information can now be recovered about the Ziriya language.

A new wordlist of TiZora was taken in March 2016, which can be compared with the one collected by Shimizu (1979) in 1973. During this period TiZora went from being spoken on a daily basis to one spoken between men over seventy in scattered settlements, under heavy pressure from Hausa. As a consequence, although speakers are quite fluent, the noun-class system has undergone sys-

3 Nominal affixing in the Kainji languages

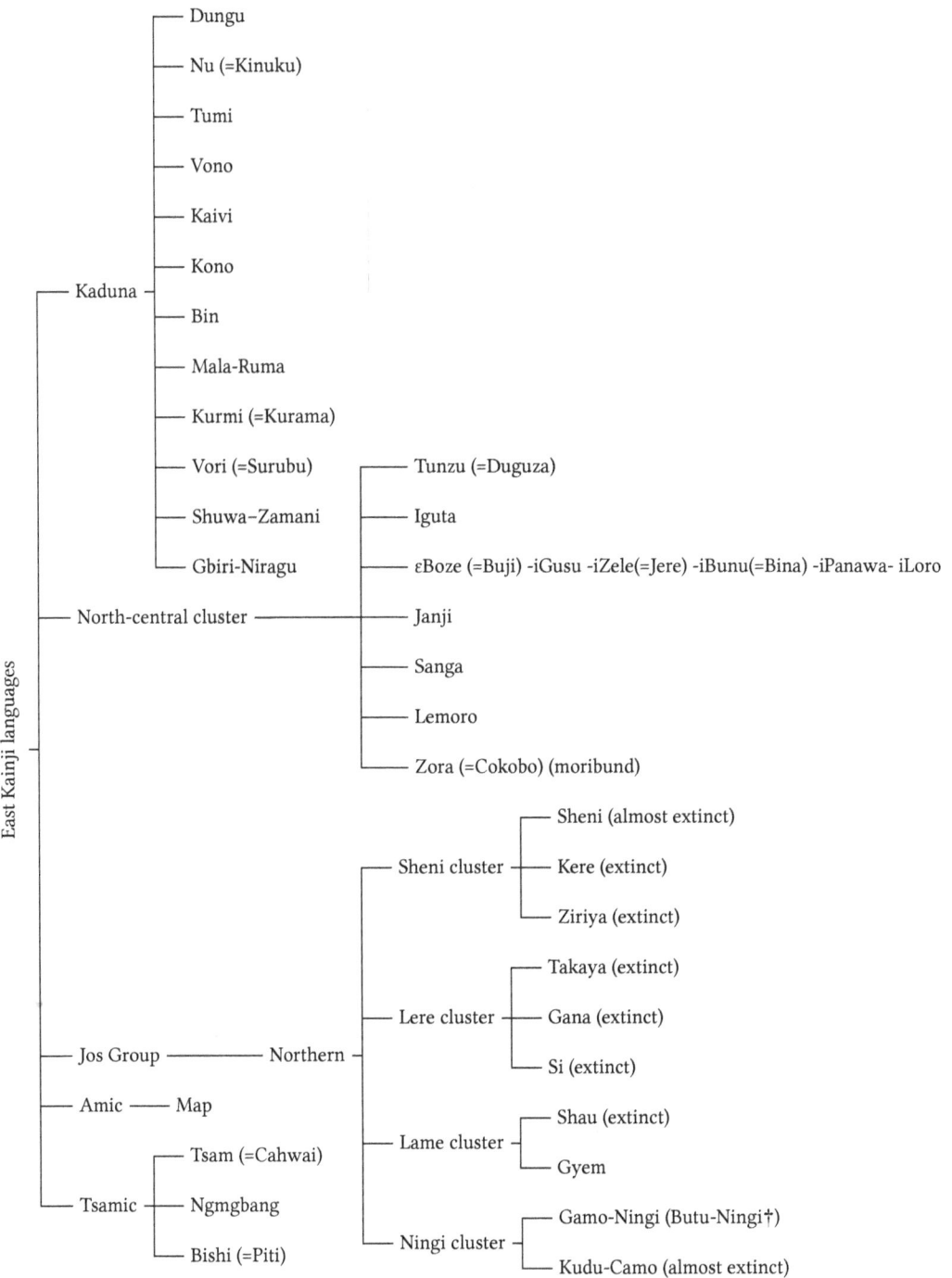

Figure 7: East Kainji languages and their internal structure

Figure 8: Sarkin Yakubu [left], the last rememberer of Ziriya, 2003

tematic collapse. This is described briefly in §3.5.4 to exemplify the rapidity with which morphological change can occur.

3.5.2 ɛBoze [=Buji]

The ɛBoze language is spoken in some seven villages west and northwest of Jos. The language has been threatened by the spread of Hausa but has recently undergone a significant revival. Boze has a rich inventory of prefixes with underspecified vowels and a variety of realisations.[6] Table 15 shows a summary of the underlying affixes and their allomorphs.

Marking tone on ɛBoze prefixes is something of a hostage to fortune and they are only noted in the table where the evidence is quite strong. Broadly speaking, ɛBoze has a rule where the singular prefix is low and the plural (both prefix and stem) tones are one level higher. However, there are many unexplained irregularities resulting from the influence of the stem tone on the prefix.

---

[6]Work on ɛBoze has been conducted since the early 2000s in conjunction with John Nengel and the Boze Literacy Committee (BLC).

3 Nominal affixing in the Kainji languages

Table 15: Prefixes and their allomorphs in ɛBoze nouns

No.	Singular Prefix	Allomorphs	Plural Prefix	Allomorphs	Semantics
1a	O-	ɔ-, o-, u-	a-		persons
1b	`VnV-	ono, OnO-, unu-, uno-	anˊV́-	ana-, ano-, anu-	persons
2	bˋV-	be-, bɛ-, bə-, bi-	i-		animals, people, tools
3	àa-		tV̀-	t-, te-, tɛ-, ti-, tu-	miscellaneous
4	ɛ-, (ə-), i-		N-	n-, ŋ-, m-	abstracts, miscellaneous
5	ø-		tV-	t-, te-, tɛ-, ti-, tu-	insects, reptiles
6a	màa-, m-, n-		ø-		mass nouns, abstracts
6b	màa-, m-, n-		i-		miscellaneous
7	Ò-	ɔ-, o-	tV-	t-, te-, tɛ-, ti-, tu-	objects
8	ùu-		ti-		plants, foods, tools
9a	rV̀-	re-, ri-	a-		miscellaneous
9b	rV̀-	re-, ri-	sV-	se-, sɛ-, si-	miscellaneous
10	ka-, kɔ-, ku-				diminutive
11	A-	a-, ə-	a-		verbal nouns

The table only represents common pairings, but ɛBoze has numerous examples of unexpected pairings, where the singular/plural gender is only represented by one or two attestations. The vowel in prefixes often harmonises with the stem, although vowels tend to be either front or back; only the allomorphs of *tV-* show the broad range of vowels. It is striking that in Class 2, the class which includes persons, the singular prefix is *bV-*, where it might be expected to mark plural.

ɛBoze shows occasional signs of a feature much more common in Plateau, the 'intrusive nasal'. In common examples a nasal is inserted between the prefix and the stem vowel in either the singular or the plural:

(13) ɛBoze: Intrusive nasal
Sg. *ituma* 'work'
Pl. *intúmá* 'works'

The likely explanation is that n- was originally a nominalisation prefix applied to a verb stem. When the verbal noun was incorporated into the nominal system, it acquired a new prefix, without the previous one being deleted.

3.5.3 Map [=Amo]

The correct name for the language of the Map people is tiMap. Its noun classes are described [under the name Amo] in (Di Luzio 1972; Anderson 1980). Table 16 shows Anderson's (1980: 156) summary of tiMap noun classes and concord. Table 17 shows the tiMap nominal prefix pairings and their semantics, where these can be identified. Nasal prefixes in tiMap do not appear to be homorganic and do not change in relation to the following consonant.

As with other Kaniji languages, tiMap has a diminutive and an augmentative. However, in striking contrast to Boze (see above) it has a very static concord system with the prefixes copying the nominal affixes directly. The underspecified vowel in Boze has been lost and tiMap prefixes are all static.

3.5.4 ìZora

The ì-Zora language was recorded in 1973 by Shimizu when it still had a functioning system of noun classes. Table 18 shows the nominal prefix pairings which were functioning at that time.

3 Nominal affixing in the Kainji languages

Table 16: tiMap nominal prefixes and concord (Anderson 1980: 156)

Class	Prefix	Map	Gloss	Concord
1	ù-	ù-là	'fire'	u
2	à-	à-fà	'leaf'	a
3	kù-	kù-fà	'leaves'	ku
4	tè-	tè-là	'fires'	te
5	lè-	lè-kpì	'rat'	le
6	ṅ-	ṅ-fép	'breath'	mi
7	kì-	kì-té	'place'	ki
8	nì-	nì-té	'places'	ni
9	fè-	fè-ʃù	'bee'	fe
10	ì-	ì-ʃù	'bees'	i
11	kà-	kà-vín	'goat'	ka
12	mà-	mà-ví	'big goats'	ma

Table 17: tiMap nominal prefix pairings and semantics

Class Pair	Prefix	Semantics
1/2	ù-/ à-	mostly humans
1/4	ù-/ tè-	unclear
3/2	kù-/ à-	unclear
5/2	tè-/ à-	body parts and diverse
5/4	lè-/ tè-	diverse
6/4	ṅ-/ tè-	mass nouns
7/8	kì-/ nì-	diverse
9/10	fè-/ ì-	animals, crops and diverse
11/8	kà-/ nì-	domestic animals and diverse
1a	ù-	uncountable
2a	à-	uncountable
4a	tè-	uncountable
6a	ṅ-	uncountable

Table 18: ì-Zora nominal prefix pairings

Paired classes	Sg.	Pl.
	ù-	à-, ì-, ʃì-, m-, mV-
	lV-	à-, ʃì-
	ì-	í-, bì-
	rì-	à-, ʃì-, sù-
	bì-	ì-, à-
	ø-	à-
	ʼN-	ì-
Unpaired classes		
	à	
	ì-	
	ò-	
	ù-	
	ø-	
	mà-	
	mi-	

Unpaired class prefixes associated with uncountable nouns are highly diverse but there is a strong correlation in (14) between the *mi-* prefix and liquids:

(14) i-Zora: *mi-* prefix and liquids
 mi-ɲùŋu 'blood'
 mi-ʃiyà 'oil'
 mi-ɲf 'water'

By 2016, the situation had changed radically. Only nineteen individuals now speak ì-Zora, and they do not live in the same location. To record the language, they had to be brought together (Figure 9). Less than ten per cent of nouns were remembered as having any plural, and the majority of nouns had acquired a 'default' singular prefix *ù-* and a plural *à-*. Table 19 shows a comparison between the forms recorded in 1973 and in 2016.

This also illustrates other changes, including the change from labial-velars to labialised velars ($kp > k^w$) and the loss of palatalised consonants ($k^y > ke$). This likely reflects the pressure from the phonology of Hausa, in which all speakers are bilingual and illustrates how rapidly morphological systems can change in particular sociolinguistic contexts.

3 Nominal affixing in the Kainji languages

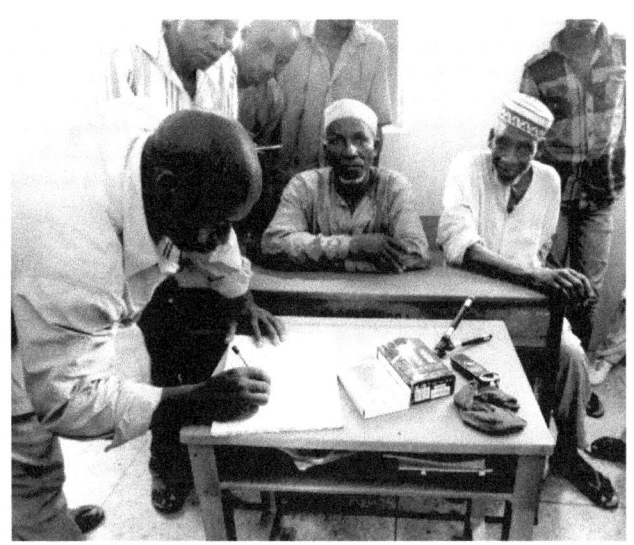

Figure 9: Recording the Zora language, 2016

Table 19: ì-Zora nominal prefix pairings compared

Gloss	Shimizu (1979)	Blench (2016)
'meat'	ǹ-námá pl. ì-	ùnámá
'fish'	ù-kpàlà pl. ì-	ùkwálá
'stone'	rì-kyàlé pl. à-	ùkélé

3.6 The Kamuku group

3.6.1 Introduction

The Kamuku peoples, following Gunn & Conant (1960) and Rowlands (1962) have conventionally been divided into 'Acipa' and 'Ucinda'. The Acipawa, correctly the Acipu, are linguistically part of the Kambari cluster, and are treated in §3.4 The whole Kamuku area consists of a complex of related languages, and each lect traces its origin to the individual hills in the Mariga area. A study of Kamuku lects has added a great deal to our understanding of these languages but also added many new possible languages (Yoder et al. 2008). Several languages seem to be either extinct or moribund, but their names and locations are known. The two languages for which there are descriptions in some depth are Hungwəryə (Hackett & Davey 2009) and Cinda (Mort 2012). Figure 10 shows the likely subgrouping of the Kamuku languages, based on speakers' impressions.

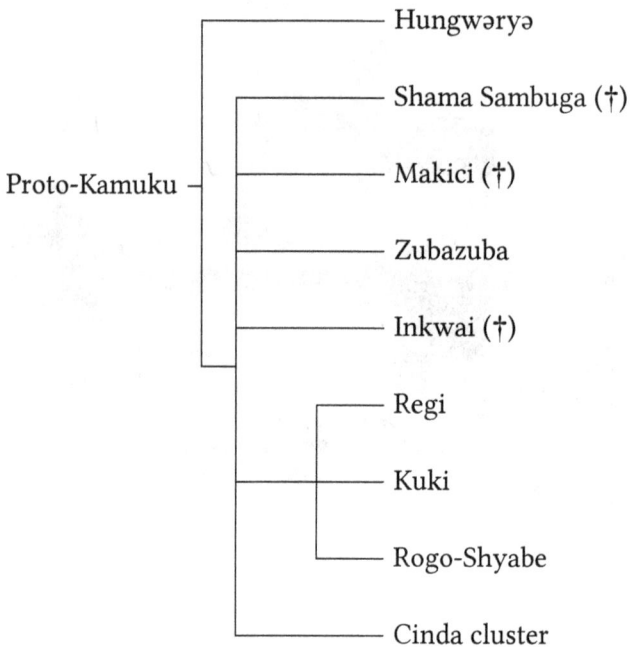

Figure 10: Subclassification of the Kamuku languages

3.6.2 Hungwəryə [=Ngwoi]

The cəHungwəryə language [Ungwai, Ngwoi in older sources] has been described in Hackett & Davey (2009). Hungwəryə has between 13 and 17 noun class affixes which encode both number and size. The feature marking of size is also reported for tHun (Bendor-Samuel et al. 1973) and its optionality may mean that it is more common than is recognised. The class marker indicates whether the referent is small, normal-sized, or large. Other features distinguish the Hungwəryə system from its neighbours, including leftwards nasal harmony of the prefixes. Where the stem vowel is nasalised, this feature spreads to the prefix vowel. In many plural prefixes the vowel has been lost and a C- prefix now abuts the stem directly, a typological change which has developed and been generalised in the Northwest Kainji languages.

Hungwəryə is characterised by extensive allomorphy of its prefixes. Table 20 shows the singular and plural class markers, re-arranged from the data in Hackett & Davey (2009). To match the mass noun affix in class 6 and the person class 1, as well as merging classes where the prefixes seem to be allomorphs, I have been obliged to re-assign their numbering.

Table 20: Hungwəryə singular and plural class markers (Restructured from Hackett & Davey (2009).)

Number	Singular	Plural	Example	Gloss
1a	bu-,	ə-,	bú-ləgəsə, ə-ləgəsə	'boy'
	bo-¨	a-¨	bó-mátā`, á-mátā`	'father-in-law'
1b	bʷ-	s-	bʷ-á:rʲè, s-á:rʲè	'husband'
1c	bi-,	i-,	bí-tʃítʃí, í-tʃítʃí	'caterpillar'
	bʲẽ	ẽ-	bʲẽ`-rʲẽ´, ẽ`-rʲẽ´	'mouse'
2a	i-,	mu-,	í-pəpì, mú-pəpì	'bat'
	e-,	mo-,	é-káŋgàzà, mó-káŋgàzà	'girl'
	ʔɛ-,	mɔ-,	ʔẽ´-hɔ´, mɔ´-hɔ´	'day'
	j-	mʷ-	j-ãˇrɔmà, mʷ-ãˇrɔmà	'chick'
2b	i-	h-:[1]	í-jɛlà, h-ɛ:là	'tooth'
3	ə-,	sə-,	ə-gúbə, sə-gúbə	'hawk'
	a-,	sə-,	á-tābɔ, sə-tābɔ	'spoon'
	ə-/a-	tʃə-	á-mʷɔnʲé, tʃə-mʷɔnʲé	'hemp leaf'
4a	u-,	hə-,	ú-kʷəgə:, hə-kʷəgə:	'chameleon'
	o-,	ha-,	ó-bʷɔmbá, há-bʷɔmbá	'leaf'
	ʔũ-,	hə-,	ʔũ´-wə´, hə´-wə´	'water monitor lizard'
	ʔɔ³,	ha-,	ʔo-tá, há-tá	'bow'
	w-	h-	w-ələmí, h-ələmí	'teacher'
4b	w-	s-	w-ã´rɔmà, s-ã´rɔmà	'chicken'
5a	ø-	sə-	-wâ:, sə-wâ:	'arm'
5b	ø-	i-	-bʷɔná, í-bʷɔná	'leg'
5c	ø-	ha-	-bʲa̰tɔ, há-bʲa̰tɔ	'medicine'
6	m-		m-ĩˇjə´	'water'
			m-əhṵtù	'burning embers'
			m-àrʲé	'food'
			m-úhʲúwə	'smoke'
			m-ɔnʲégʷà	'meat'
7	tʃí-		tʃí-lā⁻põ`	'shirt'
8a	ka-, ka-,kə-		ká-tʃɛbà	'mousetrap (karaku)'
			ká-tābɔ	'medium spoon'
			kə-zəgí	'small loud drum'
8b	kə-	sə-	kə-gúbə	'medium hawk'
8c	ki-	mu-	kí-pəpì	'small bat'
8d	ku-	hə-	kú-kʷəgə:	'large chameleon'

In some cases, what must have been a high back vowel in the prefix has now become labialisation (Table 21).

Table 21: High back prefix vowel becoming labialised

Class pair	Sg.	Pl.	Gloss
y-/mʷ-	y-ã̌ rɔmà	mʷ-ã̌ rɔmà	'chick'

Notable features are the unpaired class 7, which has few members and the prefix marking size in class 8. In other languages *kV-* is always a diminutive, but in Hungwərə there appears to be a relationship between vowel quality and size. Where the *-V-* is back, a larger size of the referent is marked, while central and front vowels seem to denote small and medium referents. Table 22 presents hypothesised abstract underlying forms for the allomorphs of singular and plural prefxes.

Table 22: Hungwərə underlying nominal affix pairings

Underlying	Singular allomorphs	Underlying	Plural allomorphs
A-	a-, ə-, ø-	S-	sə-, tʃə-
I-	i-, e-, ʔɛ-, y-	MU-	mu-, mo-, mɔ-, mʷ-
U-	u-, o-, ʔũ-, ʔɔ-, w-, ø-	hV-	hə-, ha-, hɔ-, h-
U-	w-	S-	s-
ø-	ø-	I-	i-
bU-	bu-, bo-	A-	ə-, a-
bU-	bʷ-	S-	s-

Nasalisation, although phonemic, is not treated as a feature of the underlying form. There is no trace of the nasal classes characteristic of Bantu and Bantoid.

3.6.3 The Kamuku complex

The following discussion is based on the description of Cinda in Mort (2012). Cinda noun-classes are defined by their agreement markers, shown in Table 23 but renumbered to represent allomorphy and to align the mass noun prefix with Class 6. I have entered the semantics based on lexical evidence from wordlists.

3 Nominal affixing in the Kainji languages

Table 23: Cinda noun class and agreement markers

No.	sg.	Allomorphs	No.	pl.	Allomorphs	Semantics
1	ʔA-	a-, ɨ-, ɨː-	9	ʃE-	ʃe-, ʃɛ-, ʃi-, ʃɨː-	Miscellaneous but includes numerous animals
2	E-	ɛ-, ɛː-, i-, iː-	10	mO-	mo-, moː-, mɔ-, mu-, muː-	Miscellaneous
3	O-	o-, oː-, ɔ-, u-, uː-				Plants and animals
4	bE-	bɛ-, bi-	11	E-	ɛ-, i-	Plants and animals
5	bO-	bu-, bo-, bɔ-, bʷ-	12	A-	a-, aː-, ə-, ɨ-, ø-	Persons
6	mA-	ma-, mɨ-				Mass, uncountable
7	tV-	tɛ-, tɔ-, tu-				Miscellaneous but includes body parts
8a	kA-	ka-, kɨ-				Rare
8b	kE-	kɛ-, ki-				Rare
8c	kO-	kɔ-, ku-, kʷ-				Rare

The affixes are grouped according to whether they are used for singular, plural, uncountable and as derivational prefixes.

Class markers harmonise for height with the first vowel of the root or word where they are prefixed. There may be an additional small class similar to class 1, containing singular nouns with ʔA- agreement markers, but with A- class markers on the noun. However, there is some variability between speakers, and even for the same speaker.

There is a loose semantic basis for grouping noun roots into classes and genders. Class 6 contains non-count nouns, such as *mɨ-ní* 'water', *mà-nɛbɛ* 'oil'. The gender 5/12 is used almost solely for people. Classes 2, 4, 7 and 8, forming genders 2/8, 4/8 and 4/7 are broadly associated with smaller items, although some larger things are also included, for example 'cows' bɛ-ná ɛ-ná (gender 4/7). Class 7 tU- is a derivational prefix commonly attached to a verb to create a noun, but can also be attached to a noun to derive another noun. The resultant noun behaves like other nouns, with the class marker tU-. This class is occasionally used for uncountable nouns which have no obvious derivation from a verb or another noun, like tɛgá 'porridge'. Classes 8a-c are rare, with only a total of eight examples recorded to date. The most common of these is kɔ-ɰágɔ 'food' which probably derives from ɰa 'to eat'.

3.7 The Shiroro languages

The Shiroro group consists of four languages, usually known as Rin, Fungwa, Baushi and Gurmana.[7] Baushi can be considered as language cluster with six members. The name proposed here is based on the proximity to Shiroro lake. The Shiroro languages have previously been treated as part of the Kamuku cluster, but there is no evidence for this and here they are treated as an independent branch of Kainji. The Rin (= Rĩ, formerly Pongu) language was surveyed by Dettweiler & Dettweiler (2003a) and MacDonell & Smith (2004) have circulated a phonology and grammar of Rin. For the other languages there is only wordlist data. The Rin system of nominal prefixes is quite reduced, with a bV- singular prefix predominant, and several class pairings with a zero singular prefix. Unlike many other Kainji languages, the correspondences with Niger-Congo classes have been somewhat better preserved. Figure 11 shows the likely subgrouping of the Shiroro languages.

Table 24 is a summary table of Rin nominal affixes, re-arranged from the data in MacDonell & Smith (2004) with a column listing the allomorphs of the singular prefixes which are reflected in different affix pairings. Tone is not marked in the source.

Rin has retained the Niger-Congo Class 6 prefix for liquids and mass nouns and a possible trace of the persons class (1/2). The predominance of the a- plural affix recalls the Kambari languages and the tV- prefix for mass nouns resembles the tsV- prefix also found in Kambari.

---

[7] For reasons that are unclear (perhaps typographical error?), Gerhardt (1989) placed Fungwa and Rin with Kamuku in opposition to Baushi and Gurmana. The present group was proposed and provided with some justification in Blench (1988) and has been confirmed by more detailed work (Dettweiler & Dettweiler 2003a; see especially their footnote 11).

3 Nominal affixing in the Kainji languages

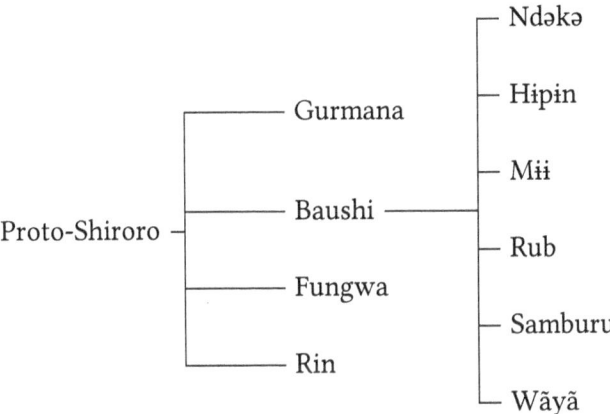

Figure 11: : The Shiroro languages

Table 24: Rin nominal affixes

No.	Singular	Allomorphs	Plural	Semantics
1	bV-	bi-	N-	animal, object
		bi-	i-	animal
		bu-	a-	human
	Ø	Ø	a-	object
		Ø	a-	animal
		Ø	N-	animal
	a-	a-	su-	animal
6	ma-		—	mass, non-count
	ri-	ri-	a-	object
	tV-	tə-	—	mass, non-count
	u-		N-	object
			a-	object

3.8 The Basa cluster

The Basa languages are spread across a wide area of central Nigeria, scattered among unrelated languages. This is probably the result of nineteenth century slave raiding. In many of the communities in the northwest, the language is moribund or only remembered by elderly speakers. As far as the fragmentary

95

evidence goes, the Basa languages are all closely related, with Table 25 showing a cluster rather than a set of distinct languages.

Table 25: The Basa languages

Basa language cluster
Basa-Kontagora (†)
Basa-Gumna (†)
Kɔrɔmba (formerly Basa-Gurmana)
Basa-Gurara
Basa-Kwali
Basa-Benue (formerly Basa-Kwomu)
Basa-Makurdi

The Basa languages probably fall into seven groups as shown in Figure 12. The subclassification is based on impressions of lexical differences.

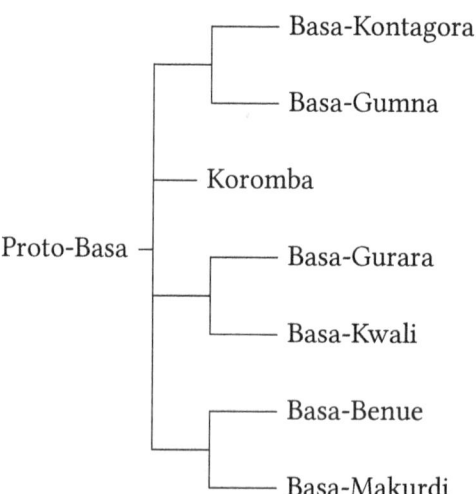

Figure 12: The subclassification of the Basa languages

Fieldwork was conducted on Basa-Benue in conjunction with Paul Imoh and the late Robert Hyslop in 1984; for other languages in the cluster only wordlist data exists. Imoh (2002) is a preliminary phonology and morphology of Basa

3 Nominal affixing in the Kainji languages

which differs somewhat from the account presented here. Tones were not marked when this data was collected.

One of the early names for West Kainji was "Basa-Kamuku", mainly because these were the languages for which data was accessible. However, the impression has remained that Basa and Kamuku have a privileged relationship, for which there seems to be no evidence. Basa-Benue noun prefixes are unique among Kainji languages in having developed three-way number marking, even if some traces of this exist in the Kambari cluster. As with Nilo-Saharan, the middle term or first plural applies to the item in general, or in an undefined quantity. In other words it is a non-countable plural where an additional plural has developed. Only a minority of nouns have three-term number marking, and those with a nasal prefix on the primary plural seem to be excluded. The second plural is countable and applies to groups or clusters of the item and, but can also be used as a distributive. The singular is a singulative, i.e. it implies a unique item. So:

(15) Basa-Benue noun prefixes: three-way number marking
a. Chili pepper
i-kpekpe 'single chili pepper'
o-kpokpo 'chili pepper(s), generic'
ʃi-kpokpo 'piles of chili peppers'

b. Broom
bi-ʃoʃo 'single broom'
i-ʃeʃe 'broom(s), generic'
n-ʃoʃo 'groups of brooms'

The prefixes are either V- or CV-. Basa permits a large number of nominal affixes and pairings, probably the consequence of the breakdown and re-analysis of the three-way number marking.

In addition, the -V in nominal prefixes in Basa can affect both the C_1 of the stem and the stem vowels. Table 26 shows the far from transparent relationship between a singular stem -a- and -E- in the plural.

However, as the second set shows, there are a variety of isolated possibilities for vowel change which do not seem to be predictable. A less common alternation is o↔(w)e. The absence of phonological conditioning is shown by the pair of words in Table 27.

Where the first syllable of the stem begins with either a palatal or a labial, the -V of the prefix can act both to delete the semi-vowel and sometimes cause changes in the vowel. Thus (16):

(16) Basa-Benue: prefixes on stems with initial palatal or labial consonants
Gloss	Singular	Plural
'guinea-fowl'	u-yogwu	ʃa-igwu
'child'	yɛ-u	myà-wɔ

Other examples of vowel mutation are more difficult to explain. Basa can also manifest intrusive nasals in the plural stem as in (17), a phenomenon more common in Plateau languages.

(17) Basa-Benue: intrusive nasals in plural stems
'large bowl'	u-gbaʤo	o-gbonʤo
'home'	u-hwɛ	n-hwan

The vowel in some CV- prefixes is underspecified and can change in order to harmonise with the 'underlying' second vowel in the noun stem. This is most

Table 26: *a/E* vowel alternations in Basa number marking

Gloss	Singular	Middle	Plural
'grass sp.'	bu-baza	tu-baza	i-bɛzɛ
'horse'	bu-dakwa	—	i-dɛkwɛ
'hand'	u-ala	—	i-ɛlɛ
'bow'	u-ta	—	i-tɛ
'dog'	u-wɛwɛ	—	ʃi-wawa
'termite'	u-da	—	i-de
'antelope sp.'	bɛ-ʃemba	—	i-ʃimbɛ
'tree'	u-'wu'wu	—	i-'wɛ'wɛ

Table 27: Non-phonologically motivated vowel alternations

Gloss	Singular	Plural
'chick'	bi-yoyo	o-yoyo
'goat' and:	bi-yoyo	i-yweywe
'rope'	u-hwohwo	i-hwehwe
'bicycle'	i-cece	n-coco

marked in the case of the ʃV- plural prefix. The prefix allomorphs are shown in Table 28.

Table 28: Prefix and stem harmony in Basa

	Example	Gloss
ʃa-	ʃa-luma	'hens'
ʃɛ-	ʃɛ-mbɛ	'grasses'
ʃe-	ʃe-jeʒe	'rays'
ʃi-	ʃi-lala	'pestles'
ʃo-	ʃo-rubo	'francolins'

There are no cases of ʃɔ- and ʃu- at present recorded. The ʃi- prefix is most common and can apparently occur with any stem vowel, synchronically. This prefix is widespread in related languages and is probably the underlying form inherited from Proto-Basa.

A similar plural prefix tV- has a more limited range of variants. In this case, the tu- form is dominant and again this corresponds to a similar prefix in other languages. The exact logic of the prefix vowels remains to be understood.

Table 29: Basa Benue variation with plural prefix tV-

Form	Example	Gloss
tɛ-	tɛ-jɛrɛka	'stone wedges'
ti-	ti-kpeku	'hills'
tu-	tu-zogu	'bush-melons'

With a few exceptions, words that have singular prefixes beginning in m-, s-, or t- do not form plurals. These affixes may originally have been applied only to uncountable nouns, such as liquids, but presently they seem to have no semantic unity and may have been generalised by analogy to countable nouns.

4 Conclusions

The Kainji languages demonstrate clear evidence for an original system of noun classes defined by nominal affixing and alliterative concord. However, the potential to reconstruct a proto-system is limited by the sparsity or absence of descriptions for many subgroups. Beyond that, however, the affix systems seem to show remarkable diversity, with only limited correspondences between branches. The observations of McGill (2009) on the noun-class system of Cicipu could apply to much of Kainji:

> It will be clear to anyone familiar with the Benue-Congo or Bantu literature that, superficially at least, the Cicipu system is very different to both the suggested Proto-Benue-Congo (PBC) reconstructions (e.g. de Wolf 1971) and the present-day Bantu systems. There are fewer classes, and the forms of the original PBC prefixes have in some cases changed beyond recognition. Nevertheless, there are also striking similarities, in particular the robust and ubiquitous alliterative agreement ... Much the same could be said about the other Kainji languages for which we have data – the prefixes and class pairings are much changed from PBC, but the mechanics of the agreement system have been retained.

The systems have eroded and been renewed in a variety of ways in different subgroups, and in particular some languages seem to have evolved highly divergent 'new' prefixes. One of the distinctive features of Kainji languages is the apparently random way singular and plural affixes shift their number marking. Thus Reshe has a Bantu-like *u-/bu-* (1/2) person marking affix pairing. Shuba has *bV-* marking plural persons but the singular prefix is the unfamiliar *do-*. In Hungwəryə the singular class marker for persons is bu- now paired with a plural ə-. A preliminary hypothesis to explain this would be that the three-way number marking found in Basa languages was formerly more widespread, and as the classes collapsed innovative class pairings resulted.

The following generalisations about Proto-Kainji seem to be supported by the data.

a) Proto-Kainji had a rich system of nominal prefixes and alliterative concord. It is possible the affixing originally showed a three-way distinction, still attested in Basa.

b) Proto-Kainji had the bilabial unpaired affix *mV-* for liquids and other mass nouns attested widely in Niger-Congo and usually assigned to Class 6.

c) Proto-Kainji had a class pair for persons, perhaps *u-/ba-* which can be treated as cognate with Bantu 1/2.

d) Proto-Kainji had underspecified vowels in a *kV*- and possibly also *tV*- and *SV*- nominal prefixes, whereby the -*V* shows harmony with the stem vowel.

e) Proto-Kainji had a diminutive (and perhaps augmentative) affix marker *kV*- (also found in some Plateau languages) which has become homophonous with a separate *kV*- marker.

f) Proto-Kainji allowed prefix swapping to indicate characteristics of the noun, marking qualities such as length or personhood.

g) If Proto-Kainji had a homorganic plural nasal prefix, the evidence is now hard to discern, since it is only clearly attested in some East Kainji and Kambari cluster languages.

Once languages where the affixes are eroded are discounted, there remains the problem of whether Reshe can be said to be part of the system. There are almost no correspondences between the Reshe system and the other branches, suggesting it is a renewed system of unknown origin. Understanding Kainji should be a priority goal in the light of its importance in the reconstruction of Proto-East Benue-Congo, but this will require a great deal more data collection and analysis.

Acknowledgements

Individual assistants and informants for particular languages are listed in the Appendix and acknowledged in particular sections, as well as in the Appendix. This chapter could not have been prepared without access to a substantial body of unpublished data, and much of the material has been re-analysed from this. However, I would also like to thank a large number of people for discussion and help in the field. These include Appollos Agamalafiya, Jennifer Davey, Steve and Sonia Dettweiler, David Heath, David & Liz Crozier, Robert (†) and Joyce Hyslop, John Nengel, Barau Kato, James McDonell, Gareth and Katherine Mort and Stuart McGill, Becky Paterson and Clark Regnier (†). Larry Hyman acted as a reviewer and made many helpful comments, as well as suggesting comparisons and extensions of these ideas. A significant update on the East Kainji material has been possible following fieldwork in Nigeria in February-May 2016. Thanks to Luther Hon and the Elm House Survey Department for help with logistics and community relations.

Abbreviations and conventions

A	any central vowel	O	any mid-back vowel
C	consonant	S	s or ʃ
E	any mid-front vowel	V	Vowel
N	any nasal		

Appendix A. Data sources for the Kainji Languages

Table 30: Principal unpublished sources for Kainji languages

Branch	Subgroup	Language	Sources
Reshe		Reshe	Harris, mss., Agamalafiya, Blench, Dettweilers
Upper Niger	Rerang	Rop	Meek, Blench, McGill
	Laru	Shuba	Blench, McGill
		Shen	Meek, Sterk, Blench, McGill
Northwest	Lela	cLela Zuru	Hoffmann, Rikoto, Dettweilers, Regnier, Blench
		cLela Ribah	Blench
	Hun	tHun	Skitch & Cressman, Regnier, Dettweilers, Heath
		sSaare	Regnier, Dettweilers, Blench
	Gwamhi	Gwamhyə	Regnier, Rowlands, Blench, McGill
		Wurə	Regnier, Blench, McGill
		Mba	Blench, McGill
	ut-Ma'in	Kag	Blench, Regnier
		Fer	Regnier
		Jiir	Regnier
		Kər	Regnier
		Koor	None
		Ror	Smith, Regnier
		Us	Regnier
		Zuksun	Rowlands
	?	Damakawa	McGill

3 Nominal affixing in the Kainji languages

Table 31: Unpublished sources for Kainji languages (continuation of Table 30)

Branch	Subgroup	Language	Sources
Kambari		CiShingini	Hoffmann, Crozier, Stark et al.
		Tsivadi	Lovelace, Blench
		Baangi	Blench
		Tsikimba	Blench, Stark et al.
		Agwara	Mierau, Stark et al.
		Cicipu	McGill, Dettweilers
East		Gbiri	Wenger
		Boze	Blench
		Sheni	Blench
		Moro	Blench
Kamuku		Shama	Regnier, Yoder et al., McGill
		Rogo-Shyabe	Regnier, Yoder et al., Blench, McGill
		Səgəmuk	Regnier
		Cinda	Regnier, Blench, Mort, Yoder et al.
		Regi	Regnier, Omanor, Yoder et al.
		Kuki	Regnier, Blench, Yoder et al.
		Zubazuba	Yoder et al., Blench, McGill
		Kagare	Yoder et al.
		Hungwəryə	Davey
Shiroro		Fungwa	Blench, McGill
		Rin	Rowlands, Regnier, Dettweilers, Blench, MacDonell & Smith
		Wəgə	Blench, McGill
		Gurmana	Johnston, Blench, McGill
	Baushi	Ndəkə	Regnier
		Hipina	McGill
		Rubu	None
		Miin	Gimba, Blench
		Samburu	None
		Wãyã	Dettweiler
Basa		Basa Kontagora	Rowlands, Blench
		Basa-Gumna	Blench
		Korɔmba	Blench
		Basa-Gurara	Sterk
		Basa-Benue	Blench
		Basa-Makurdi	Blench

References

Anderson, Stephen C. 1980. The noun class system of Amo. In Larry Hyman (ed.), *Noun classes in the Grassfields Bantu borderland* (Southern California Occasional Papers in Linguistics 8), 155–178. Los Angeles: Department of Linguistics, Univ. of Southern California.

Bendor-Samuel, John, Donna Skitch & Esther Cressman. 1973. *Duka sentence, clause and phrase.* Zaria: Institute of Linguistics.

Bertho, J. 1952. Aperçu d'ensemble sur les dialectes de l'ouest de Nigéria. *Bull Institut français de l'Afrique Noire (IFAN)* 14. 259–271.

Blench, Roger M. 1982. Social structure and the evolution of language boundaries in Nigeria. *Cambridge Anthropology* 3. 19–30.

Blench, Roger M. 1988. *The internal structure of Basa-Kamuku languages.* Paper for the 18th Colloquium on African Languages and Linguistics (CALL), Leiden.

Blench, Roger M. 2016. *Lamnso' verb extensions.* Cambridge. University of Cambridge Manuscript.

Blench, Roger M. & Boze Literacy Committee (BLC). n.d. *A dictionary of Boze.* Jos: Boze Language Committee. Unpublished manuscript.

Boettger, E. & V. Boettger. 1967. *Tsureshe grammar.* Unpublished manuscript.

Crozier, David. 1984. *A study in the discourse grammar in Cishingini.* Ibadan: Department of Linguistics & Nigerian Languages, University of Ibadan Doctoral dissertation.

Crozier, David & Roger M. Blench. 1992. *Index of Nigerian languages.* 2nd edn. Dallas, TX: SIL.

de Wolf, Paul P. 1971. *The noun class system of Proto-Benue-Congo.* The Hague: Mouton.

Dettweiler, Stephen H. 2015. *C'Lela grammar sketch.* Unpublished manuscript.

Dettweiler, Stephen H. & Sonia G. Dettweiler. 2002. *Sociolinguistic survey (level one) of the Reshe people.* http://www.sil.org/silesr/2002/SILESR2002-042.pdf. original draft 1993.

Dettweiler, Stephen H. & Sonia G. Dettweiler. 2003a. *Sociolinguistic survey (level one) of the Kamuku language cluster.* http://www.sil.org/silesr/2003/silesr2003-003.pdf. original draft 1995.

Dettweiler, Stephen H. & Sonia G. Dettweiler. 2003b. *Sociolinguistic survey of the Duka (Hun-Saare) people.* http://www.sil.org/silesr/2003/silesr2003-014.pdf. original draft 1993.

Di Luzio, Aldo. 1972. Preliminary description of the Amo language. *Afrika und Übersee* 56(3). 3–61.

Gerhardt, Ludwig. 1989. Kainji and Platoid. In John Bendor-Samuel (ed.), *Niger-Congo*, 359–376. Lanham, MD: University Press of America.

Greenberg, Joseph H. 1955. *Studies in African linguistic classification*. New Haven: Compass Publishing Company.

Greenberg, Joseph H. 1963. The languages of Africa. *IJAL* Part II, No. 1(29).

Gunn, Harold D. & Francis Paine Conant. 1960. *Peoples of the Middle Niger region of northern Nigeria*. London.

Hackett, Chris & Niffer Davey. 2009. *A phonological sketch of the C'Hungwere language*. Unpublished manuscript.

Hoffmann, Carl. 1963. The noun-class system of Central Kambari. *Journal of African Languages* 2(2). 160–169.

Hoffmann, Carl. 1967. An outline of the Dakarkari noun class system and the relation between prefix and suffix noun-class systems. In Gabriel Manessy (ed.), *La classification nominale dans les langues négro-africaines*, 237–259. Paris: CNRS.

Hyman, Larry M. & Daniel J. Magaji. 1970. *Essentials of Gwari grammar*. Ibadan.

Imoh, Philip Manda. 2002. *The phonology and morphology of Bassa language spoken in Kogi, Nassarawa, Niger States and the Federal Capital Territory of Nigeria*. Jos B.A. thesis.

Koelle, Sigismund W. 1854. *Polyglotta Africana*. London: Church Missionary House.

MacDonell, James & Philip Smith. 2004. *A phonological and grammatical sketch of the Pongu language*. London. Unpublished manuscript.

McGill, Stuart. 2007. The Cicipu noun class system. *Journal of West African Languages* 34(2). 51–90.

McGill, Stuart. 2009. *Gender and person agreement in Cicipu discourse*. London Doctoral dissertation. http://www.cicipu.org/papers/gender_and_person_agreement_in_cicipu_discourse.pdf.

McGill, Stuart. 2010. Person and gender: Competing agreement paradigms in Cicipu. In Konstantin Pozdniakov, Valentine Vydrin & Alexander Zheltov (eds.), *Proceedings of the Personal Pronouns in Niger-Congo Workshop*, 79–87. St. Petersburg: St. Petersburg State University Press.

McGill, Stuart & Roger M. Blench. 2012. Documentation, development, and ideology in the northwestern Kainji languages. In Peter K. Austin & Stuart McGill (eds.), vol. 11, 91–136. London: SOAS.

Meek, Charles K. 1925. *The Northern tribes of Nigeria*. London: Humphrey Milford. 2 vols.

Mort, Katharine. 2012. *A phonological description of the Cinda [tʃində] dialect of the Kamuku language*. Electronic ms.

Paterson, Rebecca. 2012. The semantics of Ut-Ma'in noun classes. In Roger M. Blench & Stuart McGill (eds.), *Advances in minority language research in Nigeria*, 239–272. Köln: Rudiger Köppe.

Regnier, Clark D. A. 2003. *Sociolinguistic survey of the people of Fakai district.* http://www.sil.org/silesr/2003/silesr2003-021.pdf.

Rikoto, Bulu Doro, P.N. Senchi, M. Earwicker, D. Rowbory & Renée Wenger. 2001. *K'Batksa C'Lela-C'Anasara-C'Gana*. s.l.: Lelna Language Development/Translation Project.

Rowlands, E. C. 1962. Notes on some class languages of Northern Nigeria. *African Language Studies* 3. 71–83.

Shimizu, Kiyoshi. 1968. *An outline of the I-búnú noun class system.* Ibadan: Dept. of Linguistics & Nigerian Languages Doctoral dissertation.

Shimizu, Kiyoshi. 1979. Five wordlists with analyses from the Northern Jos group of Plateau languages. *Afrika und Übersee* 62(4). 253–271.

Shimizu, Kiyoshi. 1982. Die Nord-Jos-Gruppe der Plateausprachen Nigerias. *Afrika und Übersee* 65(2). 161–210.

Shimizu, Kiyoshi. 1982a. Ten more wordlists with analyses from the Northern Jos group of Plateau languages. *Afrika und Übersee* 65(1). 97–134.

Smith, Rebecca Dow. 2007. *The noun class system of UT-Ma'in, a West Kainji language of Nigeria*. Grand Forks, ND: University of North Dakota MA thesis.

Temple, Olive. 1922. *Notes on the tribes, provinces, emirates and states of the Northern provinces of Nigeria*. Capetown: Argus Printing & Publishing Co.

Westermann, Diedrich & Margaret A. Bryan. 1952. *Languages of West Africa: Part II*. Vol. 2. London: Oxford University Press.

Williamson, Kay. 1971. The Benue-Congo languages and Ịjọ. In Thomas Sebeok (ed.), *Current trends in linguistics*, 245–306. The Hague: Mouton.

Williamson, Kay. 1989. Benue-Congo overview. In John Bendor-Samuel (ed.), *The Niger-Congo languages*, 246–274. Lanham, MD: University Press of America.

Williamson, Kay & Roger M. Blench. 2000. Niger-Congo. In Bernd Heine & Derek Nurse (eds.), *African languages: An introduction*, 11–42. Cambridge: Cambridge University Press.

Yoder, Zachariah, Katarína Hannelová, Carol Magnusson, Yakubu Oro, Linus Otronyi, Michael J. Rueck & Katharine Spencer. 2008. *Sociolinguistic survey of the 'Yara (Kamuku) people, Niger and Kaduna States, Nigeria*. Jos: Wycliffe Nigeria. (Unpublished survey report.)

Chapter 4

Nominal affixes and number marking in the Plateau languages of Central Nigeria

Roger M. Blench
McDonald Institute for Archaeological Research, University of Cambridge

> The Plateau branch of East Benue-Congo consists of between sixty and eighty languages spoken in central Nigeria, spreading from Lake Shiroro to the banks of the Benue River. Proto-Plateau is usually considered to have a system of alternating nominal affixes marking number combined with alliterative concord. The paper presents an overall internal classification and then reviews the evidence for affix systems by subgroup, taking a specific language as an exemplar, with a view to linking these to broader hypotheses about Niger-Congo nominal classes. It appears that Plateau has undergone extensive affix renewal, and thus only fragments of any more coherent system are still present. Plateau languages originally had a rich noun class system with CV- and V- prefixes and alliterative concord, but a wave of renewal and analogical re-alignment led to many of the CV- prefixes disappearing or becoming unproductive and replaced by a much smaller set of V- prefixes.

1 Introduction: Plateau languages

The Plateau branch of East Benue-Congo consists of between sixty and eighty languages spoken in central Nigeria, spreading from Lake Shiroro to the banks of the Benue River (Figure 1). Although most Plateau populations are small (2-10,000 speakers), there are probably more than a million speakers of Plateau languages, with the bulk of the numbers made up from large groups such as Berom and Eggon. Some Plateau languages, such as Sambe and Yangkam, are moribund and others are severely threatened, such as Ayu.

Plateau languages represent one of the four major branches of East Benue-Congo outside Bantoid, together with Kainji, Jukunoid and Cross River. Internally, they are divided into a large number of subgroups, whose inter-relations

Roger M. Blench. Nominal affixes and number marking in the Plateau languages of Central Nigeria. In John R. Watters (ed.), *East Benue-Congo: Nouns, pronouns, and verbs*, 107–172. Berlin: Language Science Press.
DOI:10.5281/zenodo.1314325

are not well understood. Plateau languages remain extremely poorly studied, with no complete grammar or dictionary for any language except Berom (which is in French and thus inaccessible to Nigerians). Basic overviews of their ethnography and ethnic distribution can be found in Temple (1922), Meek (1925; 1931), Gunn (1953; 1956) and Crozier & Blench (1992).

The most striking feature of Plateau is its morphological and typological diversity. It is usually assumed that Proto-Plateau would have had a system of paired nominal prefixes with semantic associations and alliterative concord, similar to but probably less elaborate than Bantu. However, these systems have collapsed and been rebuilt or in some cases disappeared completely. Compensatory morphology has evolved, including highly complex consonantal inventories and rich tone-systems. Synchronically, Plateau languages display systems of consonant mutation, contrastive length, as well as palatalisation, labialisation, lateralisation of initial consonants and combinations of all these.

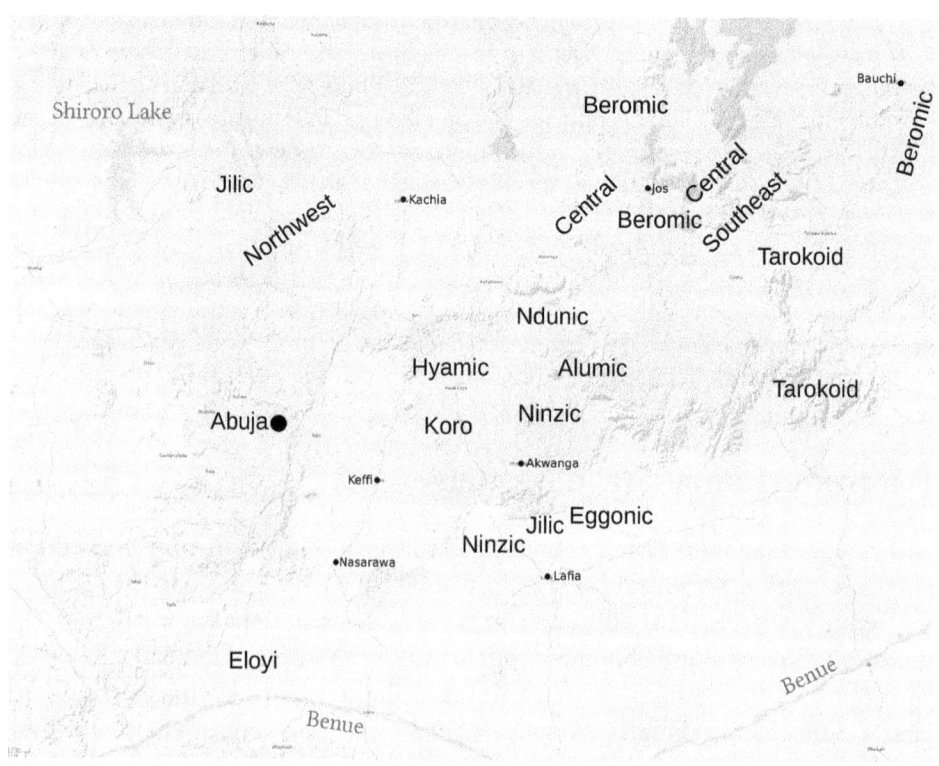

Figure 1: The Plateau languages by subgroup © OpenStreetMaps contributors

4 Nominal affixes and number marking in the Plateau languages

The origin of these diverse outcomes may lie in the characteristic marriage systems within the Plateau region. These systems often involved linguistic exogamy, which, combined with marital instability, resulted in the pervasive multilingualism which almost certainly played a role in the evolution of complex 'mixed' systems of number marking. Plateau marriage systems are discussed in considerable detail in Muller (1982). Many different systems co-existed, and there is evidence that when absolute numbers of speakers were much lower (often as little as 500 per language in the pre-colonial era) this principle of outmarriage was strongly enforced.

Plateau languages are assumed to form part of the broader unit represented by East Benue-Congo (Williamson 1971; 1989; Williamson & Blench 2000). The earliest source for Plateau, Koelle (1854) gives wordlists of Ham (Hyam), Koro of Lafia (Migili) and Yasgua (Yeskwa). Westermann (1927) assigned the few languages for which he had data to a "Benue-Cross" family, corresponding to present-day East Benue-Congo, although later in Westermann & Bryan (1952) these were classified as "isolated units". However, the modern subclassification of Plateau derives principally from the work of Joseph Greenberg (1963) who proposed dividing Westermann's "Benue-Cross" languages into seven co-ordinate groups (including modern-day Kainji and Jukunoid). With numerous emendations and additions these have been reprised in almost all subsequent works (notably Williamson & Shimizu 1968; Williamson 1971; 1972; 1989; Maddieson 1982; Gerhardt 1989; Crozier & Blench 1992; Blench 1998; 2000a). Blench (n.d.[b]) reflects the most recent understanding of Plateau subgrouping.

Comparative studies of number marking in the Plateau languages are scarce; Bouquiaux (1967) represents an initial attempt to discern commonalties across a small number of languages. Some Plateau languages retain complex systems of nominal affixes and alliterative concord, notably Kulu and other members of the northwest cluster and Tarok. However, many languages, such as Cara and the Ninzic cluster, include some affix alternation as part of a repertoire of number marking strategies, while subgroups such as Ndunic and Ake, have completely lost these systems. Other languages, such as Izere, have systems which look elaborate at first sight, but when segmental and tonal allomorphs are taken into account, the underlying number of pairings is considerably reduced. The existence of these systems certainly suggests that alternating affixes and concord were a feature of Proto-Plateau, but actual segmental correspondences between affixes are few, pointing to a continuing process of renewal. Plateau also has frequent nasal prefixes, as well as numerous examples of unproductive nasals preceding C_1 of the stem (Miehe 1991). Some of these are reflected more widely in other branches of Benue-Congo or even further afield in Kwa. However, the correspondences between noun classes and semantic subsets (humans, trees, animals, paired things) characteristic of Bantu are more tenuous.

The analytic challenge of Plateau is to account for synchronic number marking systems through the lens of the erosion of affix alternation. In the light of this, the confident assertions of authors such as de Wolf (1971) in reconstructing the prefixes of Proto-Benue-Congo seem very optimistic. Such reconstructed forms reflect a prior knowledge of Bantu and a large pool of miscellaneous data from which exemplars can be selectively chosen. This paper is an overview of nominal affixing in the Plateau languages, based principally on my own fieldwork materials.[1]. It describes the systems in individual subgroups and then asks what evidence these provide for the situation in Proto-Plateau.

None of the authors who have classified Plateau languages have presented evidence for their classifications. This is not a criticism; faced with large arrays of data it is easier to set out what appears to be the case impressionistically than to write a monograph demonstrating it. The series of publications on Plateau subgroups, especially Plateau II and IV, by Gerhardt (1969b; 1969a; 1971; 1972/3; 1972/73; 1973/4; 1974; 1983a; 1983b; 1988a; 1988b; 1989; 1994) assume the boundaries of these groups. A particular issue in the internal classification of Plateau and Jukunoid is the notion of a 'Benue' grouping. Shimizu (1975a: 415) proposed that some branches of Plateau should be classified with Jukunoid. In particular, he argued that Eggon (and by implication the other Plateau V languages, including Nungu and Yeskwa) and Tarokoid (at that time consisting only of Yergam (=Tarok) and Basherawa (=Yaŋkam)) formed a group together with Jukunoid. This emerged from his lexico-statistical tables and was further supported by five isoglosses, the words for 'drink', 'tail', 'meat', 'fire', and 'four'. This expanded group he christened "Benue". Gerhardt (1983b) questioned Shimizu's hypothesis noting both that his own lexico-statistical work (Gerhardt & Jockers 1981) did not support this, and casting doubt on the five isoglosses proposed by Shimizu. The 'Benue' group continued in a sort of half-life, appearing in Gerhardt (1989) as a subgrouping of Jukunoid and Tarokoid against the rest of Plateau. Blench (2005) has presented evidence that there is a genuine boundary between Plateau and Jukunoid, drawing on lexical and morphological evidence.

This uncertainty is a reflection of a more general problem, the evidence for a bounded group "Plateau" in opposition to Kainji, Jukunoid, Dakoid or Mambiloid, other members of the Benue-Congo complex. The relationships between Plateau languages, their coherence as a grouping and their links with Jukunoid and Kainji

---

[1]Lexical and grammatical materials are available on the author's website Blench (n.d.[g])

remain undetermined. Rowlands (1962) was the first to suggest that there was a dichotomy between certain languages of the Jos area, which he linked to West Kainji, and the remainder, but his short wordlists were far from constituting linguistic proof. Comparative analysis has produced some tentative evidence for isoglosses defining Plateau, but so far no phonological or morphological innovations that would define the group have been proposed. Some of this diversity is undoubtedly due to long-term interactions with the mosaic of Chadic languages also occurring on the Jos Plateau (Blench 2003).

With these caveats, Figure 2 presents a new subclassification of Plateau, within the context of East Benue-Congo. Evidence for this subgrouping is presented in Blench (in press). The majority of evidence is lexical, but some subgroups, such as Northwest, clearly also share considerable common elements in the noun-class system. This "tree" is clearly not final, as there are too many co-ordinate branches and too little internal structure. But until further analysis is undertaken, provisional versions of Plateau which do not promote too many unwarranted assumptions are the best that can be produced.

This paper is organised using these Plateau subgroups and listed approximately left to right. The summary Tables 1–10 also gives a list of all known Plateau languages. The great majority of material presented here is either from my own fieldwork since 1980, from manuscript sources, with a relatively small amount from published work, cited in the reference list. Where no source is cited, it can be taken this is my own data. All original wordlists can be found on my website. Some of the earliest data is not tone-marked, and the segmental transcription may be less reliable. Most Plateau languages have a three-level tone system and by convention the mid-tone is not marked. Therefore, if the data is tone-marked, a vowel without a tone is deemed to be mid. Where a standardised orthography exists, for example in the case of Mada, only the high tone is unmarked. I have noted deviations from the standard tone marking in relation to relevant examples.

The sample wordlist is usually five hundred items and of these some 350 are nouns with singular and plural recorded. Allowing for entries that cannot be elicited, the nouns available for analysis amount to around 300. Where the data has not been collected by the author, the sample may be smaller, whereas in the case of dictionaries prepared by the author, for example Berom, Izere, Mada and Tarok the sample is usually well over a thousand. For most languages only singular/plural pairs are available, but where a grammar sketch has been prepared, we also have an overview of the concord system. The reader should refer to the

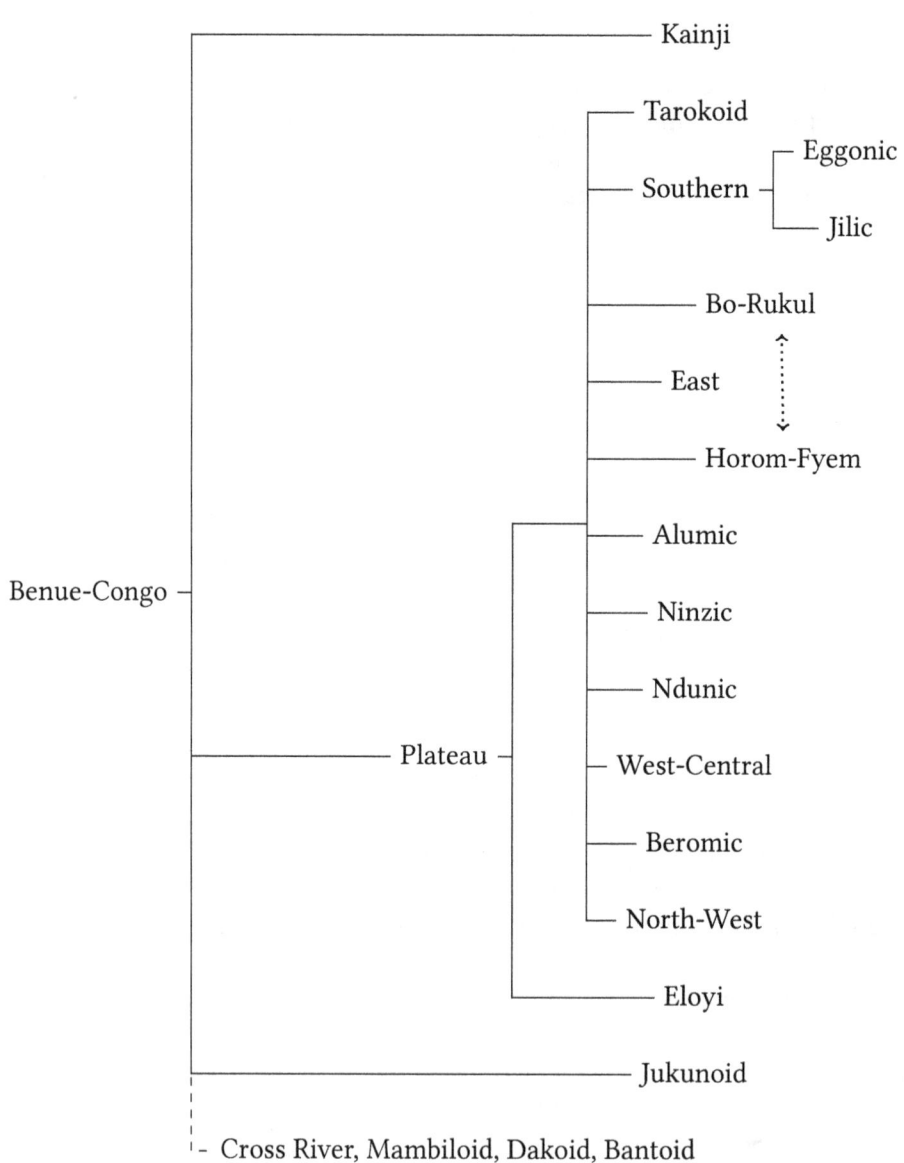

Figure 2: Proposed classification of Benue-Congo languages

original wordlist for examples of the noun-class pairings, where these are summarised in the tables below.

Plateau languages exhibit extensive allomorphy in their nominal affix systems. Allomorphs are here defined as 'one of two or more complementary morphs which manifest a morpheme in its different phonological or morphological environments' Loos et al. (2003). In Plateau, tonal allomorphs are common because the tone of the prefix may be driven by the tone of the stem, thus the V of a CV prefix may have one of three tone levels, as for example in Kulu. Sometimes claims of allomorphy in less-well-studied languages are only educated guesses, based on parallels with better known languages. The term alternation is used to apply to the change in prefix on a stem marking number, i.e. singular and either one or two plurals. Throughout the text, the tables present a summary of the prefix alternations occurring in the data, mostly wordlists. This is not ideal, as we have no evidence for the patterns of concord in many languages, but it provides a preliminary guide to the synchronic system.

2 Plateau languages by subgroup

Tables 1–10 show a comprehensive list of Plateau languages, by subgroup, and a summary of the system of number-marking, as far as it is known. Where there is a published reference on a specific language, it is given, although I do not always agree with the analysis and the text presents my own hypothesis. No entry in the reference column means the summary is based on my own fieldwork. The names of the branches are proposed by the author, since the classification is at variance with previous proposals in many areas. Further justification can be found in Blench (2000a).

Table 1: Synthesis of nominal affixing: Northwest

Language	Comments	Reference
Eda	Reduced alternating prefixes, concord	
Edra	Reduced alternating prefixes, concord	
Acro	Reduced alternating prefixes	
Obiro	Reduced alternating prefixes	
Kulu	Extensive alternating prefixes, elaborate allomorphy, concord	Seitz (1993)
Ẹjẹgha [Idon]	Extensive alternating prefixes, elaborate allomorphy, concord	
Doka	Data very poor	
Ẹhwa [Iku-Gora-Ankwe]	Reduced alternating prefixes	

Table 2: Synthesis of nominal affixing: Beromic

Language	Comments	Reference
Berom	Reduced alternating prefixes, consonant mutation, concord	Wolff (1963) Bouquiaux (1970)
Cara	Restricted alternating prefixes, stem-tone change, consonant mutation, concord	
Iten	Reduced alternating prefixes, consonant mutation, concord	Bouquiaux (1964)
Shall-Zwall	Data very poor but affix system apparently heavily eroded	

4 Nominal affixes and number marking in the Plateau languages

Table 3: Synthesis of nominal affixing: West-Central

Izeric		
Izere of Fobur of Fobur	Restricted alternating prefixes, and extensive stem-tone changes.	Blench (2000b)
Icèn, Ganàng, Fəràn	Similar to others in group	
Rigwe		
Rigwe	Innovative system, with residual concord	Anonymous (2006) Blench & Gya (2012)
Southern Zaria		
Jju	Innovative prefix system, suffixed elements	McKinney (1979) Hyuwa (1986)
Tyapic		
Tyap	Innovative prefix system, suffixed elements	Follingstad (1991)
Gworok	Innovative prefix system, suffixed elements	Adwiraah & Hagen (1983)
Atakar, Kacicere, Sholyo, Kafancan	Similar to others in group	
Koro		
Ashe	Very reduced affix alternation	
Tinɔr (Waci-Myamya)	Very reduced affix alternation	
Idũ, Gwara	Very reduced affix alternation	
Nyankpa-Barde	Very reduced affix alternation	
Hyamic		
Shamang	As Hyam cluster	
Cori	As Hyam cluster	Dihoff (1976)
Hyam	Nominal prefixes almost lost and replaced by consonant mutation and stem-tone change	Jockers (1982)
Zhire	As Hyam cluster	
Shang	Small number of alternating prefixes but probably borrowed from Koro languages	
Gyongic		
Gyong (=Kagoma)	Very restricted alternating prefixes, palatalisation, concord	Hagen (1988)
Kamanton	Similar to Gyong	

Table 4: Synthesis of nominal affixing: Ninzic

Language	Comments	Reference
Ninzo	Very restricted alternating prefixes	
Ce	Elaborate alternating prefixes and concord	Hoffmann (1976)
Bu-Niŋkada	No morphological plurals	
Mada	Very restricted alternating prefixes, some concord, multiple other number-marking strategies	Price (1989)
Numana-Nunku-Gwantu-Numbu	Information inadequate	
Ningye-Ninka	Alternating prefixes lost, tone plurals	
Anib	Very restricted alternating prefixes	
Ninkyob	Very restricted alternating prefixes	
Nindem	Very restricted alternating prefixes	
Nungu	Information inadequate	
Ayu[a]	a. prefix alternation or addition b. consonant mutation c. tone-change d. nasal insertion	

[a] Ayu is of uncertain Ninzic affiliation

Table 5: Synthesis of nominal affixing: Ndunic

Language	Comments	Reference
Ndun [=Tari]	Extremely reduced system, retaining Niger-Congo a/ba person class	Rueck et al. (2008)

4 Nominal affixes and number marking in the Plateau languages

Table 6: Synthesis of nominal affixing: Alumic

Language	Comments	Reference
Toro, Alumu-Tǝsu	No functioning noun-prefixes and a single plural suffix.	
Hasha	Innovative system, reduplicating first syllable of stem	
Sambe (†)	No functioning noun-prefixes and a single plural suffix.	

Table 7: Synthesis of nominal affixing: Southern

Language	Comments	Reference
Eggonic		
Eggon	Very reduced nominal affix pairings and concord, evolution of single pluralising prefix.	Maddieson (1982; n.d.); Sibomana (1985)
Ake	No functioning noun-prefixes	
Jilic		
Jili	Elaborate alternating prefixes and concord	Stofberg (1978)
Jijili	Elaborate alternating prefixes and concord	

Table 8: Synthesis of nominal affixing: Southeastern

Language	Comments	Reference
Fyem	Very reduced nominal affix pairings, suffixing, stem initial syllable reduplication	Nettle (1998b)
Horom	Very reduced nominal affix pairings, circumfixing	Nettle (1998a)
Bo-Rukul	Alternating prefixes with extensive allomorphy and concord	Nettle (1998a)

Table 9: Synthesis of nominal affixing: Tarokoid

Language	Comments	Reference
Tarok	Alternating prefixes and concord	Sibomana (1981), Longtau (2008)
Pe [=Pai]	Very reduced nominal affix pairings and concord	
Kwang-Ya-Bijim-Legeri	Very reduced nominal affix pairings and concord	
Yaŋkam [=Bashar]	Fragmentary nominal affix pairings, may be a problem of informant recall	
Sur [=Tapshin]	No functioning noun-prefixes	

Table 10: Synthesis of nominal affixing: Eloyi

Language	Comments	Reference
Eloyi	Elaborate alternating prefixes and concord	Armstrong (1964), Mackay (1964)

2.1 Northwest Plateau

Northwest Plateau consists of Eda/Edra, Acro-Obiro [=Kuturmi], Kulu, Idon, Doka and Iku-Gora-Ankwe. No new data has been published since this group was set up, although a wordlist of Kulu has been circulated (Moser 1982, analysed in Seitz 1993) and Shimizu (1996) has posted a grammar sketch on the Internet. Recent interest in Ẹda [=Kadara] language has resulted in an unpublished dialect survey, a preliminary alphabet book and the launching of an alphabet chart in 2009. Kadara is known to its speakers as 'Ẹda' and there is a closely related lect, Ẹdra (which is presumably the source of the common Hausa name). Two other lects for which information is recorded, Ẹjẹgha and Ẹhwa,[2] correspond to Idon and the Iku-Gora-Ankwe clusters (as named in the Benue-Congo Comparative Wordlist in Williamson & Shimizu 1968; Williamson 1972). The wordlists are so

---

[2]Thanks to Zac Yoder for sound files of wordlists of 384 items of these languages. Retranscribed by the author.

different from each other and from Ẹda that they clearly deserve separate language status. Northwest Plateau remains a high priority for further research.

Table 11 shows the singular/plural prefix pairings recorded in Kulu including tonal variants, based on Moser (1982) and Seitz (1993). A postulated 'underlying' prefix is given together with its allomorphs. The mid-front vowel shows harmony with the stem-vowel. The bracketed nasals in the plural prefixes show their sporadic appearance. They are homorganic with the following consonant and only follow /i/.

Table 11: Kulu prefix pairings. Re-analysis by author of Moser (1982) and Shimizu (1996).

Singular		Plural	
Underlying	Surface	Underlying	Surface
E-	è, e, é, ȅ, ɛ	bE-, a-	bὲ. bɛ, a
dì-	dì, di	a, be- e-	a, be, è, e
gE-	gè,ge,gé,gȅ,gɛ	bE-	be,bɛ
gì-	gì,gi,gí	E-, Ni-	be,i(m), i(ŋ), nì, ni, nǐ, ní(n), í(n)
gù-	gù,gu	E-, Ni-	ɛ,ȅ,e,ì,i(n)
ì-	ì	Ni-	m̀,mì(n)
ù-	ù,u	bE-, i-	be, i

Tonal variation in prefixes is driven by the stem-tone (as in many Plateau languages, cf. Blench 2000b) and the different surface tones do not in themselves mark distinct pairs marked for number. The numerous forms of a *gV*- prefix presumably point to these all originally having a single underspecified vowel which has gradually diverged.[3] The presence of an underspecified vowel in the V of a prefix is very common in the East Kainji languages with which Kulu is in contact and it is possible this is a borrowing.

Kulu has frequent doubled /l/ in stem-initial position, assumed to derive from nasal prefixes which have been first fossilised and then assimilated to an initial lateral. For example (1):

(1) a. Doubled /l/ in stem-initial position
    b. *gé-llam* 'water'

---

[3] One reviewer queries the directionality of this process. However, if instead this were a case of convergence, this would require ten different surface forms to come together, which is hardly an economical explanation.

c. *gu-llúrú* 'storm'
d. *gɛ-llán* 'chin'
e. *gɛ̀-llìbì* 'hyena'

Semantic associations in Kulu are weak, but the majority of nouns for persons show *E-/bE-* prefix alternation. Most domestic animals have a *gV-* singular prefix but no consistent plural marking. Wild animals, on the other hand, almost all have their singular and plural forms distinguished only by tonal differences in the stem. Trees, body parts, abstracts and even mass nouns do not form consistent sets marked by paired affixes. The *ni-* prefix for noun plurals is uncommon and surprisingly, it is strongly correlated with household items as in Table 12.

Table 12: The *ni-* plural prefix in Kulu

Gloss	Singular	Plural
'knife'	gí-ŋmáŋ	ní-ŋmáŋ
'bag'	gi-mpak	ni-mpak
'mortar (wood)'	gí-ŋklu	ní-ŋklu
'pot (generic)'	gí-nugu	nǐi-nugu
'head-board'	gí-ŋgwel	ní-ŋgwel
'basket (generic)'	gi-ndʒili⁺	ni-ndʒili⁺
'spoon'	gi-ntʃàk	ni-ntʃàk
'fish-trap'	gí-sak	nín-sak

However, Kulu does operate a principle of using prefixes to assign semantics, such as the parts of a tree, by means of prefixes, as for example in (2):

(2) Kulu prefixes used to assign semantics e.g. parts of tree
 gi-n-yoŋ 'locust tree'
 gɛ́-n-yoŋ 'locust fruit'
 u-yoŋ 'locust pod powder'

2.2 Beromic

The term 'Beromic' has been adopted here to cover former Plateau 2 languages. Beromic now consists of Berom, Iten, Cara and two closely related lects, Shall and Zwall, geographically distant in Bauchi State. The principal publications on Berom are Bouquiaux (1970; 2001) and Kuhn & Dusu (1985), and on Iten,

Bouquiaux (1964). Recent unpublished materials are dictionaries of Berom and Iten. Cara (Teriya) was reported in a mimeo paper by Shimizu (1975b), who first proposed a link with Berom. Shall and Zwall were previously classified with the Ninzic languages (Plateau 4), but are better placed with Beromic Blench (n.d.[c]). Beromic languages show a broad range of number-marking systems, although none have a full noun-class system and Shall-Zwall has lost all nominal affixing, perhaps under the influence of Chadic. A summary of Beromic number marking is shown in Table 13.

Table 13: Number-marking in Beromic.
Source: All analyses of Beromic by author based on personal fieldwork.

Language	Summary of number marking
Berom	Very restricted prefix alternations, incipient consonant mutation
Cara	Restricted prefix alternations, complex consonant mutation, tone and length contrasts
Iten	Prefix alternations, complex consonant mutation
Shall-Zwall	Nominal prefixes entirely lost

Berom itself has a complex internal structure. Central Berom includes the Du dialect described by Bouquiaux (1970; 2001) as well as both Vwang (Vom) and Ryom (Riyom). The speakers of Vwang are the most numerous, but the main dialect used for literacy and bible translation is the Eastern dialect, roughly centred on Foron, spoken by only a minority. The other minority dialect is Rim, south and east of the main centres. Data on Berom presented here is based on long-term fieldwork on the Foron dialect and shows marked differences with the Du of Bouquiaux.

Berom noun pluralisation strategies are extremely varied. The most common are:

a) prefix addition or alternation

b) tone-raising

c) (de)labialisation

d) consonant alternation

e) number marking in verbal nouns replicating corresponding verbal plurals

In some cases, two procedures can be applied to mark a plural, suggesting the dynamics of renewal. The great majority of Berom singular nouns have no prefix, while on nouns that are marked for plural, the *be-* prefix is predominant. Berom shows 'echo' concord, where a small subset of concordial adjectives exactly copy the nominal prefix of the noun they qualify. Where the noun has no prefix, the adjective shows no concord. Berom also has just three suppletive plurals in a dictionary which includes more than 2000 nouns. Due to this relatively large database, it is possible to estimate the frequency of nominal prefix alternations in Eastern Berom seen in Table 14.

Table 14: Nominal prefix alternations in Eastern Berom

Sg.	Pl.	Incidence	Semantics
ø-	be-/pe-	common	loanwords, miscellaneous
ø-	ba-	occasional	body parts, grasses
ø-	nè-	common	miscellaneous
kè-	nè-	common	diminutives
ne-/n-/ŋ-/m-	ø-	common	colours, abstracts, mass nouns, diminutives
*ra-, re-, rɛ-	ba-	common	body parts, miscellaneous
se-	ø-, ba-, ne-	rare	unpaired class marks abstracts, paired classes miscellaneous
-w-	ø-	common	miscellaneous
wò-	be-	occasional	'person of, from'
-y-	ø-	common	miscellaneous

Tone-marks show the most characteristic tone for this class, with mid-tone unmarked. However, there are numerous unexplained exceptions, which may reflect interaction with the stem-vowel. *ra-* is not attested synchronically as a productive prefix, since all singular nouns in current Berom with stem-initial *ra-* have a zero singular prefix and a plural prefix *be-*. However, many words have *ra-* as a first syllable, such as *rato* 'head' where the *ra-* is not historically part of the root, because *–to* is widely attested across Benue-Congo for 'head'.

4 Nominal affixes and number marking in the Plateau languages

The alternation *wo-/be-*, in (3), is the ethnonym for the Berom people, and is probably not originally a noun class pair. *wo* is a personal pronoun and *be-* a generic plural marker.

(3) *Wòrom* 'Berom person'
    Berom 'Berom people'

The labial and palatal infixes *-w-* and *-y-* almost certainly originally derive from *u-* and *i-* prefixes which have been incorporated into the stem, as in many other Plateau languages. Kießling (2010) has described analogous processes in the languages of the Grassfields of Cameroun. Tonal changes accompany number marking suggest that the tone of the lost prefix vowel affected the stem tone of the noun.

The nasal prefixes form a complex set. It is most likely there is a diminutive marker *ne-* which shows up both as a plural prefix and unpaired in non-count nouns, as well as in *ke-/ne-* alternations marking small entities in (15). The *ke-* is probably cognate with Bantu *ka-* which has a similar diminutive function (Maho 1999: 88).

Table 15: *ke-/ne-* alternation in Berom

Gloss	Sg.	Pl.
'small calabash'	kèkyɔ́k	nèkyɔ́k
'any small bird'	kènòn	nènòn
'little town'	kèrèpomo	nèbàpomo

ne- is also a plural marker for a set of miscellaneous nouns in Table 16.

Berom also has an *n-, ne-* unpaired marker for liquids, colours and abstracts as in Table 17, comparable to the *ma-* class 6 in Niger-Congo.

An optional *se-* prefix, noted with parentheses in Table 18, marks abstract states.

There is no trace of either Bantu class 3, *mù-* for trees and plants, or Class 9, *nì-* for animals. Berom has a small set of nouns showing initial consonant mutation in Table 19

Presumably these originally had a singulative, *fu-*, and the stem-initial *t-* was deleted, converting the high back vowel into a labial.

Table 16: ø-/ne- alternation in Berom

Gloss	Sg.	Pl.	Also
'knife'	bá	nebá	
'lie'	bɔs	nebɔs	
'household head'	dá lɔ	beda nelɔ	
'limb, place'	dèm	nedem	
'soil being dug'	fòŋol	nèfòŋol	ṅfòŋol
'spirit'	gabik	nègabik	begabik
'place'	kwɔ́n	nèkwɔ̄n	

Table 17: Unpaired n-, ne- prefix in Berom

Gloss	Berom
'brownness'	nèrós
'blackness'	nèsi
'redness'	nèsinàng
'stubbornness'	nèshágárák
'intense sweetness'	nèrókrók
'dirtiness'	nèrwĭk
'friendship, fellowship'	nèsá
'blood'	nèmí
'milk (of animal or human being)'	nèvasal
'local salt (made from acca straw)'	ṅtow
'urine'	ṅtyěk

Table 18: An optional se- abstract prefix in Berom

Gloss	Berom
'leprosy'	(se-)kwa
'madness'	(se-)loloŋ
'slavery'	(se-)sesàm
'fascination, temptation'	setógós

Table 19: Consonant mutation in Berom

Gloss	Sg.	Pl.
'hut for pounding'	*fwaŋ*	*tàŋ*
'cave'	*fware*	*tàre*
'thigh'	*fwa*	*tà*

2.3 West-Central

2.3.1 General

West-Central Plateau consists of what used to be known as the 'Southern Zaria' languages. Published and manuscript sources include Koelle (1854); Gerhardt (1971; 1974; 1983a; 1994); Adwiraah & Hagen (1983); Adwiraah (1989); McKinney (1979; 1983); McKinney (1984; 1990); Follingstad (1991); Follingstad (n.d.). Although these languages are clearly linked, no published evidence supports their coherence as a group. The languages Nandu [=Ndun] and Tari [=Shakara] were listed in Crozier & Blench (1992) as part of this group. This is erroneous; Ndun-Shakara, together with the newly discovered Nyeng, form their own group, Ndunic (§2.4). The West-Central Plateau languages are a coherent geographical clustering and undoubtedly show numerous links with one another, but their genetic unity is unproven. Gerhardt (1983a: 67ff) presents a comparative wordlist showing cognates between Rigwe, Izere and Tyap. However, with both new insights into the phonology of these languages, and in particular the large number of lects still unrecorded at that period, a new comparative analysis is still to be undertaken. Figure 3 presents the known groups of West-Central Plateau as a flat array.

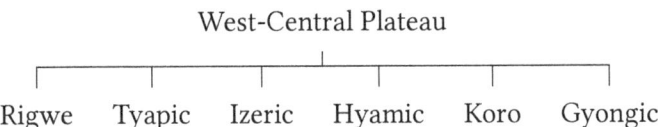

Figure 3: West-Central Plateau subgroups

2.3.2 Rigwe

The Rigwe language is spoken southeast of Jos. It is notable for an extremely complex phonology (Anonymous 2006). Any former system of extensive alternating affixes has been replaced by a standard pluralising prefix or by a variety of tonal changes. Analysis of Rigwe was undertaken by the author in co-operation with Daniel Gya. Table 20 lists the strategies for plural marking in Rigwe with their allomorphs.

Table 20: Nominal plural marking in Rigwe

No.	Strategy	Allomorph
I.	addition of ɾè- prefix	
II.	ɾV-/Ǹ alternation	ø-/Ǹ- alternation
III.	tone-raised on initial nasals with low tone	+ stem-tone raising
IV.	extra-low tone initial nasal raised to mid	extra-low stem-tone-raising

Class II nouns have a ɾV-/Ǹ- alternation. ɾV- is realized as ɾi- when the stem vowel is front, and as ɾu- when the stem-vowel is back. Ǹ- is realised as ɲ- before palatals ɲ- and j- and as ǹ- elsewhere. Table 21 presents examples of the operation of this class.

Table 21: ɾV-/Ǹ- alternations in Rigwe nouns

Gloss	Sg.	Pl.
'head'	ɾitʃí	ǹtʃì
'eye'	ɾijìî	ɲ̀jì
'tooth'	ɾiɲìî	ɲ̀ɲì
'horn'	ɾité	ǹtè
'hole'	ɾuvɔ́	ǹvɔ̀

4 Nominal affixes and number marking in the Plateau languages

As the glosses show, the nasal prefix is associated with human and animal body parts, which seems to be innovative. The Class III alternation in Rigwe is ø-/Ǹ-, where Ǹ- is homorganic with the following consonant, realised as ɲ- before palatals, ŋ- before velars and n- elsewhere. Only /a/, /e/ and /u/ have been recorded as stem vowels in Class III. Unlike the other classes, the stem tone changes and is always low, regardless of the tone in the singular. Table 22 presents examples of this class. This class is equally associated with body parts but is otherwise miscellaneous.

Table 22: ø-/Ǹ- alternation in Rigwe nouns

Gloss	Sg.	Pl.
'bone'	kú	ŋ̀kù
'corpse'	kʷé	ŋ̀kʷè
'firewood'	ekʷé	ŋ̀kʷè
'food'	jâ	ɲ̀jà
'hand'	vá	ṅvà
'leg'	tá	ṅtà
'part of'	klá	ṅklà

In Class IV, an extra-low nasal prefix is raised to mid, and an extra-low stem-tone becomes falling, shown in Table 23.

Table 23: Extra-low nasal raising in Rigwe plurals

Gloss	Sg.	Pl.
'chair'	ǹtɕṳ	ntɕû
'chief'	ŋ̰gʷɛ̰	ŋgʷê
'agama lizard'	ǹdä	ndâ
'scar'	ŋ̰mgbɛ̰	ŋ̄mgbê
'boyfriend'	ǹtɕä	ntɕâ

Rigwe has innovated in nominal affixing to such an extent that no obvious connection with postulated classes for either Niger-Congo or Bantu can be discerned.

2.3.3 Tyapic

Table 24: Tyap nominal affixes and concord (Follingstad 1991: 72)

Noun class	Number	Prefix	Tone change on root	Post-concord Element	Gloss	Sg.	Pl.
1	Sg.	ə̀		wu	'hare' 'chief'	ə̀sòm wù ə̀gwàm wù	
2a	Pl.	ə̀yə		ba	'hares'		ə̀yə́som bà
2b	Pl.	ø	+	ba	'chiefs'		ə̀gwam bà
3	Sg.	ø		ji	'cricket' 'place'	jèt jì tyàn jì	
4a	Pl.	ø	+	ji	'crickets'		jet jî
4b	Pl.	redup.		jí	'places'		tityàn jí
5	Sg.	ə̀		ka	'tree' 'farm' 'tooth'	ə̀kən ka ə̀bin ka ə̀nyuŋ kâ	
6a	Pl.	ə̀kə̀		na	'trees'		ə̀kə̀kwə̀n nà
6b	Pl.	ə̀ + redup.		hu	'farms'		bibin hu
6c	Pl.	ə̀ + redup.		ba	'teeth'		ə̀nyûnyuŋ ba
6d	Pl.	ø	+	na			
7	Sg.	ø		hu	'hand' 'root'	bwak hu ə̀nan ka	
8a	Pl.	N-		na	'hands'		mbwàk na
8b	Pl.	ə̀ + redup.		ba	'roots'		ə̀ninan bâ
9	sg/pl.	ə̀		na	'water'	ə̀sə̀khwôt nà	

The Tyapic languages are named for Tyap, or Kataf in older sources. The group consists of six languages (Tyap, Gworok, Atakar, Kacicere, Sholyo, and Kafancan), with the closely related Jju[4]. Only Tyap itself is well-described (Follingstad 1991). The prefixed elements appear to be innovative and consist of a (Ca-) and its allomorphs. However, the noun is also followed a variety of alternating CV suffixes. These are almost certainly noun-class affixes, now placed after the stem. Table 24 shows a summary of Tyap nominal affixes and concord as well as examples of nominal pairs.

---

[4] It is usual to list Jju separately from the Tyap cluster but this seems increasingly to reflect ethnic separation rather than linguistic reality.

4 Nominal affixes and number marking in the Plateau languages

The elements marked 'post-concord' in Table 24 were almost certainly former CV prefixes which have been copied at the end of the word, a procedure attested elsewhere in Niger-Congo. They are written in the orthography as distinct words as they do not show phonological merger with the root they follow.

Plurals reduplicate by doubling the first syllable of the root. Thus (4):

(4) Plurals reduplicate the first root syllable
əkwənka 'tree' əkəkwən nà 'trees'

Classes 1/2, with the suffixes *wu/ba*, probably corresponds to Bantu class 1/2 and includes many Tyap nouns for human beings. Class 9, which is unpaired, includes liquids such as *əsəkhwôt nà* 'water' and *əbààn na* 'milk' which is semantically similar to Niger-Congo Class 6. The homorganic plural nasal prefix in Class 8a is possibly to be compared with Bantu Class 6 where it is the plural of Class 5 'paired things', e.g. *mbwàk na* 'hands'.

Follingstad (1991: 79) shows that concord in Tyap is much reduced with only a few adjectives and lower numerals showing any agreement. The agreement is of the 'direct-copy' or 'echo' type, where the numeral has the same prefix as the noun it agrees with.

2.3.4 Izeric

The Izeric languages consist of northwest Izere, northeast Izere, Cèn, Ganàng and Fəràn.[5] The language which is best-known is Izere of Fobur but wordlists suggest that the affix pairings in the other languages are broadly similar.[6] Blench (2000b) is a more detailed description of Izere number marking. Nominal plurals in Izere of Fobur are formed in four ways:

a. affix alternation

b. stem-tone alternation

c. deverbal nouns that copy the alternations of verb stems

d. suppletion

---

[5]These last three are essentially single settlements, whereas the others represent clusters of villages, hence the rather asymmetric geographical names.
[6]Analysis of Izere was undertaken by the author in collaboration with Bitrus Kaze.

Affix alternation and stem-tone alternation are frequently combined producing a very large number of plural formations. Izere of Fobur has a relatively restricted set of segmental noun-class prefixes. Table 25 shows Izere nominal affix pairings.

Table 25: Izere nominal affix pairings

Singular	Plural	Semantics
a-	*a-*	persons, loanwords
i-	*i-*	miscellaneous
ka-, ki-		diminutive
ka-	*na-*	birds, trees, miscellaneous
ku-	*a-, i-*	miscellaneous
nà-	*ø-*	liquids, solids, abstracts
ri-	*a-*	miscellaneous

Tone cannot be specified for most Izere prefixes, since it reflects the tone of the stem. The unpaired mass noun prefix, corresponding to Niger-Congo Class 6, is always low tone. *ka-* and its allomorph *ki-*, realised when the noun stem contains a palatal, can function as a diminutive prefix. Paired *ka-* and *ku-* were probably allomorphs of one another historically, since there is a tendency for stem-vowels following *ka-* to be front or central and those following *ku-* to be back. However, exceptions now abound, suggesting a historical class split.

Izere has an unpaired *nà-* prefix for liquids and solids which probably corresponds to the *ma-* prefix in Niger-Congo, shown in Table 26.

Table 26: Examples of Izere unpaired prefix *nà-*

Gloss	Izere	Gloss	Izere
'breast-milk'	nàbàsang	'tears'	nànyìsi
'poison, venom'	nàdɔm	'dirt, fertiliser'	nàrìk
'gum'	nàgàng	'blood'	nàsɔk
'oil, pomade'	nàmè	'local potash'	nàtɔk
'dew'	nàming	'sap'	nàwùn

There is no evidence for a link between the common *na-* prefix in Izere and Bantu nasal prefixes.

2.3.5 Hyamic

The Hyamic languages are spoken between Kwoi and Nok, southwest of Jos and are now central to the prehistoric Nok culture. The members of the Hyamic cluster are as follows:

- Cori
- Hyam cluster (incl. Kwyeny, Yaat, Sait, Dzar, Hyam of Nok)
- Shamang
- Zhire-Shang

Many of these languages are very poorly known and existing descriptions are tonally and phonologically inadequate (e.g. Dihoff 1976; Jockers 1982).

Hyam has a wide range of strategies to mark nominal plurals. Analysis of Hyamic languages is based solely on fieldwork by the author. The most important are shown in Table 27:

Table 27: Examples of Hyam noun pluralisation strategies

Strategy	Gloss	Sg.	Pl.
Tone-raising	'tree'	ki	kí
Prefix addition	'leaf'	ʤàŋ	maʤàŋ
	'person'	nèt	mò-nèt
Prefix alternation	'blacksmith'	na-naa	fu-naa
Palatalisation	'vine'	rik	ryĭk
Depalatalisation	'seed/grain'	ʃaŋ	sáŋ
Labialisation	'fear/fright'	hyoŋ	hywoŋ
Consonant mutation	'path'	fwor	swor

Transcription of tone is best described as schematic; Hyam has a highly complex tone-system which is far from being fully understood, but which includes multiple contour tones, combining different levels of the underlying three-tone system.

All of these point to the former existence of nominal prefix alternation and palatalisation and labialisation to incorporated *i-* and *u-* prefixes. The *ma-* prefix on 'leaf' is exceptional and not linked with the Class 6 prefix. The *mò-* prefix is applied to most humans, large animals and reptiles, but not other animals, and a small scatter of miscellaneous lexemes. The *na-/fu-* singular/plural alternation is only recorded for a few nouns related to occupations as in (5), and may be some sort of reassigned relative marker ('one who') rather than a relic nominal affix.

(5) *na-/fu-* singular/plural alternation

na-hywes	'witch'	*fu-hywes*	'witches'
na-kyat kpyo	'sorcerer'	*fu-kyat kpyo*	'sorcerers'
na-naa	'blacksmith'	*fu-naa*	'blacksmiths'

Almost all verbs and adjectives have obligatory plural forms and many undergo the same phonological shifts or mutations as nouns. Adjectives agree in number, i.e. where the noun is plural, the plural adjective is obligatory, but they do not show the type of alliterative concord characteristic of noun-class languages.

The Shang language, while lexically Hyamic, has a nominal affix system resembling Tinɔr and similar Koro languages (§2.3.7) Blench (n.d.[e]). Shang has a reduced system of nominal affixes. The main noun-class pairs are between zero affixes in the singular and plural *a-* and *i-* prefixes seen in Table 28. Rare plural prefixes include *ka-*, *u-* and *ru-*. No singular affix, either productive or fossil, has been recorded. Some nouns referring to persons have a singular/plural alternation *nè-/fú-* (as in Hyam) but these are probably not old affixes but compounded terms for 'person'. The tone on the vowel of the plural affix always appears to be low.

Table 28: Shang nominal affix pairings

Affix	Sg.	Pl.	Gloss
ø-/a-	ʤàŋ	à-ʤàŋ	'leaf'
ø-/i-	tàà	ì-taa	'stone'
ø-/u-	xá	ù-xá	'load'
ø-/ka-	kwè	kà-kwè	'nose'
à-/ru-	à-bin	rù-bin	'thing'

Semantic correlations are not very clear for most of these pairings. However, there is a strong predominance of body parts with the *ka-* plural affix. Most nouns relating to persons have an *a-* prefix in the plural, but since this is statistically the most common prefix, this may not be significant. There is no trace of nasal prefixes.

2.3.6 Gyongic

Gyongic is the closest relative of Hyamic and consists of two languages, Gyong [Kagoma] and Angan [Kamanton]. Neither language is well-known but there is a description of Gyong which includes information on noun-classes (Hagen 1988). According to this, Gyong marks plurals with prefix alternation, palatalisation alternation and tone. The data tables below follow her presentation. The reduced prefix system is as follows in Table 29.

Table 29: Gyong nominal affixes

Sg.	Pl.
ø-	bɔ̀, kì-
kì-	ø-, rì-

Interestingly, liquids, abstracts and mass nouns fall into the unpaired kì- class in Table 30.

Table 30: Gyong mass noun ki- prefix

Gloss	Gyong
'blood'	kìdzí
'water'	kìmàláŋ
'oil'	kìtsɛ̀s
'death'	kìkpó
'ashes'	kìtɔ̀ŋ
'smoke'	kìdzɔ̀ŋ
'jealousy'	kìɣwúp

Stem-tone changes multiply the possible number-marking strategies. Hagen (1988: 139) gives examples of adjectival agreement in (6).

(6) Gyong adjectival agreement
    kìpèndèm kìlúm   pèndèm rúm
    large   farm   large   farms

The data is not extensive enough to fully understand the system. Demonstratives do show alliterative concord in (7):

(7) Gyong demonstrative concord
kìhá kìhɔ́nà   rìhá rìdú(nà)
house that   house those

2.3.7 Koro

The Koro cluster consists of five languages spoken in Central Nigeria, north of Keffi. The published literature is sparse and based on limited data (Gerhardt 1972/73; Goroh 2000). All the material presented on the Koro languages is based on fieldwork by the author. Figure 4 shows a tentative outline classification of the languages in the Koro cluster.

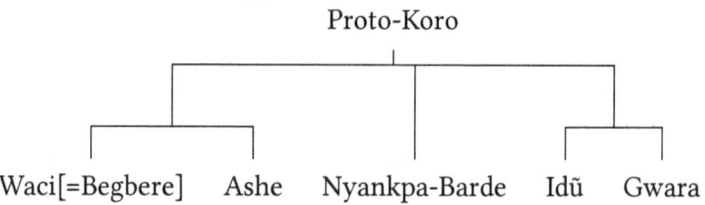

Figure 4: Classification of the Koro languages

Waci has retained a much richer noun-class system than any of the related languages, although it is in decay – see Table 31. There is a strong tendency to cite some types of nouns, especially those to do with living things, without a singular prefix and to reduce the pluralisation marker to an *a-* prefix. Moreover, there are a very large number of singular/plural pairings, many of them only occurring once suggesting a complex process of re-analysis is under way. Some prefixes have several allomorphs, probably prefiguring class merger. There is some semantic correlation with prefix pairings: for example, humans commonly have *u-/bV-* prefixes and animals most often *ì/i-*, but the correlation is far from perfect.

There is no evidence for a distinctive mass noun prefix. Some liquids, such as water (*bàm*) and blood (*bèʤí*) show no singular/plural prefix alternation, while others, such as tears, saliva and urine, have diverse singular/plural affix pairs.

The *bV-* plural prefix almost always marks persons and is usually, but not always paired with *u-* singular Table 32. The vowel is underspecified and very often copies the stem vowel, although *b*+ high vowel (i.e. *bi-* and *bu-*) is apparently not permitted.

There is a tendency for the V- of other plural prefixes to copy the ±ATR properties of the stem vowel where these are mid. See Table 33.

4 Nominal affixes and number marking in the Plateau languages

Table 31: Waci nominal affix pairings

Singular	Plural	Semantics
ø-, ì-, ù-	bV-	human beings
i-	i-	large or salient animals, trees
i-	a-, bV-, ri-	miscellaneous
gV-	ru-, ro-	miscellaneous
gV-	bV-	miscellaneous
o-	i-	miscellaneous
wu-	a-, E-, O-	miscellaneous
yV-	bV-	miscellaneous

Table 32: *bV-* plural prefixes in Waci

Gloss	Sg.	Pl.
'person/people'	ù-ndìrà	bà-ndìrà
'husband'	ù-sá	bá-sà
'wife'	ù-cɛ́	bè-cɛ́
'masquerade type'	keberè	be-keberè
'leper'	ì-kpíŋ	bè-kpíŋ
'masquerade type'	ú-kù	bó-kù
'brother'	ù-cɔ́bɔ̀	bɔ̀-cɔ́bɔ̀
'friend'	ù-dɔ́rḭ̀	bɔ̀-dɔ́rḭ̀

Table 33: (C)V- prefixes in Waci, illustrating ±ATR vowel copying

Gloss	Sg.	Pl.
'death'	gà-pú	rù-pú
'Senegal coucal'	gbodotŭtŭ	o-gbodotŭtŭ
'story'	wù-sɔ́sɔ̀gɔ̀	ɔ̀-sɔ́sɔ̀gɔ̀
'wound'	wù-sɔ̀	ɔ̀-sɔ̀

But there are exceptions as in (8):

(8) 'song' wù-vʷɔ́m ò-vʷɔ́m

wu- (*gu-* in some speakers) is a very common prefix which can be paired with almost any plural *V-* prefix as in Table 34.

Table 34: Waci *wu-* singular prefix and its pairings

Gloss	Sg.	Pl.
'leaf'	wù-yí(í)	à-yí(í)
'root'	wù-náŋ	à-náŋ
'rubbish-heap'	wù-rírí	è-rírí
'village/settlement'	wù-sέp	έ-sὲp
'arm, hand'	wù-bɔ́	ɔ̀-bɔ́
'story'	wù-sɔ́sɔ̀gɔ̀	ɔ̀-sɔ́sɔ̀gɔ̀
'wall (of room)'	wù-gúgò	ò-gúgò

u- may also be an allomorph of *wu-* in Table 35.

Table 35: Waci *u-* prefix and its plural pairings

Gloss	Sg.	Pl.
'large river'	ù-hέk	έ-hὲk
'thing'	ù-bín	è-bín
'wart-hog'	ù-jì	e-ji
'tail'	ù-sáp	ì-sáp
'load'	ù-cá	ì-cá
'day'	ù-nɔ́m	í-nɔ̀m
'night'	ù-fĩ́	έ-fĩ̀
'bark (of tree)'	ù-gùgúb	ɔ̀-gùgúb

i- prefixes alternating with other prefixes than *i-* are quite rare and somewhat inconsistent in (9):

(9) 'thorn' ì-dìdɔ́k bà-dìdɔ́k
    'year'   ì-yέ   gὲ-yέ

4 Nominal affixes and number marking in the Plateau languages

The Waci prefix *yV*- where V is always a front vowel is usually paired with *bV*- in the plural seen in Table 36, although these nouns do not refer to persons as might be expected by analogy to the pairing of *mu-/ba-* (classes 1/ 2) for persons in Bantu.

Table 36: *yV*- prefixes in Waci

Gloss	Sg.	Pl.
'star(s)'	gè-jĭ ~ yì-jĭ	bà-jĭ
'fire'	gì-rá ~ yì-rá	bà-rá
'boil'	yì-kpì	bè-kpì
'pygmy mouse'	yì-kìríko	bò-kìríko
'bird (generic)'	yè-nɔ̀	bà-nɔ̀
but:		
'faeces'	yè-bì	ru-bi

One of the most striking alternations is *gV-/rV-*, which does not seem to have any immediate parallel in other Koro languages. The -V- in *gV*- can be any vowel except the high back vowels. The vowel quality in the *gV*- prefix partly reflects stem vowels although the correlation is not perfect. Similarly, most plurals have *rV*- with a few exceptions (Table 37). Some *yV*- prefixes, such as 'faeces' in Table 36 may well be allomorphs of *gV*- to judge by the *rV*- plurals.

The Waci nominal affix system seems to have undergone major renewal. Apart from a class pair for persons and a rather weak animal class, there is no evidence for an unpaired non-count noun prefix and no evidence for semantically clustered prefix pairs elsewhere.

2.4 Ndunic (=Ahwai)

Ndunic is a new name proposed here for the languages previously called 'Nandu-Tari'. Existing sources list two languages, but a third language, Ningon, was first recorded in 2003. The Ndunic languages are spoken in a small area southwest of Fadan Karshi. The correct names for these languages are Ndun (Nandu), Shakara (Tari) and Ningon. The languages are extremely close to one another. The Ndunic peoples have recently adopted the name 'Ahwai' as a cover term for all three languages (Rueck et al. 2008). Shakara has a much reduced set of nominal affixes, but Ndun has numerous nominal singular/plural affix pairs. All the tables

Table 37: gV- prefixes in Waci

Gloss	Singular	Plural
'compound'	gá-hà	rú-hà
'forest'	gà-kwéy	rù-kwéy
'death'	gà-pú	rù-pú
'stick'	gá-tì	ró-tì
'gecko'	ge-mɛ́ kpikpi	ru-mɛ́ kpikpi
'tongue'	gè-ɽɛ́m	rù-ɽɛ́m
'rope'	gɛ-ri	ru-ri
'genet cat'	gibíkɔn	bèbikɔn
'thigh'	gì-cáy ùdà	à-cáy àdà
'stomach'	gì-nɪ́	bà-nɪ́
'sandfly'	gì-zù	bò-zù
'bag'	gò-gúr	rù-gúr
'snake (generic)'	go-sʊ	ru-sʊ

for Ndunic languages are based on fieldwork by the present author. The main attested noun-class pairings of Ndun are shown in Table 38.

However, there are also numerous plurals created by tonal change and by presence and absence of labialisation and palatalisation. Sporadic nasalisation appears between the stem and the prefix as a result of fossil nominal prefixes, although Ndun still preserves a few productive nasal prefixes. Ndun has many noun-class pairings that only occur once, in part due to the underspecified vowels. The tones are too insecurely marked to be sure that there are no additional contrasts on the V- prefixes.

Palatalisation can be applied to almost any initial consonant in singular/plural formation, often combined with primary affix alternation as in Table 39. The likely historical explanation is that there was an initial *i*- prefix which was incorporated into the stem and then a new plural affix (ironically sometimes a new *i*- prefix) was applied subsequently.

Ndun also shows numerous examples of sporadic inserted nasals in affix alternations as in Table 40.

Only a single example of an alternating *n*- prefix showing alternation has been recorded, shown in Table 41.

4 Nominal affixes and number marking in the Plateau languages

Table 38: Ndun nominal affix pairings

Sg.	Pl.
ø-	e-, i-, i(Cy)-, -y-
a-, a(n)-	i-, me-, na-
e-	ø-, be-, i(n)-
i-	be-
m-, ma-, me(n)-	ø-
n-	be-
u-	e-, i(Cy)-, n-
-y-	ø-

Table 39: Ndun nominals with contrastive palatalization

Gloss	Sg.	Pl.
'dream'	nári	ínyári
'relations'	ùgap	ìgyàp
'song'	úhwá	ihywa
'body'	ilyak	ilak

Table 40: Ndun nominals with sporadic inserted nasals in prefixes

Gloss	Sg.	Pl.
'cheek'	upăŋ	empaŋ
'grandparent'	inìnkyer	ínikyer
'chief'	ètùm	entûm
'horn'	anshem	meshèm
'spider'	tìntàn	intíntàn

Table 41: Single example of alternating n-prefix

Gloss	Sg.	Pl.
'thorn'	ùshayí	ṅshayî

In addition there are many nouns with initial homorganic nasals (*m-*, *n-*, *ŋ-*) which seem to have been incorporated during an earlier wave of prefix incorporation.

It is not uncommon for Ndun nouns for persons to be *-r* final Table 42:

Table 42: Ndun nominals with final *-r*

Gloss	Sg.	Pl.
'person/people'	ènèr	bénèr
'man'	èromir	béromír
'grandparent'	ininkyer	iníkyer
'friend'	èsamir	bésamir

In one case, the final *-r* alternates with a final nasal as in (10).

(10) 'woman' *nyaan* *nyaar*

These are probably the traces of former prefixes which have moved to final position and have almost lost their class pair alternation. Semantic correlations with noun-class affix pairings are weak at best. The *e-/be-* prefix pair includes many nouns referring to persons (Table 43).

Table 43: Ndun *e-/be-* prefixes marking persons

Gloss	Sg.	Pl.
'person/people'	ènèr	bénèr
'man'	èromir	béromír
'father'	èdâ	bédâ
'friend'	èsamir	bésamir
'guest/stranger'	èkyen	békyen

Most liquids have initial *m-* or *mV-* and this presumably reflects Niger-Congo Class 6 Table 44.

However, where *mV-* appears as a plural number marker it seems to show no semantic correlation. No other Ndun prefixes show any tendency to reflect semantic classes such as body parts, trees or salient animals.

Table 44: Ndun *mV-* prefixes marking liquids

Gloss	Ndun
'water'	mákúrì
'blood'	mémiŋ
'tear'	mémil
'saliva'	méntí
'sweat'	ḿfɔɔr
'urine'	ménfirì

Shakara now has a much reduced system, but Proto-Ndunic clearly had a wide range of nominal affix pairs, with fragmentary evidence for a suffix alternation to do with persons. Nasal prefixes were clearly very common but have become so generalised across the system it is now difficult to discern what part they may have played in the original affix alternations.

2.5 Ninzic

Ninzic, formerly Plateau IV, is probably the most difficult group to characterise and weak data on several languages make it unclear whether certain peripheral languages really belong to it. The name Ninzic is introduced here, reflecting the element *nin-*, which is part of many ethnonyms. The Ninzic languages are spoken south of Fadan Karshi in Plateau, Nassarawa and Kaduna States. The membership of Ninzic has changed quite significantly between various publications noted in Table 45.

General overviews can be found in Gerhardt (1972/3; 1983a) and materials on specific languages in Hoffmann (1976); Hörner (1980); Price (1989); Wilson (2003).

The number marking systems of Ninzic must originally have been paired affixes with alliterative concord, as fragments of such systems are found across the group. However, in most languages the system has broken down or become severely eroded and compensatory strategies have evolved. This section uses examples from Ninzo based on Hörner (1980); Ninzo Language Project Committee (1999) and fieldwork in Fadan Wate in 1995 Blench (n.d.[f]). Ninzo prefix pairings are in Table 46.

Many words have unproductive prefixes and singular and plural is now marked only by tone. Some *u-/a-* prefix alternations are co-associated with *u-/i-* alternations in the first vowel of the stem in Table 47.

Table 45: Changing composition of the Ninzic language group.
Key: Blank = not listed; + = assigned to group; – = assigned to another group; ? thus in source.

	Greenberg (1963)	Hansford et al. (1976)	Gerhardt (1989)	Crozier & Blench (1992)	This paper
Ce [=Rukuba]	+	+	+	+	+
Ninzo [=Ninzam]	+	+	+	+	+
Mada	+	+	+	+	+
Nko					+
Katanza					+
Bu-Niŋkada		–	–	–	+
Ayu	+	+	+	?	?
Nungu		–	–	–	+
Ninkyob [=Kaninkwom]	+	+	+	+	+
Anib = Kanufi		+	+	+	+
Nindem		+	+	+	+
Gwantu cluster		+	+	+	+
Ningye					+
Ninka					+
Kwanka-Boi-Bijim-Legeri		+	+	+	–
Shall-Zwall		+		?	–
Pe [=Pai]		–	+	–	–

Table 46: Ninzo prefix pairings

Sg.	Pl.
ø-	à-, ì-
ì-	à-
ù-	à-, ì-

4 Nominal affixes and number marking in the Plateau languages

Table 47: Ninzo *u-/i-* alternations in first vowel of stem

Gloss	Sg.	Pl.
'man'	ù-nùru	a-nirú
'old person'	ù-tuce	a-tice
'senior in age'	ù-nunku	a-ninku
'bow'	ù-tuta⁺	i-tita

Table 48: Ninzo prefix pairs *u-nV-/a-bV-*

Gloss	Sg.	Pl.
'guest/stranger'	ù-ni-cir	a-bi-cir
'doctor'	ù-ni-fù	a-bi-fù
'hunter'	ù-nì-zhá	à-bì-zhá
'thief'	ù-nà-yí	à-bà-yí
'blacksmith'	u-nì-là	a-bí-lá
But:		
'witch'	ù-nu-tri	a-da-tri

Other *u/a-* prefix alternations also incorporate alternations of CV syllables of the stem as in Table 48, particularly *u-nV-/a-bV-*. These suggest an unusual process, the retention of a former *ni-/bi-* alternation with the addition of an innovative prefix system preceding it. The *bV-* plural marker is reminiscent of Niger-Congo *ba-* but this may be coincidence; the core lexemes for persons in Ninzo do not have this alternation. A partial development from this is the formation of plural with *VnV-* prefixes Table 49. For example, *à-* and *ì-* singular prefixes alternate with *ànV-* plural prefixes.

As Table 49 shows there is quite a strong correlation between animals and the *anV-* plural prefix, which is highly reminiscent of the Bantu Class 9 *nì-* singular prefix for animals. Ninzo shows no obvious active or fossil morphology for non-count nouns although the word for 'water', *amasír*, has inherited the *ma-* affix from related Plateau languages.

Table 49: Ninzo prefix pairs V-/anV-

Gloss	Sg.	Pl.
'death'	ì-kfu	áni-kfu
'leopard'	ì-ce	áni-ce
'guinea-fowl'	ì-tsì	áni-tsì
'kob antelope'	à-kùrù	áná-kúrú
'cat'	à-músâ	àna-músâ
'chameleon'	a-kanda	anu-kanda

A common number marking process, which can be combined with prefix alternations, is reduplication of the first syllable of the root seen in Table 50. The vowel of the reduplicated syllable is usually /i/, but /u/ in two unexplained cases.

Table 50: Plural marking with reduplication in Ninzo

Gloss	Sg.	Pl.
'senior in status'	àŋkpyè	aŋkpikpyè
'ankle'	í-gblédzá	à-gbígblédzá
'navel'	í-mgbèkù	í-mgbímgbèkè
'liver'	ì-sur	ì-sisur
'animal (bush)'	í-názhù	í-nínazhù
'hoe'	à-kla	í-kikla
'termite'	í-yó	í-yíyó
'knife (small)'	á-njî	í-njínjî
'gown, small'	à-nkru	í-nkinkru
'basket (generic)'	à-sà	í-sísà
'arrow'	à-wyírr	i-wyiwyírr
'friend'	ù-kpà	á-kpukpà
'king'	ù-ṭû	á-túṭù

Ninzic languages have highly diverse nominal morphology and space precludes describing all of them. Many have a non-count noun prefix, but this seems to vary from one group to another. For example, Table 51 shows the prefix for liquids in Ce, bə-, which is quite consistent, but which seems to be segmentally unrelated to Niger-Congo Class 6, usually mV-.

4 Nominal affixes and number marking in the Plateau languages

Table 51: Ce prefix for liquids bə-

Gloss	Ce
'oil'	bə̀-nyì
'fat/grease'	bə̀-nhyɔ̀
'boiled sorghum'	bə̀-kɔ̀
'potash'	bə̀-tòk
'sorghum-beer'	bə̀-hi
'milk'	bə̀-nsə
'sweat'	bə̀-cilí

This is an example of metatypy, the copying of a structural feature without the associated segments.

The Mada language has undergone a striking collapse of characteristic affix alternations, which have then been rebuilt using grammaticalisation strategies, which have resulted in highly idiosyncratic marking of nominal plurals. These can be divided into six categories:

(11) I tone-change
      II initial syllable reduplication
      III prefix addition
      IV person nouns grammaticalised as pseudo-prefixes
      V diminutives grammaticalised as pseudo-prefixes
      VI suppletives

Prefixes marking size can alternate with non-prefixed nouns creating a plethora of additional forms. Some nouns usually take diminutive prefixes in speech, but these are not easy to predict. The historical layering of these number marking strategies can be detected through the existence of multiple forms, sometimes with, for example, tone-raising applied to a noun formerly which also has first syllable reduplication or prefix addition. The consequence of this has been that the tone-plurals of Mada show extremely low levels of predictability as in Table 52.

To give a sense of the variety of number marking strategies in Mada, Table 52 above shows the operation of first syllable reduplication in Mada nouns, and selected examples in Table 53 and Table 54 below display recently adopted plural strategies.

Table 52: First syllable reduplication in Mada nouns

Pattern	Sg.	Pl.	gloss
be→bə	bě	be, bəbe	'seed'
bwɔ→bə	bwɔ̌	bɔ̄bwɔ	'pocket'
cu→cu	cūn	màcùn, màcūcùn	'chief'
gbu→gbu	gbù	gbūgbu	'town, hill'
gyə→gi	gyə̌r	gigyər	'mother'
kpa→kpə	kpān	kpə̄kpàn	'friend'
kri→kə	krì	kə̄krì	'yam'
lɔ→lə	lɔn	mə̄lə̄lɔn	'husband'
ci→ci	màcī	mācici	'father-in-law'
mbə→mbə	mbə̄	mbə̀mbə̄	'wife, woman'
mgba→mə	mgban	mə̀mgbǎn	'armpit'
mkpi→mkpə	mkpìr	mkpə̄mkpìr	'hip'
mla→mə	mlà	mə̀mlǎ	'first born'
mpa→mpə	mpā	mpə̄mpà	'sore, wound'
nci→nci	nci	ncīnci	'traditional district'
nji→nji	njī	njīnji	'knife'
njo→nju	njò	njūnjo	'horn'
nkɔ→nkɔ	nkɔ̀n	nkɔ̄n, nkɔ̄nkɔ̄n	'road, way, door'
ri→ri	rì	rīrī	'day'
te→tə	tè	te, tə̄te	'father'
tse→tsɛ	tse	tsə̄tse	'town'

4 Nominal affixes and number marking in the Plateau languages

Table 53: Mada *mə̀-* prefixes where stem tone is conserved

Sg.	Pl.	Gloss
bān	mə̀bān	'law'
gɔ̄n	mə̀gɔ̄n	'back'
gā	mə̀gā	'shoulder'
gbrīn	mə̀gbrīn, gbə̄gbrìn	'spirit'
jūjū	mə̀jūjū	'hole'
kpɔ̄	mə̀kpɔ̄	'female agama lizard'

Table 54: Mada *mə̄-* prefixes where stem tone is conserved

Sg.	Pl.	Gloss
brɛ	mə̄brɛ	'grave'
ləngga	mə̄ləngga	'enemy'
mla	mə̄mla	'relation'
nē	mə̄nē	'person'
vəngga	mə̄ngga	'girl'

The most recent addition to the Mada repertoire of plural strategies is probably the *mə-* prefix. This appears to have two realisations, *mə̀-* and *mə̄-*. The low-tone form seems to have no strongly-defined semantic field in Table 53, but mid-tone *mə̄-* is applied quite strictly to persons in Table 54. The examples in these tables and in other sections show the prefix has been added, sometimes subsequently to other strategies, such as tone-raising or reduplication, providing evidence for its recent genesis. Most nouns taking a *mə̀-* prefix conserve stem-tone in Table 53.

Mada provides a striking example of how rapidly a nominal affix system can break down and then be rebuilt using processes of grammaticalisation, thereby illustrating the difficulties of tracing synchronic affixes back to a presumed protosystem.

2.6 Alumic

One subgroup of Plateau languages spoken in Central Nigeria has effectively no published data. These languages are Hasha [=Yashi], Sambe, Alumu-Təsu and Toro [=Turkwam]. Except for Sambe, they have apparently been classified in previous lists on the basis of geographical proximity. Sambe is moribund, as there were only two speakers over 90 in 2005, and none remain in 2017. The rest have at most a few hundred speakers. All data and analyses given here were the result of fieldwork by the author Blench (n.d.[a]).

The group is here named Alumic, after the language with the most speakers, but this term can be regarded as provisional. The Alumic languages are now scattered geographically, and isolated among the Ninzic (=Plateau IV) languages. The very different sociolinguistic histories may explain their striking morphological diversity. The internal structure of the Alumic group is shown in Figure 5.

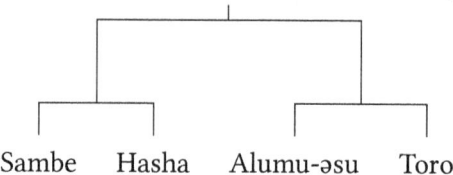

Figure 5: The relation of Sambe to Hasha and the Alumic languages

Alumu, Toro and Sambe no longer have functioning noun class systems, but the nouns have transparent fossil prefixes. Hasha has developed a highly idiosyncratic system of reduplicating the first syllable of the stem to mark plurality in both nouns and verbs, apparently under the influence of a neighbouring Chadic language, Sha. Təsu has entirely converted to a system of a single plural suffix, with no functioning noun-prefixes. Nonetheless, these can be recovered in part from the existing nouns, especially by comparison with cognate forms in other Plateau languages. Although many nouns have zero prefixes, fossil V- and N- prefixes are quite widespread. The most common prefix is à- and ə̀- is probably its allomorph. Table 55 shows some characteristic examples.

Table 55: Təsu à-/ə̀- prefixes

a-	Gloss	Təsu	ə-	Gloss	Təsu
	'tree (generic)'	à-gbè		'song'	ə̀-humu
	'mushroom'	à-wá		'leaf'	ə̀-ʃu
	'thorn'	à-tɔ̀tɔ̀		'road'	ə̀-ki
	'sand'	à-seŋge			
	'farm'	à-yi			

Nouns for persons typically have an à- prefix as in Table 56.

4 Nominal affixes and number marking in the Plateau languages

Table 56: Təsu à- prefix for persons

Gloss	Sg.
'man, husband'	à-tsìyà
'child'	à-yà
'woman, wife'	à-meré
'father'	à-da

Other fossil prefixes are given in Table 57.

Table 57: Fossil prefixes in Təsu

Təsu e- & i-					
e-	Gloss	Təsu	i-	Gloss	Təsu
	'cloud'	è-vírí		'algae'	ì-bu
	'mouth'	è-né		'tomorrow'	í-kyá
	'grasshopper'	é-sɔ		'large stone'	ì-tre
	'spear'	é-mbè		'cloud'	ì-ve
Təsu Ǹ- & u-					
Ǹ-	Gloss	Təsu	u-	Gloss	Təsu
	'smoke'	ǹ-zu		'bush-fowl'	úgrɔ́
	'evening'	ŋ-vìʃì			
	'work'	ǹ-dɔmɔ			
	'land/country'	ǹ-zimbɔrɔ			
	'navel'	ŋ-bu			

There is no trace of a semantic association for other prefixes. Liquids and non-count nouns show no characteristic morphological pattern.

Sambe no longer has a functioning noun-class system, perhaps a consequence of the switch to Ninzo. However, it clearly existed until recently and many words were cited with fossil prefixes. Indeed, sometimes a word would be cited in one elicitation with the prefix and again without it, showing the language in transition prior to its inevitable death. The tones marked are best characterised as approximate, with speakers varying between elicitation sessions. Three prefixes can be discerned in the data, *kV*-, *bV*- and *tV*-, each with an underspecified or 'hollow' vowel. In some languages this shows concord with the stem vowel, but this does not seem to have been the case with Sambe.

The most common prefix is *kV̀*- in Table 58.

Table 58: *kV*- fossil prefixes in Sambe

Prefix	Gloss	Attestation
ka-	'basket'	kàjese
ke-	'jar for local 'beer'	kèγa
	'head'	kècu
ki-	'spear'	kìnkwar
	'divination (types)'	kìtsu
ku-	'winnowing tray'	kùhûn
	'mortar (wood)'	kùtù
	'skink'	kùva
	'faeces'	kùbwà

Table 59 shows words with a *bV*- fossil prefix.

Table 59: *bV*- fossil prefixes in Sambe

Prefix	Gloss	Attestation
ba-	'sorghum-beer'	bàfù
	'ant (generic)'	bàtúnú
	'ancestors'	bàgúgó
be-	'fat/grease'	bènkun
bi-	'small hoe'	bíkíta
bu-	'today'	búrùmi
	'salt'	bùwan
	'rib'	bùkyέ

4 Nominal affixes and number marking in the Plateau languages

Table 60 shows words with a *tV-* fossil prefix.

Table 60: *tV-* prefixes in Sambe

Prefix	Gloss	Attestation
ta-	'name'	tánásè
	'breath'	tawùrì
ti-	'guinea-fowl'	tìmìsì
	'word'	tìmĭvən
	'squirrel (tree)'	títɔ
to-	'hippo'	tòbárì

Sambe probably also had a nasal prefix which was homorganic with the following consonant, see Table 61.

Table 61: *N-* prefixes in Sambe

Gloss	Sambe
'hair'	mfu
'brother/sister'	mlànà
'Senegal coucal'	mpàlàn
'leaf'	ŋgbá ʃì
'cock'	ŋgwà
'vervet monkey'	njînjèhun
'sheep'	ntùmà

Many nouns referring to persons have an *a-* prefix and some which are naturally plural, such as 'ancestors' have a *ba-* prefix, see Table 62.

From this we can conclude that Sambe originally had an *a-/ba-* noun class pair for humans. No other fossil prefixes have any semantic associations, and neither mass nouns nor liquids show any common features. The strong presence of CV- prefixes with underspecified vowels is extremely rare in this area, although common in Kainji languages (Blench, Chapter 3 this volume).

Table 62: *a/ba-* prefixes in Sambe

Gloss	Sambe
'man'	àróro
'woman'	àhìn
'father'	adídá
'mother'	aya
'relations'	bàruhwin ninamláni
'ancestors'	bàgúgó

2.7 East

The three languages constituting Greenberg's Plateau 6, Fyem, Bo-Rukul [=Mabo-Barkul] and Horom were placed together as Southeastern Plateau in the Benue-Congo Comparative Wordlist Williamson & Shimizu (1968); Williamson (1972). Although named Southeastern (e.g. in Crozier & Blench 1992) it is here named 'East Plateau' as a better reflection of its direction in relation to the Plateau centre of gravity. However, it is highly uncertain that they do indeed form a coherent group as Bo-Rukul is very distinct from Fyem and Horom. In Figure 1 they have been separated as branches of Plateau with a tentative linkage marked. Nettle (1998b) is a sketch grammar of Fyem, and Nettle (1998a) short wordlists of all three languages, but Bo-Rukul and Horom remain virtually unknown (although see Blench 2003 for their relation with the Ron (Chadic) languages). Since Horom has the most elaborate system of nominal affixing, it is discussed in detail in this section. Data and analysis are based on fieldwork by the author.

Number marking in Horom nouns is characterised by a great diversity of strategies. V-/CV- prefix alternation is the most characteristic process and the possibilities are numerous. Of these, the *i-* plural prefix is applied in the majority of cases. The singular and plural class/pairings identified so far are shown in Table 63.

Horom also demonstrates some striking semantic unities with respect to plural markers. Singulars are diverse, but almost all animals, from mammals to insects, have *i-* plural prefixes. Similarly, nouns referring to persons have a *ba-* prefix (and sometimes a suffix) but with no corresponding singular prefix. Mass nouns and liquids have no defining morphological character. Horom shows no evidence for nasal prefixes; in one apparent case the widespread Plateau root for 'person' has grammaticalised as an affix.

4 Nominal affixes and number marking in the Plateau languages

Table 63: Singular/plural affix pairings in Horom

Singular	Plural	Comment
ø-	à-, bà-, bὲ-, ɗî-, ì-, ù-	
a-	bà-, i-	
ɗi-	a-, bà-	
ɗu-	à-, bà-, be-	
ì-	bà-	
nà-	bὲnὲ	A single example
ò-	bà-	A single example
ù-	à-, bà-, bὲ-	

The most striking typological feature of Horom is the evolution of a nominal suffixing system, characterised either by vowels or –NV structures. The singular nouns are diverse, with either zero or a wide array of prefixes. The plurals are all prefixed with *ba-*, and a vocalic or –NV segment. Table 65 on the following page shows the nouns so far recorded with both prefixes and suffixes.

Horom also has "broken plurals". In words with stems of CVCCV(C) structure, an epenthetic vowel, either *-i-* or *-ə-*, is inserted between the two syllables of the stem as in Table 64.

Table 64: Horom 'broken' plurals

Gloss	Sg.	Pl.
'okra'	zabla	i-zab-i-la
'shoe'	paksak	i-pak-ə-sak
'sweet potato'	damʃik	i-dam-ə-ʃik
'gourd-bottle (*L. siceraria*)'	yóktál	í-yók-tí-tál

These may be infixes or simply a phonological extension of the syllable. None of these words are transparent compounds, but this may be their historical origin, in which case each element of the compound would have retained its plural prefix, with the second prefix undergoing centralisation in some environments.

Table 65: Horom nominal suffixes

Suffix	Gloss	Sg.	Pl.
a	'river'	u-lap	ba-lab-a
a	'bush'	ù-háp	bà-háb-à
á	'bundle'	dí-bwát	bá-bwád-á
e	'moon/month'	u-fel	ba-pel-e
è	'song'	u-sem	ba-sem-e
è	'sore / wound'	u-cel	ba-cel-e
ɛ̀	'compound'	kyèn	bà-kyèn-ɛ̀
ɛ̀	'door'	kèn kubok	bà-kèn-ɛ̀ kubok
i	'root'	u-liŋ	bè-liŋ-i
i	'fireplace'	a-fik	ba-fik-i
ì	'mat (cornstalk)'	ú-jír	bá-jír-ì
ì	'canoe'	u-bit	ba-bit-i
ye	'needle (thatching)'	bwi	ba-bwi-ye
ɔ	'skin'	hɔr	bà-hɔr-ɔ
ɔ	'rope'	ù-zɔr	bà-zɔr-ɔ
ɔ	'sorghum'	pɔl	bà-pɔl-ɔ
u	'knife'	mbok	ba-mbuk-u
nè	'mother'	wɔ	bà-wɔ-nè
nè	'father, grandfather'	tè	bà-tè-nè
mɔ	'friend'	ɗìsì	bà-ɗìsì-mɔ

2.8 South

2.8.1 General

South Plateau is named for two language groups, Jilic and Eggonic, which are here put together. "Southern" was applied to Jilic alone in Crozier & Blench (1992). Figure 6 shows this new proposal.

The Jilic or Koro languages are spoken in scattered communities across a wide swathe of Central Nigeria and this is usually attributed to persistent slave-raiding in the nineteenth centuries. As speakers have lost contact with one another, their languages have rapidly diversified.

4 Nominal affixes and number marking in the Plateau languages

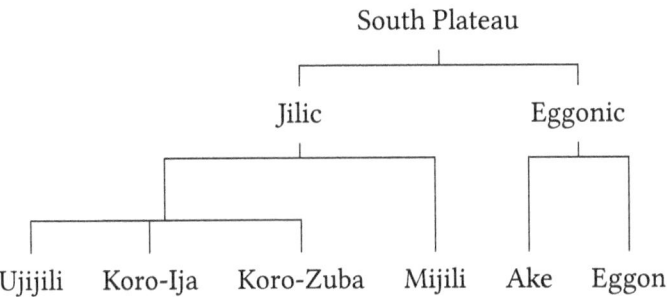

Figure 6: Classification of the Jilic-Eggonic languages

2.8.2 Jilic

Jilic consists of at least two languages, Mijili [=Koro of Lafia] and Ujijili [=Koro Huntu], now separated by a considerable geographic distance, but clearly related Blench (n.d.[h]). There is a microfiched grammar of Mijili by Stofberg (1978), while Ujijili is known from an unpublished wordlist. Koro Ija and Koro Zuba, two languages spoken northwest of Abuja, are said to be nearly intelligible with Ujijili, although no language data exists to demonstrate this. This section will focus on Mijili as described by Stofberg (1978), but with additional material from fieldwork in 2003. Mijili has a system of number marking on nouns based on prefix alternations. Table 66 is a matrix showing the possible pairings of singular and plural prefixes.

Once allomorphy of the prefixes is taken into account, the number of underlying prefixes is considerably reduced. As elsewhere in Plateau, singular nouns referring to human beings have variable morphology. Many nouns for persons have a former ɲV- prefix, now apparently lexicalised, but still in alternation in one root, the word for 'young man' in Table 67. Plural prefixes in Mijili nouns for persons are either mV- or a-.

The ɲV- prefix in singulars is unlikely to be a "true" prefix but a recent grammaticalisation of the nouns for 'person' (12):

(12) ǹnyɛ 'person'   mínyɛ 'person/people'

Almost all liquids and non-count nouns have an unpaired ń- prefix as in Table 68.

No other semantic correlations with noun class pairs have been detected.

Table 66: Matrix showing matching of singular and plural prefixes in Mijili. Adapted from Stofberg (1978: 316)

	á-	à-	àmà-	í-	mí-	mì-	mú-	mù-	Ń-
cù-							+		
jì-						+			
kí-	+			+					
kú-	+								
lú-				+				+	
mí-				+					
mú-				+					
Ń-				+					
Ǹ-			+		+		+		
ò-/ɔ-	+			+			+	+	
rí-	+								+
rú-									+
ø-	+	+		+	+		+	+	

(Singular prefixes on rows)

Table 67: Singular and plural prefixes for person nouns in Mijili

Gloss	Sg.	Pl.
'old person'	nyɛkúkɔ́	mínyɛkúkɔ́
'in-laws'	nyélɔ́	mínyélɔ́
'doctor'	nyɛmũgá	minyɛmũgá
'man'	nyɛvɛlè	mínyɛvɛlɛ
'guest/stranger'	nyɛ̀zɔ̃́	minyɛ̀zɔ̃́
'young man'	nyézhò	ázhò
'woman'	nyinyrà̃	mínyinyrà̃
'uncle'	òcã	múcã
'male ancestor'	òco	múco
but:		
'thief'	oyi	áyi

4 Nominal affixes and number marking in the Plateau languages

Table 68: Mass nouns with n- prefixes in Jili

Jili	Gloss	Jili	Gloss
ńcḛ̀	'saliva'	ńsá̰	'salt'
ńjẽ	'fat/grease'	ńsí	'tear'
ńkwálḕ	'water'	ńswàná	'hair'
ńnoro	'mud'	ńzẽ	'blood'
ńnɔ	'oil'	ńzɔ̃	'smoke'

2.8.3 Eggonic

Eggonic consists of just two languages, Eggon and Ake, spoken around Akwanga. These have previously been put together with Ninzic, although this is more a supposition based on geography than historical linguistics. The Eggon people are numerous and their language is divided into numerous dialects, while Ake (=Aike) is spoken in only three villages. Although the languages share enough common glosses to be put together, they are still quite distant from one another. Eggon has a limited system of nominal morphology, while Ake has lost its system entirely. All data and analyses in this section are based on fieldwork by the author.

Ake nouns no longer have morphologically marked plurals, with a few exceptions in the case of persons. However, there is considerable evidence for prior systems of CV prefixes, many of which survive in frozen form preceding the stem. The key to detecting such affixes is external cognates. Many words appear with different prefixes in related languages. Thus, although Proto-Ake almost certainly had a *ki-* prefix, in the word *kipindye* 'village/settlement' the *ki-* is not a prefix, since it is cognate with forms in remote Plateau languages such as Hyam *khep*, Jili *kúpɔ̰*, and the *–ndye* element would then be a compounded element. Such evidence is not available for all the terms with potential affixes, so only more elaborated morphological comparisons will increase certainty. The former V- prefixes often have two distinct tones and may therefore be ultimately of different origins or it may be that this is the result of a now-lost morphophonemic process. However, since they exist in high-low pairs for almost all the hypothetical prefixes reconstructed in Table 69.

Ake has a variety of *kV-* prefixes which constitute possible evidence for an original affix with an underspecified vowel, such as occur both in Sambe (§2.6)

Table 69: Ake fossil noun prefixes

Prefix	Allomorphs
a-	à-, á-
i-	ì-, í-
kV-	kà-, kè-, kì-, kí-, kù-, kú-
mu-	mù-, mú-
O-	ɔ̀-, ɔ́-, ò-, ó-
rV-	rì-, rí-, rù-, rú-
u-	ù-, ú-

Table 70: Ake *kV*- prefixes

Gloss	Ake
'world'	kàyùnzà
'ground'	kàʃe
'masquerade'	kàŋgìrì
'grave'	kèmì

and East Kainji languages such as Boze (see Blench 2018 [this volume], §3.5.2). Examples are given in Table 70.

An intriguing feature of Ake prefixes, not apparently found in related or nearby Plateau languages, is semantic clustering around specific segments. Some examples are found in (13):

(13) Ake prefixes semantic clustering around specific segments

    a. ɔ̀-/ɔ́-
       This prefix is strongly associated with body parts:
         'mouth'   ɔ̀mu
         'tongue'   ɔ̀lɛ́
         'neck'   ɔ̀lwa
         'shoulder' ɔ́kyɛ
         'armpit'   ɔ́ŋgwɔ

4 Nominal affixes and number marking in the Plateau languages

b. ò-/ó-
This prefix is strongly associated with animals:
'calf' òyèna
'castrated small ruminant' òkì
'colobus monkey' òkpesɛ̀
'hare' òzwè
'electric fish' òrĭ
'fish sp.' ópò

c. ŋ̀-

Strikingly, and in contrast to most other Plateau languages, the velar nasal prefix is not homorganic synchronically. Almost all the words with ŋ- prefixes are in the same semantic area, reptiles, crustaceans and insects. See (14):

(14) Ake ŋ- prefix
'hammer' ŋ̀bùkù
'fish sp.' ŋ̀gásɔ́ré
'river turtle' ŋ̀gyáklà
'skink' ŋ̀bɔ́klɔ́
'toad' ŋ̀báwù

Ake has almost certainly reprefixed stems with former velar nasal prefixes in words such as those in Table 71.

Table 71: Reprefixed stems in Ake

Gloss	Ake
'chameleon'	íŋbrŭ
'bee'	ìŋwè
'giant snail'	ìŋgìrà

It is conceivable this is related Bantu Class 9, nì-, for animals, although large salient species in Ake do not have an ŋ- prefix.

There is weak evidence for an *mV-* prefix defining liquids in Table 72.

Nouns referring to persons do not have any morphologically unifying characteristics.

Roger M. Blench

Table 72: Ake *mV-* prefix defining liquids

Gloss	Ake
'blood'	mìʃe
'tear(s)'	mínyi
'urine'	màŋgbà

2.9 Tarokoid

The Tarokoid languages consist of four distinct languages and the Kwang cluster. Tarok is numerically the most dominant, spoken in a large area around Langtang, while the others are spoken in small communities isolated from one another between Langtang and Jos. Yangkam is moribund, spoken only by men over fifty years of age. Figure 7 shows the internal structure of Tarokoid.

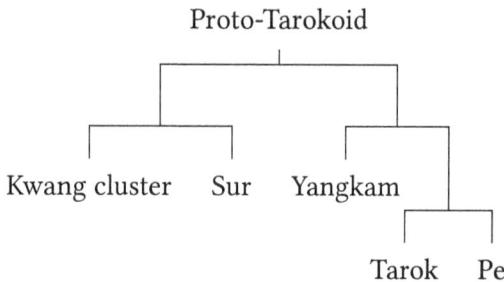

Figure 7: Internal structure of Tarokoid

Within Tarokoid there is a considerable range of nominal morphology. Tarok itself has both the most complete prefix system and alliterative concord. Yangkam has lost functioning affix alternation but has partially developed a system of reduplicating the initial syllable of the stem. Sur has also lost any functioning affixes without the evolution of a compensatory process, perhaps under the influence of the Chadic language Ngas.

Kwang marks number with singular/plural prefix pairings, but these are extremely reduced compared with Tarok or Pe Blench (n.d.[i]). With very few exceptions, all plurals are marked with an *à-* prefix. Kwang has a small number of nouns where plurality is marked with a tone-change, Low/High or Mid/High, and some irregular plurals which may be examples of residual consonant mutation. Changes in the stem vowel occur in the plurals of some lexemes connected

4 Nominal affixes and number marking in the Plateau languages

with persons. Table 73 shows the nominal prefixes of Kwang, and by far the most common singular prefix is ø- and plural à-.

Table 73: Kwang nominal prefixes

Singular	Plural
ø-	à-
ì-	kí-
kì-	
ǹ-	

However, the large number of palatalised and labialised stems in Kwang suggests that i- and u- prefixes were formerly present. By far the most common singular/ plural alternation is ø-/à-, as shown in Table 74.

Table 74: Kwang ø-/à- prefix pairing

Gloss	Sg.	Pl.
'root'	liŋ	àliŋ
'bark'	púr	àpur
'thorn'	rèk	àrèk
'mountain'	ʃiʃ	àʃiʃ
'relations'	zyɛŋ	àzyɛŋ
'name'	sàk	àsàk

Kwang seems to have deleted the prefixes on singular nouns very extensively, as most of these now show only the root with no fossil morpheme. Nouns referring to persons all take à- plurals, but the singulars have no distinctive features. Some nouns copy the number marker at the end of the word, and assimilate the stem vowel if it is not the same –a as in Table 75.

The next most common pairing is ǹ-/á- as in Table 76.

Kwang also has occasional stem-initial consonant mutation as in Table 77.

Despite the example of 'blood' there is no association between mass nouns or liquids and nasal prefixes.

The noun classes of Tarok have been described in Sibomana (1981) with additional material in Longtau (2008). Sibomana (1981) sets up 6 singular and plural noun classes for Tarok (Figure 8).

Table 75: Kwang ø-/à- prefix pairing with suffixed copy vowel

Gloss	Sg.	Pl.
'wall (of room)'	lâr	àlárà
'person/people'	sùm	àsùmà
'strength'	sɔ̀tɔn	sɔ̀tɔna
'woman'	yì	àya
'husband'	dìmà lɔ̀g	àdàmà lɔ̀g

Table 76: Kwang ǹ-/á- prefix pairing

Gloss	Sg.	Pl.
'feather'	ǹzùna	ázùna
'gum/glue'	ǹdúr	ádúr
'forehead'	ǹjan	ájan
'catfish (spp.)'	ǹdurum	ádurum
'blood'	ǹjì	––

Table 77: Kwang stem-initial consonant mutation

Gloss	Sg.	Pl.
'child'	fàn	àmàn
'young girl'	fàyì	àwàyì

```
1.  ù-     →   2.  o-
3.  ì-     →   4.  i-
5.  m̀/ǹ-  →   6.  m/n-
7.  a-     →   8.  agá -
9.  i-     →  10.  igá -
11. m/n-   →  12.  m/nggá -
```

Figure 8: Tarok noun-class pairings

4 Nominal affixes and number marking in the Plateau languages

The order of the numbers seems less than ideal, but since it is reprised in Longtau (2008) it is also used here. Historically, these pairings must result from the merger of a more complex system, as in many singular/plural pairs there are changes in the stem tone. Some of these seem to show semantic correlations, others do not, again suggesting class merger. Tarok also has a rich inventory of adjectives with concordial prefixes. Nasal prefixes are homorganic with the following consonant, with *m-* preceding bilabials and *n-* all others.

Persons in Tarok are almost exclusively in Class 1/2, i.e. with a *u-/o-* prefix alternation, as shown in Table 78.

Table 78: Tarok *u-/o-* prefix alternations

Gloss	Sg.	Pl.
'husband'	ùɓar	oɓar
'wife, woman'	ùcár	ocár
'ancestors'	ùkà	okà
'mother'	ùnaŋ	onáŋ
'man, person'	ùnəm	onəm
'father'	ùpò(n)	opó
'ancestor'	ùrìm	orìm
'soldier'	ùshózhà	oshózhà
'child'	ùyèn	ován

There is a strong tendency for mass nouns, liquids and abstracts to have the unpaired homorganic *N-* prefix as in Table 79.

Table 79: Tarok *N-* prefixes on mass nouns

Gloss	Tarok
'oil'	m̀mì
'urine'	m̀pə̀ng
'fat'	m̀pì
'blood'	ǹcìr
'water'	ǹdəng
'smoke'	ŋ̀gù

No other semantic set, such as large animals, trees or body parts, shows a tendency to cluster around a particular prefix pairing.

163

2.10 Eloyi

The Eloyi or Afo language is spoken in about twenty villages in Nassarawa State, Nigeria. The principle sources on the language are Mackay (1964) and Armstrong (1964; 1983; 1984).[7] The classification of Eloyi has been disputed, all the more so because the lexical database for comparison has been so weak. All the preliminary sources classified Eloyi as Plateau 2, i.e. together Izere, Tyap etc. (e.g. Greenberg 1963; Williamson & Shimizu 1968; de Wolf 1971). Armstrong (1983) set out the case for classifying Eloyi as Idomoid, which is a West Benue-Congo or Volta-Niger subgroup, classified together with Yoruba, Igbo, Nupe and Ẹdo. However, in Armstrong's (1984: 29) final published discussion of the subject he expresses some doubts, concluding "Eloyi does not now seem as close to Idoma as it did when only Varvil's list was available". Eloyi has a rich system of alternating nominal prefixes, in contrast to the remainder of Idomoid, and is provisionally treated here as Plateau, though with significant influence from Idomoid. The analysis here is based on the cited published sources, and an unpublished wordlist collected by Barau Kato at the request of the author Blench (n.d.[d]).

Despite the complex affix-pairings, many words have zero prefixes, perhaps due to the impact of extensive bilingualism with Idomoid languages. Many alternations have only one or two cases so far recorded, which makes setting up the system highly provisional. Table 80 shows the nominal prefix pairings in Eloyi.

kV- prefixes are probably the most common in Eloyi singulars and *lV-* for plurals. Although usually some type of stem harmony would be expected to operate there is no evidence for this in Eloyi.

Eloyi noun-class pairings do not show much semantic clustering. Most nouns referring to persons have diverse singulars, and plurals in *a-* or *e-*. Mother and father have an exceptional class prefix pair which may reflect the Niger-Congo persons class seen in Table 81. There is no evidence for a distinctive morphology for non-count nouns and no trace of nasal prefixes.

3 Conclusion: Plateau nominal affixing

The numerous examples illustrate the problems of making any generalisations about nominal affixes in Plateau and only weak conclusions can be drawn about its relationship with other branches of Benue-Congo. This represents a common problem of historical linguistics in such a significant contact zone. Traces of prefixes familiar from Bantu and Niger-Congo are found scattered across the family,

---

[7]Despite the title of the 1984 publication, this is about Eloyi.

4 Nominal affixes and number marking in the Plateau languages

Table 80: Nominal prefix pairings in Eloyi

Underlying	sg.	Underlying	Pl.
a-	a-	mba-	mba-
ɛ-	ɛ-	mbɛ-	mbɛ-
O-	o-, ɔ-	a-	a-
O-	o-, ɔ-	E-	e-, ɛ-
O-	o-	i-	i-
u-	u-	a-	a-
u-	u-	i-	i-
kV-	kO-	a-	a-
kV-	ko-	e-	e-
kV-	ko-	lV-	lo-
kV-	kɔ-	O-	ɔ-
kV-	ku-	E-	e-, ɛ-
kV-	ka-	lV-	lɔ-
kV-	ki-	lV-	lu-
kV-	ke-	lV-	lo-
kV-	kɛ-	lV-	lu-
rE-	rɛ-	a-	a-
rE-	re-	e-	e-

Table 81: Eloyi prefixes V-/mba-

Gloss	Sg.	Pl.
'father'	á-da	mbá-da
'mother'	éné	mb-éné

and in the light of external data it might seem likely that these were present in Proto-Plateau. However, on the basis of synchronic data in Plateau alone it would be rash to reconstruct them. Taking the data as a whole we can conclude that:

a) Plateau languages originally had a rich noun class system with CV- and V- prefixes and alliterative concord

b) A wave of renewal and analogical re-alignment led to many of the CV- prefixes disappearing or becoming unproductive and replaced by a much smaller set of V- prefixes.

c) There is some evidence for underspecified vowels in CV- prefixes showing concord with stem vowels although this is too rare to be conclusive.

d) There is evidence for a class pair for persons, probably V-/bV-, although the segment in the singular prefix are less certain (e.g. Tables 43 and 48). This can be compared with the Niger-Congo person class.

e) Proto-Plateau almost certainly had an unpaired nasal class marking liquids, mass nouns and abstracts, corresponding to Niger-Congo (e.g. examples 14, 34). Unlike Kainji, this is rarely realised as *ma-* and several branches of Plateau have *nV-*. Ndun in Table 44 does display *ma-*, *me-*, and *m-*. Other unpaired classes exhibit quite different segments which may be innovative.

f) There is strong evidence that Proto-Plateau had *N-* prefixes, homorganic with the following consonant, and present in most branches. However, there is no evidence for any consistent semantic association.

g) There is weak evidence that the Bantu Class 9 prefix, *nì-*, existed in early Plateau (cf. Table 49).

Based on the synchronic evidence from Plateau, the connection with Niger-Congo noun classes remains tenuous. Only the non-count nouns and the person class show similarities and even these are obscured by innovative affixes. Similarly, there is no single affix alternation that provides evidence for the genetic unity of Plateau. This can only be deduced from lexical isoglosses (e.g. in Blench 2000a). The paper presents a summary of what is known about number marking strategies on nouns in the Plateau languages. Further work will enrich the picture, but it is unlikely to contribute to a coherent reconstruction, as affix renewal has been very extensive.

Acknowledgements

It would be impossible to list all those who have acted as informants, but Barau Kato, Daniel Gya and Selbut Longtau have been my principal co-workers on field data collection. Bitrus Kaze, Deme Dang, Ruth Adiwu, Barnabas Dusu (†), Gideon Asuku, Alex Maikarfi and Wayo Bai have been crucial to the development of extended materials in their languages. Staff members at NBTT and SIL Jos have been always helpful in giving me access to unpublished materials and to discuss issues relating to particular languages. I would particularly like to thank Mark Gaddis for arranging workshops on the Koro cluster languages.

Abbreviations and conventions

A any central vowel
C consonant
E any mid-front vowel
N any nasal

O any mid-back vowel
S s or ʃ
V vowel

References

Adwiraah, Eleonore. 1989. *Grammatik des Gworok (Kagoro)*. Frankfurt am Main: Peter Lang.

Adwiraah, Eleonore & Eva Hagen. 1983. Nominalklassensystem des Gworok und des Gyong. In R. Voßen & U. Claudi (eds.), *Sprache, Geschichte und Kultur in Afrika*, 17–33. Hamburg: Helmut Buske.

Anonymous. 2006. *How to read and write Irigwe*. Jos: Irigwe Language & Bible Translation Project & Nigeria Bible Translation Trust.

Armstrong, Robert G. 1964. A few more words of Eloyi. *Journal of West African Languages* 1(2). 57–60.

Armstrong, Robert G. 1983. The Idomoid languages of the Benue and Cross River valleys. *Journal of West African Languages* 13(1). 91–149.

Armstrong, Robert G. 1984. The consonant system of Akpa. *Nigerian Language Teacher* 5(2). 26–29.

Blench, Roger M. 1998. The status of the languages of Central Nigeria. In M. Brenzinger (ed.), *Endangered languages in Africa*, 187–206. Köln: Köppe Verlag.

Blench, Roger M. 2000a. Revising Plateau. In Ekkehard Wolff & Orin Gensler (eds.), *Proceedings of 2nd WOCAL*, 159–174. Köln: Rüdiger Köppe.

Blench, Roger M. 2000b. Transitions in Izere nominal morphology and implications for the analysis of Plateau languages. In Antje Meißner & Anne Storch (eds.), *Nominal classification in African languages* (Frankfurter Afrikanische Blätter 12), 7–28. Köln: Rüdiger Köppe Verlag.

Blench, Roger M. 2003. Why reconstructing comparative Ron is so problematic. In H. Ekkehard Wolff (ed.), *Topics in Chadic linguistics. 1st Biennial International Colloquium on the Chadic Language Family (Leipzig, July 5-8, 2001)*, 21–42. Köln: Rudiger Köppe.

Blench, Roger M. 2005. *Is there a boundary between Plateau and Jukunoid?* http://www.rogerblench.info/Language/Niger-Congo/BC/Plateau/General/Vienna%202005%20paper.pdf, accessed 2018-06-04. Paper presented at the workshop on Jukunoid languages, November 18-21st. Vienna.

Blench, Roger M. 2018. Nominal affixing in the Kainji languages of northwestern and central Nigeria. In John R. Watters (ed.), *East Benue-Congo: Nouns, pronouns, and verbs*, 59–106. Berlin: Language Science Press. DOI:10.5281/zenodo.1314337

Blench, Roger M. n.d.(a). *Alumic*. http://www.rogerblench.info/Language/Niger-Congo/BC/Plateau/Alumic/AluOP.htm, accessed 2018-06-04.

Blench, Roger M. n.d.(b). *An atlas of Nigerian languages*. http://www.rogerblench.info / Language / Africa / Nigeria / Atlas % 20of % 20Nigerian % 20Languages - %20ed%20III.pdf, accessed 2018-06-04.

Blench, Roger M. n.d.(c). *Beromic*. http://www.rogerblench.info/Language/Niger-Congo/BC/Plateau/Beromic/Comparative%20Beromic.pdf, accessed 2018-06-04.

Blench, Roger M. n.d.(d). *Eloyi*. http://www.rogerblench.info/Language/Niger-Congo/BC/Plateau/Eloyi%20wordlist%20paper.pdf, accessed 2018-06-04.

Blench, Roger M. n.d.(e). *Hyamic/Shang*. http://www.rogerblench.info/Language/Niger-Congo/BC/Plateau/Hyamic/Shang/Shang%20wordlist.pdf, accessed 2018-06-04.

Blench, Roger M. n.d.(f). *Ninzic/Ninzo*. http://www.rogerblench.info/Language/Niger-Congo/BC/Plateau/Ninzic/Ninzo%20wordlist.pdf, accessed 2018-06-04.

Blench, Roger M. n.d.(g). *Plateau*. http://www.rogerblench.info/Language/Niger-Congo/BC/Plateau/PlOP.htm, accessed 2018-06-04.

Blench, Roger M. n.d.(h). *Plateau/South*. http://www.rogerblench.info/Language/Niger-Congo/BC/Plateau/South/SouthOP.htm, accessed 2018-06-04.

Blench, Roger M. n.d.(i). *Tarokoid/Kwanka*. http : / / www . rogerblench . info / Language / Niger - Congo / BC / Plateau / Tarokoid / Kwanka % 20wordlist % 20paper%20Unicode.pdf, accessed 2018-06-04.

Blench, Roger M. & Daniel Gya. 2012. Rigwe pronouns. In Anne Storch, Gratien Atindogbé & Roger M. Blench (eds.), *Copy pronouns: Case studies from African languages*, 19–138. Köln: Rüdiger Köppe.

Bouquiaux, Luc. 1964. A wordlist of Aten (Ganawuri). *Journal of West African Languages* 1(2). 5–25.

Bouquiaux, Luc. 1967. Le système des classes nominales dans quelques langues (Birom, Ganawuri, Anaguta, Irigwe, Kaje, Rukuba) appartenant au groupe «Plateau» (Nigéria Central) de la sous-famille Benoué-Congo. In G. Manessy (ed.), *La classification nominale dans les langues Negro-Africaines*, 133–156. Paris: CNRS.

Bouquiaux, Luc. 1970. *La langue Birom (Nigeria septentrional) – phonologie, morphologie, syntaxe*. Paris: Société d'édition Les Belles Lettres.

Bouquiaux, Luc. 2001. *Dictionnaire Birom, 3 vols.* Louvain: Peeters.

Crozier, David & Roger M. Blench. 1992. *Index of Nigerian languages.* 2nd edn. Dallas, TX: SIL.

de Wolf, Paul P. 1971. *The noun class system of Proto-Benue-Congo.* The Hague: Mouton.

Dihoff, Ivan. 1976. *Aspects of the grammar of Chori.* Madison: University of Wisconsin Doctoral dissertation.

Follingstad, Carl. n.d. *Tyap database.* Unpublished manuscript.

Follingstad, Joy A. 1991. *Aspects of Tyap syntax.* Arlington: University of Texas MA thesis.

Gerhardt, Ludwig. 1969a. *Analytische und vergleichende Untersuchungen zu einigen zentralnigerianischen Klassensprachen.* Hamburg: Universität Hamburg Doctoral dissertation.

Gerhardt, Ludwig. 1969b. Über sprachliche Beziehungen auf dem zentralnigerianischen Plateau. In W. Voigt (ed.), *ZDMG Supplementa I. VXII Deutscher Orientalistentag,* 1079–1091. Wiesbaden: Steiner Verlag.

Gerhardt, Ludwig. 1971. Stammweiterungen in den Verben einiger zentralnigerianischer Klassensprachen. In Veronika Six, Norbert Cyffer, Ekkehard Wolff, Ludwig Gerhardt & Hilke Meyer-Bahlburg (eds.), *Afrikanischen Sprachen und Kulturen - Ein Querschnitt* (Hamburger Beiträge zu Afrikakunde Band 14), 95–101. Hamburg: Deutsches Institut für Afrikaforschung.

Gerhardt, Ludwig. 1972/3. Das Nominalsystem der Plateau-4 Sprachen: Versuch einer Rekonstruktion. *Afrika und Übersee* 56. 72–89.

Gerhardt, Ludwig. 1972/73. Abriß der nominalen Klassen in Koro, North-Central State, Nigeria. *Afrika und Übersee* 56. 245–266.

Gerhardt, Ludwig. 1973/4. Proto-Benue-Congo und Kagoma. *Afrika und Übersee* 57. 81–93.

Gerhardt, Ludwig. 1974. *Pi-, hi-, fi-,* und *bu-* in den Plateausprachen Nordnigerias: Klasse neun/zehn oder Klasse neunzehn? *Zeitschrift der Deutschen Morgenländischen Gesellschaft* Supplementa 2. 574–582.

Gerhardt, Ludwig. 1983a. *Beiträge zur Kenntnis der Sprachen des Nigerianischen Plateaus.* Glückstadt: Verlag J. J. Augustin.

Gerhardt, Ludwig. 1983b. The classification of Eggon: Plateau or Benue group? *Journal of West African Languages* 13(1). 37–50.

Gerhardt, Ludwig. 1988a. Auf- und Abbau von nominalen Klassensystemen. In Siegmund Brauner & Ekkehard Wolff (eds.), *Progressive traditions in African and Oriental studies,* 69–77. Berlin: Akademie Verlag.

Gerhardt, Ludwig. 1988b. Bemerkungen zur Morphologie des Kwoi. In *Afrikanische Arbeitspapiere, Sondernummer 1988*, 53–65.

Gerhardt, Ludwig. 1989. Kainji and Platoid. In John Bendor-Samuel (ed.), *Niger-Congo*, 359–376. Lanham, MD: University Press of America.

Gerhardt, Ludwig. 1994. Western Plateau as a model for the development of Benue-Congo noun-class system. *Afrika und Übersee* 77. 161–176.

Gerhardt, Ludwig & Heinz Jockers. 1981. Lexikostatistische Klassifikationen von Plateausprachen. *Berliner Afrikanistische Vorträge* 1. 25–54.

Goroh, Martin K. 2000. Koro orthography. In A. U. Okwudishu & O. S. Salami (eds.), *Orthographies of Nigerian languages, VII*, 76–97. Lagos: Nigerian Educational Research & Development Council.

Greenberg, Joseph H. 1963. The languages of Africa. *IJAL* Part II, No. 1(29).

Gunn, Harold D. 1953. *Peoples of the Plateau area of Northern Nigeria*. London: IAI.

Gunn, Harold D. 1956. *Peoples of the Central area of Northern Nigeria*. London: IAI.

Hagen, Eva. 1988. *Die Gong: Monographische Studie der Kultur und Sprache der Gong (Kagoma), Zentralnigeria*. Hamburg: Dr. R. Krämer.

Hoffmann, Carl. 1976. *Some aspects of the Che noun class system*. Ibadan. Ms.

Hörner, Elisabeth. 1980. *Ninzam: Untersuchengen zu einer Klassensprache des zentralnigerianischen Plateau*. Hamburg: Universität Hamburg Magisterarbeit.

Hyuwa, Daniel D. 1986. Kaje orthography. In Robert G. Armstrong (ed.), *Orthographies of Nigerian languages*, 72–99. Lagos: Ministry of Education.

Jockers, Heinz. 1982. *Untersuchungen zum Kwoi-Dialekt des Hyam/Jaba*. Hamburg: Universität Hamburg Magisterarbeit.

Hansford, Keir L., John Bendor-Samuel & Ronald Stanford. 1976. *An index of Nigerian languages*. Ghana: SIL.

Kießling, Roland. 2010. Infix genesis and incipient initial consonant mutations in some lesser known Benue-Congo languages. In Armin R. Bachmann, Christliebe El Mogharbel & Katja Himstedt (eds.), *Form und Struktur in der Sprache: Festschrift für Elmar Ternes*, 188–220. Tübingen: Narr.

Koelle, Sigismund W. 1854. *Polyglotta Africana*. London: Church Missionary House.

Kuhn, Hanna & B. Dusu. 1985. Berom orthography. In Ayo Banjo (ed.), *Orthographies of Nigerian languages*, vol. 3, 44–61. Lagos: Ministry of Education.

Longtau, Selbut R. 2008. *The Tarok language: its basic principles and grammar* (Language Monograph Series 1). Jos: Kay Williamson Educational Foundation.

Loos, Eugene, Susan Anderson, Jr. Dwight H. Day, Paul C. Jordan & J. Douglas Wingate (eds.). 2003. *Glossary of linguistic terms.* Dallas, TX. https://glossary.sil.org/.

Mackay, H. D. 1964. A word-list of Eloyi. *Journal of West African Languages* 1(1). 5–12.

Maddieson, Ian. N.d. *The noun-class system of Eggon.* Ibadan. Mimeo.

Maddieson, Ian. 1982. Unusual consonant cluster and complex segments in Eggon. *Studies in African Linguistics, Supplement* 8. 89–92.

Maho, Jouni Filip. 1999. *A comparative study of Bantu noun classes.* Gothenburg: Acta Universitatis Gothoburgensis.

McKinney, Carol. 1979. Plural verb roots in Kaje. *Afrika und Übersee* 62. 107–117.

McKinney, Carol. 1983. A linguistic shift in Kaje, Kagoro and Katab. *Ethnology* 22(4). 281–293.

McKinney, Norris. 1984. The fortis feature in Jju (Kaje): An initial study. *Studies in African Linguistics* 15(2). 177–188.

McKinney, Norris. 1990. Temporal characteristics of fortis stops and affricates in Tyap and Jju. *Journal of Phonetics* 18. 255–266.

Meek, Charles K. 1925. *The Northern tribes of Nigeria.* London: Humphrey Milford. 2 vols.

Meek, Charles K. 1931. *Tribal studies in Northern Nigeria.* London: Kegan Paul, Trench, Trübner & Company. 2 vols.

Miehe, Gudrun. 1991. *Die Präfixnasale im Benue-Congo und im Kwa: Versuch einer Widerlegung der Hypothese von der Nasalinnovation des Bantu.* Berlin: Reimer.

Moser, Rex. 1982. *Ikulu wordlist.* Hamburg. Unpublished manuscript.

Muller, Jean-Claude. 1982. *Du bon usage du sexe et du mariage: Structures matrimoniales du haut plateau nigérien.* Quebec: l'Harmattan.

Nettle, Daniel. 1998a. Materials from the South-Eastern Plateau languages of Nigeria (Fyem, Hórom and Mabo-Barukul). *Afrika und Übersee* 81. 253–279.

Nettle, Daniel. 1998b. *The Fyem language of Northern Nigeria.* Munich: Lincom Europa.

Ninzo Language Project Committee. 1999. *Reading and writing Ninzo.* Fadan Wate: Ninzo Language Project Committee.

Price, Norman. 1989. *Notes on Mada phonology.* Dallas, TX: SIL.

Rowlands, E. C. 1962. Notes on some class languages of Northern Nigeria. *African Language Studies* 3. 71–83.

Rueck, Michael J., Katarína Hannelová & Zachariah Yoder. 2008. *Sociolinguistic survey of the Ahwai people, Kaduna State, Nigeria.* Jos. Unpublished manuscript.

Seitz, Gitte. 1993. *Ikulu: Untersuchungen zu einer zentralnigeriansichen Klassensprache*. Hamburg: University of Hamburg MA thesis.

Shimizu, Kiyoshi. 1975a. A lexicostatistical study of Plateau languages and Jukun. *Anthropological Linguistics* 17. 413–418.

Shimizu, Kiyoshi. 1975b. *The languages of Jos Division* (Linguistic Survey of Benue-Plateau State Part I). Kano: Bayero University College.

Shimizu, Kiyoshi. 1996. *A Kulu vocabulary and fragments of Kulu grammatical structures*. http://www.aa.tufs.ac.jp/~P_aflang/TEXTS/june96/shimizu.txt.

Sibomana, Leo. 1981. Tarok II: Das Nominalklassensystem. *Afrika und Übersee* 64. 25–34.

Sibomana, Leo. 1985. A phonological and grammatical outline of Eggon. *Afrika und Übersee* 68. 43–68.

Stofberg, Yvonne. 1978. *Migili grammar* (Language Data microfiche, African Series 12). Dallas, TX: FLSIL.

Temple, Olive. 1922. *Notes on the tribes, provinces, emirates and states of the Northern provinces of Nigeria*. Capetown: Argus Printing & Publishing Co.

Westermann, Diedrich. 1927. *Die Westlichen Sudansprachen und ihre Beziehungen zum Bantu*. Berlin: de Gruyter.

Westermann, Diedrich & Margaret A. Bryan. 1952. *Languages of West Africa: Part II*. Vol. 2. London: Oxford University Press.

Williamson, Kay. 1971. The Benue-Congo languages and Ịjọ. In Thomas Sebeok (ed.), *Current trends in linguistics*, 245–306. The Hague: Mouton.

Williamson, Kay. 1972. *Benue-Congo comparative wordlist*. Vol. 2. Ibadan: West African Linguistic Society.

Williamson, Kay. 1989. Niger-congo overview. In John Bendor-Samuel (ed.), *The Niger-Congo languages*, 3–45. Lanham, MD: University Press of America.

Williamson, Kay & Roger M. Blench. 2000. Niger-Congo. In Bernd Heine & Derek Nurse (eds.), *African languages: An introduction*, 11–42. Cambridge: Cambridge University Press.

Williamson, Kay & Kiyoshi Shimizu. 1968. *Benue-Congo comparative wordlist*. Vol. 1. Ibadan: West African Linguistic Society.

Wilson, Janet E. 2003. *Transparency and spreading of tense, aspect, and mood in Kuche narrative discourse*. Arlington, TX: University of Texas at Arlington MA thesis.

Wolff, Hans. 1963. Noun classes and concord in Berom. In *Actes du seconde colloque internationale de linguistique négro-africaine*, 86–96. Dakar: Université de Dakar.

Chapter 5

Common Bantoid verb extensions

Larry M. Hyman

University of California, Berkeley

> In this paper I survey verb extensions within different Bantoid languages and subgroups, comparing them to Cameroonian Bantu zone A. Extending my survey of Niger-Congo extensions (Hyman 2007), I show that there is a band of contiguous languages in the Grassfields area where a number of contrastive verb extensions have relative productivity (cf. the studies in Idiata & Mba 2003). Interestingly, the languages in question belong to several subgroups: Limbum (NE Eastern Grassfields Bantu), Noni (Beboid), Kom and Babanki (Ring Western Grassfields Bantu), Bafut and Mankon (Ngemba Eastern Grassfields Bantu). Other languages in these same subgroups are not in this geographical band and have very few extensions. The above-mentioned languages allow a possible reconstruction of *CV extensions with *s, *t, *n, *l, *k, and *m. A major property of Bantoid extensions is the relative frequency of aspectual-type extensions, especially marking different types of pluractionality (iterative, frequentative, distributive, repetitive), diminutive (attenuation of action), and intensive (augmentation of action) semantics. In many languages the same suffix form covers two or more of these functions. The hypothesis is that the original system was more like Proto-Bantu, with extensions being more valence-related, but over time these very same extensions became reinterpreted as aspectual. However, the great variety of extensions in and outside of Bantoid suggests that there may have been more extensions at a pre-Proto-Bantu stage.

1 Introduction

While the presence and identity of Proto-Bantu verb extensions has long been established, with relatively little controversy (Meeussen 1967; Schadeberg 2003), we do not have a clear sense of the verb extension system(s) that existed at pre-Proto-Bantu stages.[1] My goal in this paper is to consider some of the issues aris-

---

[1]This paper was first presented at the Workshop on Bantu and its Closest Relatives, Berlin Bantu Conference (B4ntu), April 6-9, 2011.

Larry M. Hyman. Common Bantoid verb extensions. In John R. Watters (ed.), *East Benue-Congo: Nouns, pronouns, and verbs*, 173–198. Berlin: Language Science Press.

ing in NW Bantu, Grassfields Bantu, and some of their closest Bantoid relatives. The questions I shall be concerned with are:

(i) What are Bantoid verb extensions like?

(ii) What can be reconstructed at a Bantoid Pre-Proto-Bantu level?

(iii) What, if anything, do they tell us about Proto-Bantu?

My goal in this chapter is to evaluate our current knowledge to determine what the Common Bantoid verb extensions are that might be considered for such reconstruction.[2]

2 Grassfields Bantu

It is often remarked that the comparative study of Bantu (and Niger-Congo) verb extensions has been neglected in favor of noun classes. The same has been true in Bantoid studies. As a case in point, let us consider Grassfields Bantu. In (1) I present two subclassifications of what we might identify as "Narrow Grassfields Bantu", i.e. ignoring Ndemli (cf. Stallcup 1980a; Watters & Leroy 1989; Piron 1995; Watters 2003):

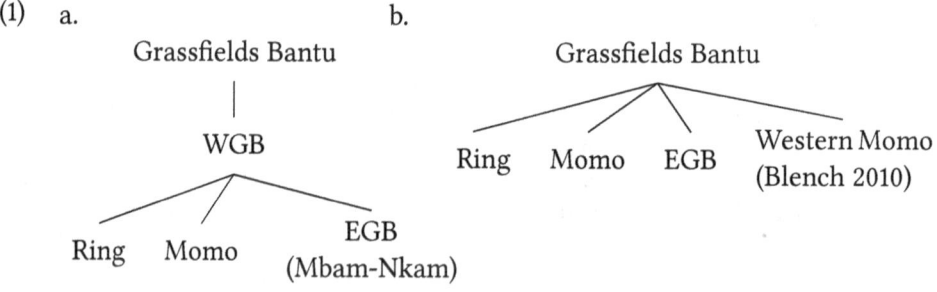

As seen, the older subclassification in (1a) recognizes a binary split between Western vs. Eastern Grassfields Bantu (WGB, EGB), while (1b) presents all of the subbranches as coordinate. Identification of some of the languages are as follows (Hyman & Voorhoeve 1980; Watters 2003):

(2) a. Ring: Aghem, Isu, Weh, Bum, Bafmeng, Kom, Oku, Babanki, Lamnso', Babungo, Babessi

---

[2]For a recent overview of the languages considered to be Bantoid, see Blench (2015).

b. Momo: Moghamo, Metta, Menemo, Ngembu, Ngamambo, Ngie, Oshie, Ngwo, Mundani, Njen
c. EGB: Ngemba (e.g. Mankon, Bafut), Bamileke (e.g. Yemba, Ghomala, Medumba, Fe'fe'), Nun (e.g. Bamun, Bali), North (e.g. Limbum, Adere)

Early on, the Grassfields Bantu Working Group discovered significant differences which seemed to motivate the division between EGB and WGB. As seen in Table 1a-g, most of the criteria for such a split concerned noun class marking (Stallcup 1980a: 55).

Table 1: Criteria for distinguishing Eastern from Western Grassfields

	Eastern Grassfields Bantu	Western Grassfields Bantu
a.	nasal prefix in class 1 and class 3 nouns	absence of the nasal
b.	no distinction between class 6 and class 6a	distinction between class 6 a- and class 6a mə-
c.	nasal prefix on all 9/10 nouns	nasal prefix only on some 9/10 nouns
d.	absence of classes 4 and 13; class 19 rare	presence of classes 4 and 13; class 19 frequent
e.	noun prefixes all carry a /L/ tone	most noun prefixes carry a /H/ tone
f.	no noun suffixes	many noun suffixes, e.g. plural -tí, -sí
g.	class 2 or 6a generalizes to mark plural	class 10 or 13 generalizes to mark plural
h.	innovation of síŋə́ 'bird', -kìə́ 'water'	maintenance of *-nɔ̀ní 'bird', *-díbá 'water'
i.	maintenance of *-úmà 'thing'	*-úmà is lost, other roots come in
Plus:	maintenance of inherited 3rd person pronouns	introduction of new 3rd person pronouns (Hyman 2018b [this volume])

A major question we continue to face is the extent to which Proto-Bantu (PB) is representative of pre-PB, e.g. "Proto-Bantoid", which includes Proto-Grassfields Bantu. It is commonly assumed that PB is conservative, preserving many features of Proto-Niger-Congo (PNC). Concerning the criteria in (1a-c), it was once generally accepted that Narrow Bantu innovated nasals in the noun prefixes for classes 1, 3, 4, 6, 9 and 10. However Miehe (1991) argued that the nasals are archaic, which Williamson (1993: 43-44) accepts, but which is still somewhat unsettled.[3] All this to say that attention has largely been on noun classes, which have often served not only as the major criterion for inclusion within Niger-Congo, but also subgrouping.

Concerning verb extensions, the PB system has been reconstructed as in (3), where it is useful to distinguish three sets (Meeussen 1967; Schadeberg 2003):

(3) a. productive extensions
   i. *-i- 'causative'   iv. *-ɪk- 'neuter/stative'
   ii. *-ɪc-i- [-ɪs-] 'causative'   v. *-an- 'reciprocal/associative'
   iii. *-ɪd- [-ɪl-] 'applicative'   vi. *(-ɪC-)-ʋ- 'passive' (-ɪbw-, -ɪgw-)

   b. unproductive extensions often restricted to post-radical position or specific combinations
   i. *-ɪk- 'impositive'   iv. *-ad- (-al-) 'extensive'
   ii. *-am- 'positional'   v. *-at- 'tentive' (contactive)
   iii. *-a(n)g- 'repetitive'   vi. *-ʋk-/*-ʋd- (-ʋl-) 'reversive/separative' (intr./trans.)

   c. frozen, mostly unidentifiable -VC- expansions
   i. *-u-, *-im-, *-un-, *-ing-   iii. *-ɪm-, *-ɔm-, *-ɔng- (but only after CV-)
   ii. *-ang-, *-ab-, *-ag-, *-ak-   iv. *-ʋt-

Attempts to reconstruct extensions in PNC and certain other branches of NC have been few, but typically produce forms resembling PB (Table 2).

It is however possible that PB may have lost (merged) earlier distinctions. When one compares Bantu with some of the Atlantic languages, for instance, one observes that the latter often distinguish more than one applicative extension where Bantu typically has only *-ɪd- (Hyman 2007: 157).[4]

---

[3] Cf. the recent workshop "Nasal Noun Class Prefixes in Bantu: Innovated or Inherited?" which I co-organized with Gudrun Miehe at the Paris Bantu Conference (Bantu5) on June 12, 2013. See Hyman (2018a [this volume]).

[4] Nuba mountain languages also typically distinguish benefactive vs. locative applicatives, in addition to other extensions not distinguished in Bantu. An overview of Nuba mountain verb extensions (Hyman 2014) is available upon request.

5 Common Bantoid verb extensions

Table 2: Proposed reconstructions of verb extensions

		Proto-Niger-Congo (Voeltz 1977)	Proto-Bantu (Schadeberg 2003)	Proto-Atlantic (Doneux 1975)
a.	applicative	*-de	*-ɪd-	*-ed
b.	causative	*-ci, *-ti	*-ic-i-	(*-an)
c.	contactive	*-ta	*-at-	
d.	passive	*-o	*-ɪb-ʊ-	*-V [+back]
e.	reciprocal	*-na	*-an-	*-ad
f.	reversive (tr.)	*-to	*-ʊd-	*-t
g.	reversive (intr.)	*-ko	*-ʊk-	
h.	stative/neuter	*-ke	*-ɪk-	
i.	stative/positional	*-ma	*-am-	

Table 3: Comparing Chichewa (Bantu) with two Atlantic languages

	Chichewa (Hyman & Mchombo 1992)	Temne (Wilson 1961; Kanu 2004)	Fula (Arnott 1970)
causative	-is-	-s	-n-
allative	-ir-	-r	-r- ?
locative	-ir-	-r	-r-
recipient	-ir-	-r	-an-
benefactive	-ir-	-a̰	-an-
circumstance	-ir-	-a̰	-an-
manner	-ir-	-a̰	-r-
instrument	-ir-	-a̰-nɛ	-r-

However, Grassfields Bantu and even Bantu zone A may diverge from PB, as seen in Table 4 (Hyman 2007: 160):[5]

Table 4: Comparing Bantu Zone A (Mokpe & Gunu) with Grassfields (Mankon & Bafut)

Mokpe A22 (Connell 1997; Henson 2001)		Gunu A62 (Orwig 1989)		Mankon (EGB) (Leroy 1982)		Bafut (EGB) (Tamanji & Mba 2003)	
-an-ɛ	reciprocal	-anIn	réciproque	-nə	réciproque	-nə	reciprocal
-an-a	instrumental	-an	pluriel, iteratif	-nə	stative, réfl	-nə	stative/intr
-o-a	reversive	-Ug	réversif intr.	-kə	intransitif	-kə	stative/intr
		-Ig	intensif	-kə	itératif	-kə	iterative
-is-ɛ	causative	-i	causatif	-sə	causatif	-sə	causative
		-Id	diminutif	-tə	diminutif	-tə	attenuative/ iterative
-e-a, -ɛl-ɛ	applicative	-In	applicatif			-lə	random
-am-a	positional	-Im	statif				
-av-ɛ	passive	=VIÚ	passif				
á-...-ɛ	reflexive	bá-	réfléchi				

Within NW Bantu it is not uncommon for certain notions to be expressed by a sequence of verb suffixes, sometimes with a specific final vowel (FV). This is especially the case with the reciprocal and the instrumental, the latter not having a distinct form in most Bantu.[6] Note that the -an- of the 'instrumental' might better be identified as 'associative' which, in its reciprocal use, is found in the sequence -ang-an- sporadically throughout the Bantu zone. See also Bostoen & Nzang-Bie (2010) for the development of such "double suffixes" in A70. Thus, in addition to the above, Kwasio (A81) distinguishes -al-a 'recip.' vs. -ɛl-ɛ 'instr.' (Ngue Um 2002: (< *-an-a, *-an-ɛ), while Mpompon (A86c) has instrumental -él-è vs. reciprocal tí-...-là (Ngantcho Lebika 2003: 38). In addition, the -ɪd and -tə diminutive extensions in zone A and Bantoid do not have an obvious cognate in what I will refer to as a central or canonical Bantu (CB). They are, for instance, not obviously related to the unproductive tentive or extensive extensions in (3b).

---

[5]The capitals I and U indicate harmonizing vowels in Gunu.

[6]As seen in Table 3, some Bantu languages use the applicative suffix for instruments; others may use the causative extension, while still others require a preposition to express an instrument.

In fact, once we move out into Bantu's closest relatives, we run into a number of problems:

(i) Many Bantoid languages have few extensions, often limited to one per verb root. In addition, although Bantu languages typically allow more than one extension in sequence, many of the Bantoid languages allow only one extension per verb root.

(ii) The forms or functions of the extensions may not correspond to those in Narrow Bantu, as I have already noted concerning the diminutive extension.

(iii) The forms may be polysemous, the semantics difficult to characterize, and the functions contradictory. I will give several examples of this below.

(iv) The roots of "formally" extended verbs often do not occur unextended. While this is sometimes the case even with productive extensions in CB, the problem is exacerbated in Bantoid, where the extensions are less productive (and their function harder to characterize).

(v) Such "formal extensions" pose problems of segmentation. It is often hard, if not impossible to tell if a *CVte* verb stem should be segmented as *CV-te* or *CVt-e*.

(vi) There is considerable, rather impressive variation vs. the relative stability of CB extensions.

These problems will become further evident from the data presented in the following section.

3 Survey of Bantoid verb extensions with focus on Grassfields

As a result of all of the above, Blench (2011: 1) quite accurately appraises our current understanding: "In contrast to Bantu, verbal extensions in Bantoid languages remain very poorly known." For the purpose of attempting a reconstruction, I therefore had to first conduct a reasonably comprehensive survey of Bantoid verb extensions based on available literature. I present the forms that were found in the following composite table—which should be considered a "first pass", with some amalgamations (Table 5).

Table 5: Survey of Bantoid verb extensions

		PLUR	DIM	INTENS	CAUS	APPL	REC	ASSOC	SEP	INTR	PASS	STAT
Kenyang	Btd	ti, ka		ka	si, ti							ɛ
Mbe	Btd									li,ri	li	
Tikar	Btd	k/ga'			si, li						li	
Vute	Btd				tɨ, hɨ, lɨ	na	an				lɨ	
Kemezung	Btd				sə		nə					
Noni	Btd	yɛ kɛn	cɛ		se, ke		ɛn, nɛn, sɛn, yɛn		tEn			m
Babanki	Ring	tə, kə, lə, m'	tə, nə		sə			(nə)		(mə)		
Kom	Ring	tə, lə, nə	tə, lə		sə		nə					
Lamnso'[a]	Ring	kir, ti(n), ri	ti	si(n), ti(n)	si, ir		nen			in	(im)	
Babungo	Ring				sə, (tə)		nə		nə	nə		
Isu	Ring	i, lə		i, lə	i							
Meta	Mo	ri, ni	ri, ni		ri, ni	ri	ri, ni	ri	ri			
Mundani	Mo	t	t							t		
Baba I	Nun	tə										
Limbum	NE	ni, shi, se, te, nger	ri		si		ni		ni	ti, té		

PLUR = pluractional (multiplicity), iterative, repetitive, frequentative; DIM = diminutive, attenuative; INTENS = intensive, quantity, effort, completely; CAUS = causative, transitive; APPL = applicative, benefactive; ASSOC = associative (together) with, manner or instrumental, simultaneity; SEP = separative, ablative, reversive, bifurcative; INTR = detransitivizing, spontaneous ('by itself'), PASS = Passive; STAT = stative, positional. Btd = Bantoid, Mo = Momo, NE = NE Grassfields, Ng = Ngemba (EGB), Bk = Bamileke (EGB), Ada = Adamawa.

[a]For a slightly different, fuller identification of the Lamnso' verb extensions along with examples, see Blench (2016).

5 Common Bantoid verb extensions

		PLUR	DIM	INTENS	CAUS	APPL	REC	ASSOC	SEP	INTR	PASS	STAT
Yamba	NE				sə							
Bafut	Ng	tə, kə	tə	kə	sə		nə	nə		nə, kə		
Mankon	Ng	kə	tə		sə		nə			kə		nə
Ngombale	Bk	té										e
Ngwe	Bk	te					(ŋe)					
Yemba	Bk	ti			ni		ni			ti		ni
Ngiemboon	Bk	tɛ					tɛ					e?
Bangwa	Bk	sə										
Shingu	Bk	sə			ni		ni			ti		ni
Balong	A10				il	il				il		
Mokpe	A20				isɛ	ea, ɛlɛ	anɛ	ana	oa		avE	ama
Bakoko	A40				le		lán	lán			bE$, lE$	
Basaa[a]	A40				¨s, ¨ha	¨l, nɛ	na				¨(b)a	í
Tunen	A40			Vl	In, on	i, si	In	Inan		Un		Im
Nomaante	A40			It, ItIt	ak	i, si	In	an		Vl		Im
Bafia	A50	tɨ, kə		tɨ	sɨ		Cɛn				i, ɛn	
Gunu	A60	an	Id	Ig	i	In	Inan			Ug	VlU	Im
Tuki	A60			iy	en	an				érí		
	A70			lá	(l)a		(a)ni			ba		
	A80				gù		àlà	na, ElE		a		
	A80			ug, ula	al		la, ya				ow	ya
	A80				əzə	éà	àlà		bà?	ówà		
Mpompon	A80				sèl		là			ì...yâ		
Kako	A90				s, id'y		in			in		

[a]The umlaut in the Basaa extensions indicate that the given suffix causes vowel height to rise.

From the above we can make the following observations:

(i) Verb extensions are most widespread in a contiguous area including Limbum (EGB), Noni (Beboid), Central Ring (WGB), and Ngemba (EGB), indicated by the ellipse I have drawn over the following map.

(ii) Areas outside the oval area on the map have undergone considerable reduction in their extensions, sometimes dramatically. Ejagham, for example, only has a stative suffix -*am* and a few frozen relics of causative -*i*, e.g. Western Ejagham -*ríg* 'to be burn', -*ríg-i* 'to burn something' (Watters 1981: 444, fn. 1).

(iii) Related Grassfields languages outside the oval have fewer extensions, e.g. Western Ring (Kiessling 2004), Momo, and Bamileke—often few forms with considerable polysemy and unpredictability.

One language which shows a wide range of verb extensions is Babanki (Kejom). Out of 434 verbs, 324 from Jisa (1977) and 122 from Akumbu (2008), I have counted the following number of entries for each of six extensions, whose meanings are also identified (Table 6).

Table 6: Babanki (Kejom) verb extension

	-tə	-sə	-mə	-lə	-kə	-nə
Total number	203	142	56	37	33	19
independent root	150	100	30	22	24	8
"formal"	53	42	26	15	9	11
Primary meaning	attenuative 'a little'	causative 'cause to V'	associative 'with, together'	augmentative 'a lot'	repetitive 'time and again'	(varies)

I have also separately indicated those entries for which an independent root exists vs. those which are "formal" extensions without a corresponding independent root. As seen, attenuative -*tə* is the most attested, followed by causative -*sə*.[7] Bila (1986: 39-44) identifies the following extensions in Bafut (EGB) which occur with independent roots, often with different, overlapping meanings (Table 7).[8]

---

[7] -*tə* has another common meaning: iterative 'one after another'.

[8] Bila uses the term "spontaneous" to refer to what I have identified as "middle" (voice), which he says "indicates that the action suggested by the verb is capable of going on without the assistance of an external agentive force." (p.42)

5 Common Bantoid verb extensions

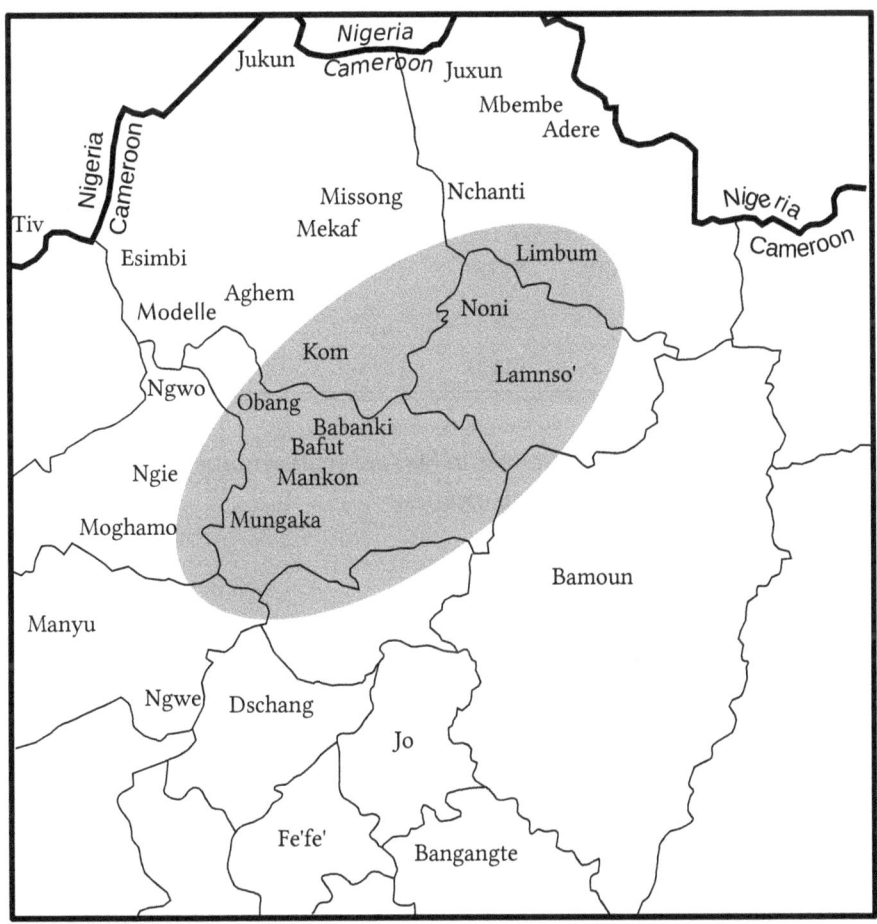

Figure 1: Map adapted from Jean-Marie Hombert from Hyman (1979: xii)

Table 7: Bafut verb extensions

-kə	-tə	-nə	-sə	-lə
388	338	171	117	112
distributive (320)	diminutive (314)	reciprocal (52)	causative	randomness (66)
repetitive (28)	repetitive (16)	simultaneous (72)		roughness (22)
middle (16)	distributive (8)	middle (47)		on several parts (7)
quantitative (20)				

Another extension that Bila mentions is perfective -mə, which being inflectional can occur on all 600 verbs in his corpus. Even ignoring this suffix, the comparison between Bafut and Babanki in Table 8 shows that the lexical frequency of the extensions can vary considerably in different languages.

Table 8: Lexical frequency of extensions in Bafut and Babanki

Bafut	n=600	mə (600)	>	kə (388)	>	tə (338)	>	nə (171)	>	sə (117)	>	lə (112)
Babanki	n=434	tə (203)	>	sə (142)	>	mə (56)	>	lə (37)	>	kə (33)	>	nə (19)

Returning to Babanki, the examples in (4a) are representative of the 80+ verbs found to have a very clear causative meaning:

(4) a. vì 'come' vì-sɔ́ 'bring near'
fɛ́n 'be black' fɛ́n-sɔ́ 'make black'
dhú 'go' dhú-sɔ́ 'carry away'
zhɨ́ 'eat' zhɨ́-sɔ́ 'feed'
búŋ 'melt' búŋ-sɔ́ 'cause to melt'
lyɔ́m 'hurt self' lyɔ́m-sɔ́ 'hurt s.o.'

b. vì 'come' vì-nɔ̀ 'come with'
tsí 'spend night' tsí-nɔ́ '... with a woman'

c. cò 'pass' cò-mɔ̀ 'meet and pass'
kwè?è 'think' kwè?-mɔ̀ 'think together'
gè 'share' gè-mɔ̀ 'share equally'
táŋ 'count' táŋ-mɔ́ 'quarrel'
shɨ̀? 'measure' shɨ̀?-mɔ̀ 'compare measures'

From (4a) there is no question, then, that Babanki -sə is related to PB *-ɪc-i-. Of the 19 verb roots which take -nə only the two examples in (4b) show a clear comitative meaning, suggesting cognacy with PB *-an-. Finally, (4c) illustrates the

5 Common Bantoid verb extensions

'associative' meaning of *-mə*, which may ultimately be related to PB positional **-am-*, which has a passive function in zone C (cf. the stative function of Gunu *-Im-* in Table 4).

While the above and other specific meanings can be identified for individual extensions, any of the six suffixes can be used with varying pluractional meanings:

(5) a. *-tə* (23)
    bɛ́n 'dance'   *bɛ́n-tɔ́* 'dance time and again'
    bɔ́ŋ 'pick up'   *bɔ́ŋ-tɔ́* 'pick up many things one by one'
    bwìɛ̀ʔɛ̀ 'carry'   *bwìɛ̀ʔ-tɔ̀* 'carry (lots of people, lots of things)'
    cɔ́ʔ 'borrow, lend'   *cɔ́ʔtɔ́* 'lend continuously to lots of people, borrow from lots of sources'
    gè 'share'   *gè-tɔ̀* 'share one by one'
    shù 'stab'   *shù-tɔ̀* 'stab lots of things one by one or one thing many times'

b. *-lə* (12)
    zhwí 'kill'   *zhwí-lɔ́* 'kill one after the other, lots of people'
    mì 'swallow'   *mì-lɔ̀* 'swallow fast, gulping, too much in mouth'
    té 'abuse'   *té-lɔ́* 'abuse lots of people or abuse one person with lots of abuse'
    bwìʔì 'hit'   *bwìʔ-lɔ̀* 'give blows a lot'

c. *-kə* (7)
    dì 'cry'   *dì-kɔ̀* 'cry time and again'
    fʌ́ŋ 'fall'   *fʌ́ŋ-kɔ́* 'fall time and again'
    pfɨ́ 'die'   *pfɨ́-kɔ́* 'die one after the other'
    tsɔ́ʔɔ́ 'jump'   *tsɔ́ʔ-kɔ́* 'jump time and again'

d. *-mə* (4)
    lám 'marry'   *lám-mɔ́* 'marry a lot'
    shwíé 'sink'   *shwíé-mɔ́* 'sink & surface and sink & surface'
    tsɔ́ʔɔ́ 'jump'   *tsɔ́ʔ-mɔ́* 'jump time and again'

e. -sə (2)
   bvù 'grind' bvù-sə̀ 'grind & mix lots of things'
   gè 'divide, share' gè-sə̀ 'separate into more parts'

f. -nə
   lém 'bite' lém-nə́ 'bite and leave and bite another spot' (= the only example)

Several verbs have two or three different pluractional forms:

(6) a. tsɔ́ʔɔ́ 'jump' tsɔ́ʔ-mə́ 'jump one after the other'

   tsɔ́ʔ-kə́ 'jump time and again'

   tsɔ́ʔ-lə́ 'jump across things'

   cf. tsɔ́ʔ-tə́ 'jump gently' (= attenuative—see below)

b. dì 'cry, cackle' dì-mə̀ 'lots of children crying'

   dì-kə̀ 'cry time and again'

   dì-lə̀ 'lots of chickens cackling'

c. zhwí 'kill' zhwí-tə́ 'kill one by one, bit by bit'

   zhwí-lə́ 'kill lots of people, one after the other'

d. sù 'stab' sù-tə̀ 'stab lots of things one by one, or one thing many times'

   sù-lə̀ 'stab with lots of things at one time'

For an understanding of the possible meanings, compare Wood's (2007) distinction between "event-internal" vs. "event-external" pluractionality, e.g. in Yurok:

> ...the Repetitive (event-internal) prefix refers to repetitions which are closely-spaced in time on a single occasion, which may indicate plurality of a transitive object or an intransitive subject... and which commonly have an implied completion or result. The Iterative (event-external) pluractional, in contrast, can refer to repetition on one or more occasions, including habitual repetition, and can indicate distributive plurality of any argument. An interesting

additional property of the Iterative is that it has an apparent intensification meaning in certain cases. I have suggested that such uses be analysed as instances in which a standard of comparison or lower bound of a gradable predicate is pluralised by the pluraction, rather than an event argument. (Wood 2007: 255)

In Babanki also there is thus a relatedness and potential overlap of the different notions of pluractionality (many participants, many actions, over and over, one after the other, bit by bit, etc.). These meanings spill over into others. Pluractionality may straightforwardly lead to augmentative or intensive interpretations, e.g. with *-lə*:

(7) a. *sáʔá* 'spring forward'   *sáʔ-lə́* 'spring, jump for joy'

　　b. *sù* 'stab'   *sù-lə̀* 'stab with lots of things at one time'

　　c. *fósé* 'force'   *fó-lə́* 'be too tight (space), crowded, congested'

　　d. *gàʔà* 'speak'   *gàʔ-lə̀* 'talk as if crazy'

　　e. *mì* 'swallow'   *mì-lə̀* 'swallow fast, gulping, too much in mouth'

There also is a potential relatedness between pluractionality and attenuation ("diminutivizing"), e.g. with *-tə*:[9]

(8) a. *cíʔ* 'close, shut'   *cíʔ-tə́* 'shut, close lots of things one after the other or a bit'

　　b. *ló* 'lick'   *ló-tə́* 'lick time and again or little by little, slowly'

　　c. *tyɛ́f* 'advise'   *tyɛ́f-tə́* 'advise one by one or a little'

　　d. *shù* 'wash'   *shù-tə̀* 'wash lots of things or a little, part(s) of body'

　　e. *kwíʔ* 'tie'   *kwíʔ-tə́* 'tie in different bundles or gently'

　　f. *nyǔ* 'drink'   *nyǔ-tə́* 'drink bit by bit or a little bit'

---

[9]Some of these meanings are reminiscent of Bantu frequentative/distributive verb stem reduplication which typically has the meaning 'do something a little here and there'.

g. ghɔ́ʔ 'become fat'   ghɔ́ʔ-tɔ́ 'get fat little by little'

h. fwìè 'rot (intr.)'   fwìè-tɔ̀ 'rot in bits' vs. fwìè-kè 'rot time and again'

Such semantic relatedness may lead to massive conflation/merger, as in Meta (in the Momo subgroup), which has two different extensions, /-dɨ/ (→ -rɨ) and /-nɨ/. The following examples drawn from the 262 verbs from Ngum (2004) show the realizations of the two extensions (attenuatives are given where possible):

(9) a. kwí 'grow'   kwí-rɨ 'grow a bit'

　　　 sob 'cut'   sob-rɨ 'cut small'

　　　 mèd 'swallow'   me-rɨ 'swallow in small quantities' (d → Ø / __r)

　　　 mìg 'measure'   mìg-rɨ 'measure with, comparatively'

　　　 kɔʔ 'climb'   kɔʔ-rɨ 'climb a bit'

　　b. nyɔ̀m 'push down'   nyɔ̀m-bɨ 'press down gently' (d → b / m __)

　　　 tàn 'delay'   tàn-dɨ 'delay a bit'

　　　 fàŋ 'be fat'   fàŋ-gɨ 'be a bit fat' (d → g / ŋ __)

　　c. cɔ̀b 'pinch'   cɔ̀p-ɨ 'pinch a bit'

　　　 ghàd 'pour'   ghàt-ɨ 'pour a bit'

　　　 jíg 'eat'   jík-ɨ 'eat a bit'

　　d. wà 'be rough'   wàà-nɨ 'be a bit rough'

　　　 cɔʔ 'borrow'   cɔʔ-nɨ 'borrow from'

　　　 wèm 'tie'   wèm-nɨ 'tie loosely'

　　　 bin 'dance'   bi-nɨ 'dance a bit' (n → Ø / __ n)

　　　 màŋ 'seize'   màŋ-nɨ 'seize several objects'

From the above examples it appears that there are two different attenuative extensions, each with two allomorphs whose distribution can be predicted. This is confirmed in the following distributions of Meta extensions, where T = a voiceless stop, D = a voiced stop or glottal stop, and N = a nasal consonant).

5 Common Bantoid verb extensions

Table 9: Distribution of Meta extensions and their functions based on Ngum (2004)

	CV(D)-rɨ	CVN-Dɨ	CVT-ɨ	CV(N)-nɨ	totals
attenuative	12	10	6	3	31
repetitive/completely	10	10	6	1	27
random/roughly	0	1	0	5	6
reciprocal/reflexive	5	2	2	4	13
associative	6	2	1	2	11
instrumental	2	3	1	1	7
ablative/separative	4	5	1	1	11
causative	4	6	1	7	18
applicative ('to, for')	4	1	1	0	6
totals	47	40	19	24	

The first two columns show that -rɨ appears after CV and /CVD/ roots, while -Dɨ appears after /CVN/ roots. We can assume underlying /-rɨ/ with a rule that converts the /r/ into a homorganic voiced stop after a nasal. The third and fourth columns show that -ɨ appears after /CVD/ roots (whose D becomes devoiced), while -nɨ appears after /CV/ and /CVN/ roots. Assuming /-nɨ/, we would have to say that /b, d, g/ → p, t, k and the nasal drops out. (Perhaps the language once had geminate stops which devoiced and then degeminated.) In any case this odd allomorphy likely results from an earlier stage where there were more extensions, e.g. *-tɨ, *-dɨ, *-nɨ, *-sɨ etc., as in Babanki and Bafut.

4 Significance of Grassfields extensions for Bantoid and Bantu

At this point I would like to raise two questions. First, what does the above mean for Proto-Bantoid? In response I would venture the following: (i) Given the rather large set of suffixes in Limbum, Ring, and Ngemba, it is likely that we can reconstruct at least six extensions at the Proto-Grassfields level, e.g. *-s, *-t, *-n, *-l, *-k, and *-m. (ii) Noni and Vute suggest that most or all of these existed at an earlier Bantoid stage as well. (iii) The functions that clearly can be reconstructed are *-s 'causative' and *-n 'reciprocal/associative'. (iv) Pluractional meanings are extremely widespread, hence tempting to reconstruct, but they have clearly spread areally throughout the Nigeria-Cameroon area, including Chadic (Newman 1990).

(v) The attenuative/diminutive function is quite widespread, even spilling over into A40 and A60!

The second question is: What is the relation of these reconstructions to PB? It is tempting to reconstruct parallel functions and forms of each of the PB extensions in (3) above. However, I have been able to document the applicative only in two languages (Meta and Vute). In Meta I have found only six examples of -rɨ having various applicative-like functions (recipient, circumstance, directional):

(10) ghàb 'share'   ghàb-rɨ 'share to'
      wí 'refund'   wíí-rɨ 'reply, refund to'
      cob 'donate'   cob-rɨ 'donate for'
      wub 'crave'   wub-rɨ 'crave for'
      sòm 'cut'   sòm-bɨ 'cut into'
      dìì 'pity'   dìì-rɨ 'pity for'

Since -rɨ has other functions, it is not clear if this suffix is cognate with PB applicative *-ɪd-. The situation is much less ambiguous in Vute, where applicative -nà is innovative:

> -nà is added to a verb to indicate that there is an indirect object or benefactive NP present in the clause. Its function is similar to a Bantu applicative extension in this way. -nà is derived from the verb nà-ni 'to give'. (Thwing 2006: 8)

5 The shift from valence to aspectual extensions

It cannot have escaped notice that most of the extensions which have (possibly lexicalized) aspectual meanings such as pluractional, attenuative/diminutive etc., resemble the valence extensions of Bantu (and other Niger-Congo). Thus consider the following examples from Bangwa (Bamileke) which show that the repetitive suffix -sɨ, clearly cognate with the causative extension found throughout Bantu, marks "une action ou une situation qui se répète plusieurs fois" in this language (Nguendjio 1989: 243):

(11) ghὲ 'partager'   → ghὲ-sə́ 'partager plusieurs fois'
      sò 'laver'   → sò-sə́ 'laver plusieurs fois'
      cí- 'casser'   → cí-sə́ 'casser plusieurs fois'

fák 'tourner'	→	fák-sə́ 'tourner plusieurs fois'
yàʔ 'couper'	→	yàʔ-sə̀ 'couper plusieurs fois'

The same could be seen from -sə in closely related Shingu (Ndawouo 1990: 88) and -si in Fe'fe' (Ngangoum 1970) and the phenomenon extends into Bantu and other Benue-Congo languages in Nigeria. As Gerhardt (1988: 5) puts it, "What is remarkable about these [verb extensions in Jarawan Bantu] is that those with syntactic functions have been lost, while aspect-like VEs are still present." I would differ only in not assuming that the current meanings are proto. Instead, I would like to propose that valence extensions, i.e. those that have to do with argument structure, generally become pluractional, attenuative etc. by a three-stage process:

(12) *Stage I*   *Stage II*   *Stage III*
      valence ⊃ aspect >   aspect ⊃ valence   >   aspect

First, valence marking affixes start to acquire aspectual meanings, which have spread areally. Then the aspectual meanings become primary, with gradually lexicalized, residual valence functions. The final stage is for the extensions to have only an aspectual function. According to this model, PB is at stage I, zone A Bantu is somewhere between stage I and stage II, and Bantoid is somewhere between stage II and stage III.

The evidence for such a valence > aspect realignment is considerable. First, there is the phonetic similarity already alluded to. Second, aspectual extensions may correlate with valence: In Bafut the iterative/repetitive extension -kə is used with intransitives, while the "contextual variant" -tə is used with transitives (Tamanji & Mba 2003: 22; Bila 1986: 99). This is strikingly reminiscent of the PB reversive ("separative") suffixes *-ʊk- (intr.) vs. *-ʊd- (tr.). Other forms also suggest that transitivizing extensions tend to be coronal, while detransitivizing ones tend to be velar (cf. PB applicative *-ɪd- vs. stative *-ɪk-). Finally, there are natural semantic pathways for these developments, e.g. causative > intentional/intensive (Kiessling 2004).

The final question is: Why does this happen? The reason can be seen in the fact that the change of valence to aspect suffixes correlates with phonological, morphological and syntactic changes within Bantoid. In Table 10 I contrast the situation in Canonical Bantu vs. Bantoid.

If we assume that Proto-Bantoid was also head-marking in the sense of Nichols (1986), where valence operations are indicated by verb suffixes, the driving force behind the change likely was phonological: While CB languages have no upper

Table 10: Canonical Bantu contrasted with Bantoid

	Canonical Bantu	Bantoid
phonology	minimum word = 2 syllables	maximum stem = 2 or 3 syllables
morphology	highly synthetic, agglutinative	less so, gradual move towards analyticity
unmarked objects	multiple	one per verb
marked objects	head marking on verb	prepositions, serial verbs

limit on word size (in fact, many require words to have at least two syllables), many NW Bantu and Bantoid languages place an upper limit on the number of syllables that a word (and especially a verb stem) can have. By so doing, this limits the availability of suffixes, since a verb that already has exhausted, say, a three-syllable maximum size will not be able to take a causative or applicative extension. Instead, some other, specifically analytical marking will be required: a periphrastic causative ('make that S'), prepositions 'for' and 'with'. and so forth. The newly introduced mechanisms then come to be the preferred structures. We already see some of this happening in languages that still have some valence-related extensions, e.g. a causative. While the causative can also be added to transitive and ditransitive verbs in Canonical Bantu, what happens in many Bantoid languages is that *s is mostly restricted to intransitive verbs. That is, while it can make an intransitive transitive, it cannot make a transitive verb ditransitive. Those relatively few transitive verbs that can take a causative extension restructure their arguments, as in the following Babungo (Ring) and Bafut (Ngemba) examples.

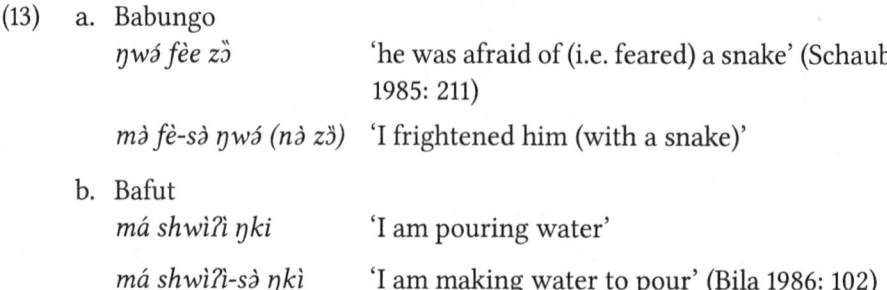

(13) a. Babungo
  ŋwɔ́ fèe zɔ̀   'he was afraid of (i.e. feared) a snake' (Schaub 1985: 211)
  mɔ̀ fè-sɔ̀ ŋwɔ́ (nɔ̀ zɔ̀)   'I frightened him (with a snake)'
  b. Bafut
  má shwìʔì ŋki   'I am pouring water'
  má shwìʔì-sɔ̀ ŋkì   'I am making water to pour' (Bila 1986: 102)

A causativized transitive verb cannot take two objects. Thus, after pointing out that the causative adds a valence to intransitive verbs, Bila (1986: 102) notes: "This suffix however does not add to the valency of the [transitive] verb but it rather modifies the meaning of the verb by adding the causative meaning to the basic meaning of the verb."

6 Summary and conclusion

In the preceding sections we have seen the following:

(i) Proto-Bantoid definitely had multiple verb extensions, probably at least *-s, *-t, *-n, *-l, *-k, *-m.

(ii) Languages within the "oval" on the map provided above show the greatest number of contrasts.

(iii) Bantoid languages outside the oval have simplified the situation considerably.

(iv) There is an unmistakable tendency for valence-related extensions to become aspectual.

(v) Contributing factors to the change and loss of extensions (and their ability to combine) are phonological (maximal size constraints), morphological (drift towards analyticity) and syntactic (change from head- to dependent-marking of arguments).

I conclude with some final observations and speculations:

(i) Most of the Bantoid languages restrict verbs to one extension, mostly of the shape *-CV.

(ii) -CVC shapes such as Noni -kɛn, -nɛn, -sɛn, -yɛn and Lamnso' -sin, -tin, -kir suggest that these were originally two extensions which fused.

(iii) Such a process is particularly common in Bantu when PB reciprocal *-an- is involved (see Bostoen & Nzang-Bie 2010 for documentation in A70).

(iv) Interestingly, different shapes of -(C)ɛn can mark reciprocals in Noni (Hyman 1981: 39–40), suggesting -C-ɛn- (cf. Guarisma 2000: 62ff re -Cɛn in Bafia (A53)).

(v) Many Bantoid languages have productive aspectual suffixes not mentioned above, e.g. perfective *-mV*, probably related to PB **-mad* 'finish', realized with various vowels in Grassfields Bantu.

The most puzzling question to me is where diminutive/attenuative **t* is from, especially the *-It-/-Id-* in A40 and A60. This has no obvious source in PB or cognates in CB and can therefore be an areal innovation. The phonetic similarity to plural diminutive noun class 13 *ti-* is intriguing, as it becomes suffixal *-tí* in some WGB. About this class in the Momo languages, Stallcup (1980b: 209) notes: "19/13 was originally a diminutive gender…. This gender also contains a number of items [in Moghamo] which occur generally in profusion — 'star, fly, bird' etc." Here again we have the relation between plural and diminutive! While nominalization often results in a verb extension appearing on a noun, the reverse has not been established. Could sound symbolism be involved somehow? Cf. Basaa (A43) *títígí* 'small'.

I opened this paper by posing three questions of which I have addressed the first two:

(i) What are Bantoid verb extensions like?

(ii) What can be reconstructed at the Proto-Bantoid level?

(iii) What, if anything, do they tell us about Proto-Bantu?

The third question presents a more different problem of interpretation. As we have seen, there is a considerable number of cognate extensions between the two and, indeed, further out at least within Benue-Congo and Gur. It is thus likely that some of what has been hypothesized for Proto-Bantoid is considerably older, as Voeltz (1977) originally supposed. Unfortunately, because of the kinds of the functional changes, mergers, and losses that have occurred within Bantoid, we can only speculate as to what the system looked like at the earliest stages. The great variety of extensions that we see outside of Bantu does, however, raise the possibility that Bantu itself may have lost earlier contrasts (e.g. between different types of applicatives which merged to **-id-*), not just that Proto-Bantu is conservative from the point of view of Niger-Congo.

Acknowledgement

My thanks to John Watters and Roger Blench for valuable comments on an earlier version of this paper.

References

Akumbu, Pius Wuchu. 2008. *Kejom (Babanki) - English lexicon (Kay Williamson Educational Foundation)*. Bamenda: Ga'a Kejom Development Committee.

Arnott, D. W. 1970. *The nominal and verbal systems of Fula*. Oxford: Clarendon Press.

Bila, Emmanuel Neba. 1986. *A semantic-syntactic study of the Bafut verb*. University of Yaounde Dissertation, Post-Graduate Diploma in Linguistics.

Blench, Roger M. 2010. *Revised subclassification of Benue-Congo languages*. Email, 13 October 2010.

Blench, Roger M. 2011. *Ngiemboon verbal extensions: A new analysis*. Ms. Kay Williamson Educational Foundation.

Blench, Roger M. 2015. *The Bantoid languages* (Oxford Handbooks Online). Oxford: Oxford University Press. http://www.oxfordhandbooks.com/view/10.1093/oxfordhb/9780199935345.001.0001/oxfordhb-9780199935345-e-17?rskey=MiYuUo&result=1.

Blench, Roger M. 2016. *Lamnso' verb extensions*. Cambridge. University of Cambridge Manuscript.

Bostoen, Koen & Yolande Nzang-Bie. 2010. On how "middle" plus "associative/reciprocal" became "passive" in the Bantu A70 languages. *Linguistics* 48. 1255–1307.

Connell, Bruce. 1997. *Mòkpè (Bakweri)-English dictionary/materials collected by Edwin Ardener*. Köln: Rüdiger Köppe Verlag.

Doneux, Jean L. 1975. Hypothèses pour la comparative des langues atlantiques. *Africana Linguistica* 6. 41–129.

Gerhardt, Ludwig. 1988. Note on verb extensions in Jarawan Bantu. *Journal of West African Languages* 18. 3–8.

Guarisma, Gladys. 2000. *Complexité morphologique, simplicité syntaxique: Le cas du bafia, langue bantoue périphérique* (SELAF A 50). Paris: Peeters.

Henson, Bonnie. 2001. *The -an- extension and diachronic language change in Mòkpè*. Paper presented at the Workshop on Comparative Benue-Congo, Berkeley, CA, March 26-27, 2001.

Hyman, Larry M. (ed.). 1979. *Aghem grammatical structure: With special reference to noun classes, tense-aspect and focus marking* (Southern California Occasional Papers in Linguistics 7). Los Angeles: University of Southern California Department of Linguistics. http://gsil.sc-ling.org/pubs/SCOPILS_6_7_8_9/Aghem_grammatical_structure.pdf.

Hyman, Larry M. 1981. *Noni grammatical structure: With special reference to verb morphology* (Southern California Occasional Papers in Linguistics 9). Los Angeles: University of Southern California Department of Linguistics. http://gsil.sc-ling.org/pubs/SCOPILS_6_7_8_9/Noni_grammatical_structure.pdf.

Hyman, Larry M. 2007. Niger-Congo verb extensions: Overview and discussion. In Doris L. Payne & Jaime Peña (eds.), *Selected Proceedings of the 37th Annual Conference on African Linguistic*, 149–163. Sommerville, MA: Cascadilla Proceedings Project.

Hyman, Larry M. 2014. *Nuba mountain verb extensions in African perspective*. Paper presented at the 2nd Nuba Mountain Languages Conference, Paris, August 28-30, 2014. Handout + table of Nuba Mountain extensions.

Hyman, Larry M. 2018a. More reflections on the nasal classes in Bantu. In John R. Watters (ed.), *East Benue-Congo: Nouns, pronouns, and verbs*, 223–236. Berlin: Language Science Press. DOI:10.5281/zenodo.1314331

Hyman, Larry M. 2018b. Third person pronouns in Grassfields Bantu. In John R. Watters (ed.), *East Benue-Congo: Nouns, pronouns, and verbs*, 199–221. Berlin: Language Science Press. DOI:10.5281/zenodo.1314329

Hyman, Larry M. & Sam A. Mchombo. 1992. Morphotactic constraints in the Chichewa verb stem. In Laura Buszard-Welcher, Lionel Wee & William Weigel (eds.), *Proceedings of the Eighteenth Meeting of the Berkeley Linguistics Society, General Session and Parassession*, 350–363. Berkeley: Berkeley Linguistics Society.

Stallcup, Kenneth L. 1980a. La géographie linguistique des Grassfields. In Larry M. Hyman & Jan Voorhoeve (eds.), *L'expansion bantoue: Actes du colloque international du CNRS, Viviers (France) 4–16 avril 1977. Volume I: Les classes nominales dans le bantou des Grassfields*, 43–57. Paris: SELAF.

Hyman, Larry M. & Jan Voorhoeve (eds.). 1980. *L'expansion bantoue: Actes du colloque international du CNRS, Viviers (France) 4–16 avril 1977. Volume I: Les classes nominales dans le bantou des Grassfields*. Paris: SELAF.

Stallcup, Kenneth L. 1980b. The Momo languages. In Larry M. Hyman & Jan Voorhoeve (eds.), *L'expansion bantoue: Actes du colloque international du CNRS, Viviers (France) 4–16 avril 1977. Volume I: Les classes nominales dans le bantou des Grassfields*, 193–224. Paris: SELAF.

Idiata, Daniel Franck & Gabriel Mba (eds.). 2003. *Studies on voice through verbal extensions in nine Bantu languages spoken in Cameroon, Gabon, DRC, and Rwanda*. Munich: Lincom.

Jisa, Harriet. 1977. *Filecards of Babanki verbs*. Those with extensions digitized by LMH in Filemaker Pro™.

Kanu, Sullay Mohamed. 2004. *Verbal morphology of Temne*. University of Tromsø MA thesis.

Kiessling, Roland. 2004. Kausation, Wille und Wiederholung in der verbalen Derivation der westlichen Ring-Sprachen (Weh, Isu). In Raimund Kastenholz & Anne Storch (eds.), *Sprache und Wissen in Afrika*, 159–181. Köln: Rüdiger Köppe Verlag.

Leroy, Jacqueline. 1982. Extensions en mankon. In Gabriel Nissim Gladys Guarisma & Jan Voorhoeve (eds.), *Le verbe bantou*, 125–138. Paris: LACITO.

Meeussen, A. E. 1967. Bantu grammatical reconstructions. *Africana Linguistica* 3. 79–121.

Miehe, Gudrun. 1991. *Die Präfixnasale im Benue-Congo und im Kwa: Versuch einer Widerlegung der Hypothese von der Nasalinnovation des Bantu*. Berlin: Reimer.

Ndawouo, Martine. 1990. *Esquisse phonologique du Shingu*. University of Yaounde Mémoire for the Maitrise en Linguistique.

Newman, Paul. 1990. *Nominal and verbal plurality in Chadic*. Dordrecht: Foris.

Ngangoum, R. P., Bernard. 1970. *Le bamileke des fe'fe': grammaire descriptive usuelle*. Saint-Léger-Vauban: Abbaye Sainte-Marie de la Pierre-Qui-Vire.

Ngantcho Lebika, Francine. 2003. *Verb morphology and the structure of Mpumpuŋ*. University of Yaounde I. MA thesis.

Ngue Um, Emmanuel. 2002. *Morphologie verbale du Mvùmbɔ*. University of Yaounde I. Mémoire de Matrise.

Nguendjio, Emile-Gille. 1989. *Morphologie nominale et verbale de la langue baŋgwa*. Université de Yaounde Thèse de Doctorat de Troisième Cycle en Linguistique.

Ngum, Comfort Che. 2004. *Verbal extensions in Meta'*. University of Yaounde I Dissertation, Maîtrise in Linguistics.

Nichols, Johanna. 1986. Head-marking and dependent-marking grammar. *Language* 62. 56–119.

Orwig, Carol. 1989. Les extensions verbales en nugunu. In Daniel Barreteau & Robert Hedinger (eds.), *Descriptions de langues camerounaises*, 283–314. Paris: ORSTOM.

Piron, Pascale. 1995. Identification lexicostatistique des groupes bantoïdes stables. *JWAL* 25. 3–30.

Schadeberg, Thilo C. 2003. Derivation. In Derek Nurse & Gérard Philippson (eds.), *The Bantu languages*, 71–89. London: Routledge.

Schaub, Willi. 1985. *Babungo* (Croom Helm Descriptive Grammars). Beckenham, England: Croom Helm.

Tamanji, Pius & Gabriel Mba. 2003. A morphological study of verbal extension in Bafut. In Daniel Franck Idiata & Gabriel Mba (eds.), 15–38.

Thwing, Rhonda Ann. 2006. *Verb extensions in Vute*. Unpublished manuscript.

Voeltz, Erhard. 1977. *Proto Niger-Congo extensions*. University of California, Los Angeles dissertation.

Watters, John R. 1981. *A phonology and morphology of Ejagham – with notes on dialect variation*. Los Angeles: University of California at Los Angeles Doctoral dissertation.

Watters, John R. 2003. Grassfields Bantu. In Derek Nurse & Gérard Philippson (eds.), *The Bantu languages*, 225–256. London: Routledge.

Watters, John R. & Jacqueline Leroy. 1989. Southern Bantoid. In John Bendor-Samuel (ed.), *The Niger-Congo languages*, 430–449. Lanham, MD: University Press of America.

Williamson, Kay. 1993. The noun prefixes of Benue-Congo. *Journal of African Languages & Linguistics* 14. 29–45.

Wilson, W. A. A. 1961. *An outline of the Temne language*. London: School of Oriental & African Studies.

Wood, Esther Jane. 2007. *The semantic typology of pluractionality*. University of California, Berkeley dissertation. http://linguistics.berkeley.edu/~survey/resources/dissertations/wood-2007.pdf.

Chapter 6

Third person pronouns in Grassfields Bantu

Larry M. Hyman
University of California, Berkeley

> "In linguistic theory, the 3rd person has had bad luck." (Pozdniakov n.d.: 5)

In this paper I have two goals. First, I propose a reconstruction of the pronoun system of Grassfields Bantu, direct reflexes of which are found in Eastern Grassfields, with a close look at the pronoun systems, as reflected across this varied group. Second, I document and seek the origin of innovative third person pronouns in Western Grassfields. While EGB languages have basic pronouns in all persons, both the Momo and Ring subgroups of WGB have innovated new third person (non-subject) pronouns from demonstratives or perhaps the noun 'body'. However, these languages show evidence of the original third person pronouns which have been restricted to a logophoric function. I end with a comparison of the Grassfields pronouns with nearby Bantoid and Northwest Bantu languages as well as Proto-Bantu.

1 The problem

While Eastern Grassfields Bantu, like Narrow Bantu, has an old and consistent paradigm of pronouns, Western Grassfields Bantu has innovated new third person forms, often keeping the original forms as logophoric pronouns. The major questions I address in this chapter are: (i) Where do these new third person pronouns come from? (ii) Why were they innovated? (iii) What is the relation, if any, to logophoricity? In the following sections I first briefly introduce the subgrouping of Grassfields Bantu that I will be assuming, then successively treat third person pronouns in the different subgroups: Eastern Grassfields, Ring Grassfields, and Momo Grassfields. I then consider some examples from outside Grassfields Bantu. The last section provides a brief summary and conclusion.(For a broader discussion of East Benue-Congo noun class systems, their morphological behavior, and, in particular, the place of third-person pronouns in those systems, see Good, Chapter 2 of this volume, and in particular §4 on domains of concord.)

2 Grassfields Bantu

In (1), I present two subclassifications of Grassfields Bantu, ignoring the possible inclusion of Ndemli (cf. Stallcup 1980, Watters & Leroy 1989, Piron 1995, Watters 2003).

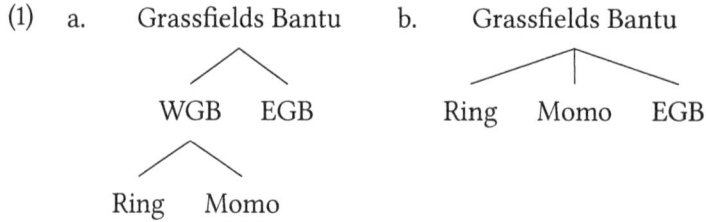

The subgrouping of (1a) shows a split between Western Grassfields Bantu (WGB) and Eastern Grassfields Bantu (EGB), where WGB consists of two further subgroups, Ring and Momo. In (1b) these two subgroups are considered coordinate with EGB. Some of the major languages of each subgroup are identified in (2).

(2) a. Ring: Aghem, Isu, Weh, Bum, Bafmeng, Kom, Oku, Babanki, Lamnso', Babungo, Babessi

b. Momo: Moghamo, Metta, Menemo, Ngembu, Ngamambo, Ngie, Oshie, Ngwo, Mundani, Njen

c. EGB: Ngemba (e.g. Mankon, Bafut), Bamileke (e.g. Yemba, Ghomala, Medumba, Fe'fe'), Nun (e.g. Bamun, Bali), North (e.g. Limbum, Adere)

Although the two subgroupings in (1) differ in whether a WGB unit is recognized, I will assume the classification in (1a) for the purpose of the present discussion. The following table in (3) summarizes the significant differences between EGB and WGB (Stallcup 1980: 55):

(3)

	Eastern Grassfields Bantu	Western Grassfields Bantu
a.	nasal prefix in class 1 and 3 nouns	absence of the nasal
b.	no distinction between class 6 and class 6a	distinction between class 6 *a-* and class 6a *mə-*
c.	nasal prefix on all 9/10 nouns	nasal prefix only on some 9/10 nouns
d.	absence of classes 4 and 13; class 19 rare	presence of classes 4 and 13; class 19 frequent
e.	noun prefixes all carry a /L/ tone	most noun prefixes carry a /H/ tone
f.	no noun suffixes	many noun suffixes, e.g. plural *-tí, -sí*
g.	class 2 or 6a generalizes to mark plural	class 10 or 13 generalizes to mark plural
h.	innovation of *-síŋɔ́* 'bird', *-kìɔ́* 'water'	maintenance of **-nɔ̀ní* 'bird', **-díbá* 'water'
i.	maintenance of *-úmà* 'thing'	**-úmà* is lost, other roots come in
Plus:	maintenance of inherited 3rd person pronouns	introduction of new 3rd person pronouns

As seen, the differences in (3a-g) all have to do with noun classes. Significant to this chapter is the last difference, which I have added: As we shall see in the following sections, EGB languages maintain the inherited Proto-Grassfields Bantu (PGB) third person pronouns, while WGB languages have innovated new pronouns.

Larry M. Hyman

3 Eastern Grassfields Bantu

In this section I begin with EGB pronoun systems, since they directly reflect the reconstructions proposed by Hyman & Tadadjeu (1976) and others subsequently. In each section we need to consider subject, object and possessive pronouns. I will often illustrate the forms with human third person pronouns, i.e. singular class 1 *(m)u-, plural class 2 *ba-. Thus, unless otherwise noted, "third person" will refer to class 1 (sg) and class 2 (pl).

In (1) I present the human (class 1/2) subject and object pronouns in selected EGB languages:

Table 1: Class 1/2 subject & object pronouns in some EGB languages

	subject pronouns							object pronouns					
	1sg	2sg	3sg	Log	1pl	2pl	3pl	1sg	2sg	3sg	1pl	2pl	3pl
Mankon	mà	ò	à	zɨɨ́	tɨ̀	nɨ̀	bɨ́	ɣə̂	ɣô	ɣɛ́	wɨ́ɨɣɔ́	wɨɨŋɔ́	wá
Dschang	mə̀ŋ/Ǹ	ò	à	yí	pɛ̀k	pɛ̀	pɔ́	ga	wu	yí	wek	wɛ	wɔp
Fe'fe'	Ǹ	ò	à	—	pàh	pɛ̀n	pō	ā	ō	ī	yɔ̄h	yēɛ	yaa
Bangangte	mə	o	a	—	bag	bi	bo	ám	ó	é	yág	zín	yób

In the above forms 1pl = first person plural exclusive.

As seen, the plural subject pronouns generally begin with class 2 p- or b- while the corresponding object pronouns all begin with class 1 w- or y- = class 1 (cf. the possessive forms in Table 2). As seen in the table, the subject logophoric pronoun is identical to the 3sg object pronoun yí in Dschang (Yemba) (Harro & Haynes 1991: 22). In Mankon, on the other hand, the subject logophoric pronoun corresponds to the distinct 3sg independent pronoun zɨɨ́ (Leroy 2007: 209).

In Table 2 I present the class 1/2 possessive pronouns in a wide range of EGB languages, where ˷ = nasalization and ° = a level L tone (contrasting with a L that downglides from L to a lower L before pause). For the proposed Proto-Grassfields Bantu (PGB) reconstructions, indicated below these forms, see Hyman & Tadadjeu (1976: 85).

Important for our purposes is that the PGB possessive pronoun reconstructions directly correspond to the morphologically complex independent pronominal stems proposed for Proto-Bantu (PB) by Kamba Muzenga (2003: 215): *-a-mi-e, *-u-bɪ-e, *-a-i-, *-i-cu-e, *-i-ɲu-e, *-a-ba-o (cf. Table 20). The story is quite different in the Ring and Momo subgroups, at least in the third person.

Table 2: Class 1/2 possessive pronouns in various EGB languages

	class 1 *gù-						class 2 *bɔ́-					
Language	1sg	2sg	3sg	1pl	2pl	3pl	1sg	2sg	3sg	1pl	2pl	3pl
Mankon	ɣà	yò	yìé	wàyɔ́	wàŋɔ́	wàá	bɔ̂	bô	byé	báyɔ́	báŋɔ́	báá
Mbui	wà	yò	wì°	wìì°	wə̀°	wʌ̀°	bá	búó	bí	bíí	bɔ́	bʌ́
Bamenyan	wìè	yò	yĕ	wɯ́ɯ̀	wŏ	wŏ	píè	pô	pé	pɯ́ɯ̀	pó	pó
Babadjou	ɣà	yò	yè°	wɔ̀°	wèì°	ɣàp°	pâ	pô	pé	pɔ́	péí	páp
Dschang	ɣà	wù	yì°	wək̀°	wè°	wòp°	pá	pú	pí	pák	pé	póp
Ngwe	ɣà	yò	gyè°	wə̀°	wʌ̀°	wʌ̀p°	bá	bó	bé	bák	bʌ́	bʌ́p
Babete	à	è°		wək̀°	wɯ̀ɯ̀°	wɔ̀p°	pá	pú	pé	pák	pɯ́ɯ̀	póp
Bati	à	ù	ì	pɔ̀	yì	yàp°	pá	pú	pí	pɔ̀	yí	yáp
Bagam	à	ò	è°	wíŋì	wùŋ°	wɔ̀p°	pá	pó	pé	píŋì	púŋ	pɔ́p
Bangang	à̰	ò	ì°	wək̀°	ɯ̀ì°	wɔ̀p°	pá̰	pú	pé	pák	pí	pɔ́p
Baloum	à	ò	ì°	wʰɯ̀ɯ̀	wè°	wɔ̀p°	pá	pú	pí	pʰɯ́ɯ̀	pé	pɔ́p
Fomopea	à	ò	ì°	wək̀°	wè°	wɔ̀p°	pá	pú	pí	pák	pé	pɔ́p
Bamendjou	à	ò	ì°	wək̀°	wɯ̀ɯ̀°	wòp°	pá	pó	pí	pák	pɯ́ɯ̀	póp
Baleng	à	ò	è°	wək̀°	wè°	wùp°	pá	pú	pyé	pák	pé	púp
Bandjoun	à	ò	è°	yɔ̀k°	yɔ̀°	yàp°	pă	pŭ	pyɔ́	pɔ́k	pɔ́	páp
Batie	à	ò	è	yɔ̀k°	yèè°	yàp°	pé	pó	pé	pɔ́k	péé	páp
Bangou	à	ù	ì	yɔ̀h	yɯ̀ɯ̀	yòp	pē	pō	pɔ́	pɔ́h	pɯ́ɯ̀	póp
Bangwa	è~à	ù~ò	ì~è	yɔ̀	ʒyə̀	ʒùp	pé	pú	pí	pɔ́	pyɔ́	púp
Batoufam	à	ù	ì	wɔ̀	wɯ̀ɯ̀ɣə̀	wùp	pē	pū	pɔ́	pɔ́	pɯ́ɯ̀ɣɔ́	púp
Fotouni	à	ɔ̀	ì	yɔ̀°	yè°	yàp°	βá	βɔ́	βí	βɔ́	βé	βáp
Fondanti	à	ò	ì	yɔ̀	yì	yàp	bá	bó	bí	yɔ́	yí	yáp
Fe'fe'	à	ò	ì°	yɔ̀h°	yìì°	yàà°	bă	bɔ̆	bī	bɔ̆h	bīī	bāā
Bali	à	ù	ì	yɯ̀ɯ̀?	yìn	yàp	bá	bú	bí	bɯ́ɯ́?	bín	báp
Bamun	à	ù	ì	ɯ̀ɯ̀	ɯ̀m	àp	pá	pú	pí	pɯ́ɯ́	pɯ́m	páp
Bapi	á	ú	í	yú?	yɯ́m	yɔ́p	pá	pú	pí	pú?	pɯ́m	pɔ́p
Bangangte	àm	ò	è°	yàg°	zìn°	yòb°	cám	có	tsɔ́	cághɔ̀°	tsínɔ̀°	cóbɔ̀°
Limbum	yà	yò	yì	yèr	yèè	yàb	wá	wó	ví	wér	wéé	wáb
Adere	wàm	wɔ̀	wì°	-wùt°	-wùn°	-wɔ̀	bám	bɔ́	bí	-wùt°	-wùn°	-wɔ̀
PGB:	*gù-àmɔ̀	*gù-ò	*gù-í	*gù-ítɔ́	*gù-ínɔ́	*gù-ábɔ́	*bɔ́-àmɔ̀	*bɔ́-ò	*bɔ́-í	*bɔ́-ítɔ́	*bɔ́-ínɔ́	*bɔ́-ábɔ́

4 Ring Grassfields Bantu

While the EGB languages provide a "baseline" for Proto-Grassfields Bantu, Ring and Momo have innovated new third person pronouns. Thus, in the Ring languages, Babanki *wén* and Aghem *wɨ́n* 'him/her, his/her' are quite different from the PGB 3sg *-í* reconstruction. In past literature I have considered two different historical scenarios (to which we will return below):

> The third person pronoun 'his/hers' is derived from the noun /əwén/ 'body' (Hyman 1980a: 245)

> … the form 'his/her' is related to the demonstrative root -*ɨ́n* 'this/these'. His-

torically, a form such as [Aghem] *nwín ⁺fɨ⁺ wín* 'his/her bird' meant 'bird of this one'. (Hyman 1979: 29)

In other words, it is possible that the new third person pronouns came either from a noun such as 'body' or from the near speaker demonstrative. In order to observe the phonetic resemblances, compare in Table 3 the following Babanki and Kom pronouns and 'near speaker' demonstratives with their words for 'body': Babanki *ə̀-wɛ́n*, Kom *ɔ̄-wúīn* (Hyman 1980b, Kom notes; Jones 2001).

Table 3: Babanki and Kom pronouns and 'near speaker' demonstratives

		Babanki				Kom			
a.		mò	'me'	yès	'us'	mā	'me'	ɣʌ̀s	'us'
		wù	'you sg.'	ɣʌ̀ŋ	'you pl.'	vvà	'you sg.'	zɨ̀	'you pl.'
b.	cl.	'him, them, it'		'this/these'		'him, them, it'		'this/these'	
	1	wɛ́n		ə̀-ɣɛ̀n		ŋwēn		ɔ̄-wên	
	2	və̀-wɛ́⁺n-ə́		ə̀-vɛ́n-ə́		à-ŋɔ̄ná		ɔ̄-yên°	
	3	ə̀-wé⁺é-ɣə́		ə̀-ɣɛ́n-ə́		ə̀-ŋwēn		ɔ̄-wên°	
	5	ə̀-wé⁺é-zə́		ə̀-ʒɛ́n-ə́		ì-ɲēn-ɨ̄		ī-yén-ì°	
	6	à-wé⁺é-ɣə́		à-fɛ́n-ə́		à-ŋkə̄n-ā		ā-kə́n-à°	
	7	kə̀-wɛ́n(-kə́)		ə̀-kɛ́n-ə́		à-ŋkɔ̄n-ā		ā-kə́n-à°	
	8	ə̀-wé⁺é-və́		ə̀-vɛ́n-ə́		ə̀-ŋwēn		ɔ̄-wên°	
	9	wɛ́n		ə̀-ʒɛ̀n		ɲēn		ɔ̄-yên	
	10	sə̀-wɛ́n(-sə́)		ə̀-sēn-sə́		ǹsēn-sɔ̄		ɔ̄-sén-sə̀°	
	13	tə̀-wɛ́n(-tə́)		ə̀-tēn-tə́		ǹēn-tɔ̄		ɔ̄-tén-tə̀°	
	19	fə̀-wɛ́n(-fə́)		ə̀-fēn-fə́		ǹfēnfɔ̄		ɔ̄-fén-fə̀°	
	6a	ŋ̀-wéé-mə̀		ə̀-mɛ̀n-ə̀		ə̀mēǹ		ɔ̄-mên	

While phonological rules obscure some of the forms (e.g. by deleting an intervocalic [n] in some of the pronominal forms in Babanki), the phonetic resemblance of the new third person pronouns to both the demonstrative 'this/these' and the word for 'body' is striking. (The Kom form *ɔ̄-wúīn* 'body' shows labialization into the root from the historically prior form *ú-wín*; cf. Oku, to which we now turn.)

In Table 4 the first and second person possessives are shown for the different noun classes in Oku (from my notes). Although the second person singular

6 Third person pronouns in Grassfields Bantu

forms have the unrounded diphthong [iɛ] and final *t has become [s] in the first person plural forms, the above pronominal forms clearly resemble those reconstructed in PGB Table 2. In addition, there is an initial underlying /ə-/ on the pronoun, corresponding to PGB *ə-CV-PRON, which however can become obscured by phonology, e.g. kēkém əkɔ́m → kēkém̀ kɔ́m 'my crab'.

Table 4: Oku 1p and 2p possessives for each Oku noun class

cl.	noun	gloss		'my'	'your sg'	'our (excl)'	'your pl'
1	wān	'child'	wāǹ	wɔ́m	vīɛ̀	wēs	wēn
2	yɔ́n	'children'	yɔ́n	əyɔ́m	əyíɛ̀	əyɛ́s	əyɛ́n
3	ēblēŋ	'bamboo'	ēblēŋ	wɔ́m	víɛ̀	wɛ́s	wɛ́n
4	īléŋ	'bamboos'	īléŋ	èyɔ́m	èʒíɛ̀	əyɛ́s	əyɛ́n
5	ī∫ɔ́ŋ	'tooth'	ī∫ɔ́ŋ	èyɔ́m	èʒíɛ̀	əyɛ́s	əyɛ́n
6	ēsɔ́ŋ	'teeth'	ēsɔ́ŋ	əyɔ́m	əyíɛ̀	əyɛ́s	əyɛ́n
7	kēkém	'crab'	kēkém̀	kɔ́m	kīɛ̀	kɛ́s	kɛ́n
8	ēbkém	'crabs'	ēbkém̀	wɔ́m	vīɛ̀	wɛ́s	wɛ́n
9	ɲâm	'animal'	ɲâm	yɔ́m	ʒīɛ̀	yɛ́s	yɛ́n
10	ɲámsɔ̄	'animals'	ɲâm	sɔ́m	∫íɛ̀	sɛ́s	sɛ́n
13	tɔ̄bíì	'kolanuts'	tɔ̄bíì	tɔ́m	tíɛ̀	tɛ́s	tɛ́n
19	fə̄nə̂n	'bird'	fə̄nə̂n	fɔ́m	fíɛ̀	fɛ́s	fɛ́n
6a	m̄nə̂n	'birds'	m̄nə̂n	mɔ́m	míɛ̀	mɛ́s	mɛ́n

Oku third person possessives are again quite different, as seen in the forms in Table 5 compared with those from EGB in Table 2.

As indicated, in the third person singular, Oku distinguishes both anaphoric and logophoric possessive pronouns, the latter cognate with the EGB pronominal forms seen above in Table 2. This WGB pattern was already noted by Voorhoeve:

> Une comparaison entre les deux types de langues met en évidence que le pronom logophorique sg correspond avec le pronom anaphorique sg dans les langues [EGB] sans pronom logophorique. (Voorhoeve 1980: 192, describing Ngwo, a Momo language—see §5).

As also noted, instead of a uniform L tone ə̀-, an associative marker 'of' occurs between the noun and third person "pronoun": ə̀- after class 1, sé- after class 10, mè- after class 6a, and ɔ́-. This follows the same pattern as in 'Noun₁ of Noun₂' genitive constructions in Table 6, which is greatly simplified compared to other Ring languages:

205

Table 5: Oku 3p possessives for each Oku noun class

cl.	noun	gloss	'his/her'		'their'		'his/her (log.)'	
1	wān	'child'	wāṅ	wēṅ	wāṅ	yēṅ	wāṅ	vī
2	yɔ́n	'children'	yɔ́n	ɔ́ wēṅ	yɔ́n	ɔ́ yēṅ	yɔ́n	èyí
3	ēblɛ́ŋ	'bamboo'	ēblɛ́ŋ	ɔ́ wēṅ	ēblɛ́ŋ	ɔ́ yēṅ	ēblɛ́ŋ	èví
4	īlɛ́ŋ	'bamboos'	īlɛ́ŋ	ɔ́ wēṅ	īlɛ́ŋ	ɔ́ yēṅ	īlɛ́ŋ	èʒí
5	īʃɔ́ŋ	'tooth'	īʃɔ́ŋ	ɔ́ wēṅ	īʃɔ́ŋ	ɔ́ yēṅ	īʃɔ́ŋ	èʒí
6	ēsɔ́ŋ	'teeth'	ēsɔ́ŋ	ɔ́ wēṅ	ēsɔ́ŋ	ɔ́ yēṅ	ēsɔ́ŋ	èfí
7	kēkém	'crab'	kēkém	ɔ́ wēṅ	kēkém	ɔ́ yēṅ	kēkém	ekí
8	ēbkém	'crabs'	ēbkém	ɔ́ wēṅ	ēbkém	ɔ́ yēṅ	ēbkém	èví
9	ɲâm	'animal'	ɲâm	wēṅ	ɲâm	yēṅ	ɲâm	ʒī
10	ɲâmsē	'animals'	ɲâmsē	wēṅ	ɲâmsē	yēṅ	ɲâmsē	èsí
13	tēbíí	'kolanuts'	tēbíí	ɔ́ wēṅ	tēbíí	ɔ́ yēṅ	tēbíí	tí
19	fēnún	'bird'	fēnún	ɔ́ wēṅ	fēnún	ɔ́ yēṅ	fēnún	fí
6a	m̄nún	'birds'	m̄nún	mè wēṅ	m̄nún	mè wēṅ	m̄nún	mèmī

Table 6: Oku 'Noun₁ of Noun₂' genitive constructions

cl.	noun₁ of noun₂		cl.	noun₁ of noun₂	
1	wán ə̀ kèkɔ̀s	'child of slave'	2	yɔ́n ɔ́ kèkɔ̀s	'children of slave'
3	ēblɛ́ŋ ɔ́ kèkɔ̀s	'bamboo of slave'	4	īlɛ́ŋ ɔ́ kèkɔ̀s	'bamboos of slave'
5	īʃɔ́ŋ ɔ́ kèkɔ̀s	'tooth of slave'	6	ɛsɔ́ŋ ɔ́ kèkɔ̀s	'teeth of slave'
7	kēkém ɔ́ kèkɔ̀s	'crab of slave'	8	ēbkém ɔ́ kèkɔ̀s	'crabs of slave'
9	ɲàm ə̀ kèkɔ̀s	'animal of slave'	10	ɲám sē kèkɔ̀s	'animals of slave'
13	tēyúm ɔ́ kèkɔ̀s	'eggs of slave'			
19	fēnún ɔ́ kèkɔ̀s	'bird of slave'	6a	m̄nún mè kèkɔ̀s	'birds of slave'

As in other African languages, logophoric pronouns refer back to person(s) reporting indirect discourse (/yi/ → ʒi):

(4) a. Subj:

    èb sōí gē èb gwí yè   'he$_i$ says that he$_j$/she$_j$ is coming'
    èb sōí gē ʒī gwí yè   'he$_i$ says that he$_i$ (LOG) is coming'
    s/he say that PRON come PROG

  b. Obj:

    èb sōí gē mɛ ne lɔ̂ yēn wīṅ   'he$_i$ says that I saw him$_j$/her$_j$'
    èb sōí gē mɛ ne lɔ̂ yēn ʒi   'he$_i$ says that I saw him$_i$ (LOG)'
    s/he say that I PAST ASP see PRON

c. Poss:

    èb sōí gē ʒī yénó kēkém ó wīǹ 'he_i says that he_i sees his_j crab (cl. 7)'
    èb sōí gē ʒī yénó ēbkém ó wīǹ 'he_i says that he_i sees his_j crabs (cl. 8)'
    èb sōí gē ʒī yénó kēkém òkí 'he_i says that he_i sees his_i (LOG) crab (cl. 7)'
    èb sōí gē ʒī yénó ēbkém òví 'he_i says that he_i sees his_i (LOG) crabs (cl. 8)'

While the reconstructed 3sg. *-í pronoun serves both an anaphoric and logophoric function in EGB, the innovated third person anaphoric pronouns in the Ring languages have clearly replaced the inherited *-í forms (as will be seen again in the Momo languages in §5). But where did the new pronouns come from, and why?

In order to get a fuller picture, relevant comparative data from different Ring languages are presented in Table 8 on the next page (logophors in parentheses are identical to the anaphors). As can be observed, in most of their paradigm, Ring languages have replaced the inherited third person anaphoric pronouns seen in EGB in Table 2 above. Class 2 'they, them' is often derived from the singular, at least in some cases, e.g. Babanki và-wén'-ó; Babungo và-ŋwó > vǎŋ (?). In addition we can observe the following:

(i) Neither 'body' nor 'this/these' provides a perfect phonetic source for the third person sg. pronoun.

(ii) The root for 'body' is identical in Babanki and Lamnso'; however, class 3 'body' would require new forms to be developed in the other classes (its own plural is in class 4 (Aghem, Kom), 13 (Aghem, Kom) or 6a (Mbizinaku, Bafmeng, Bum, Weh)).

(iii) Class 1 'this' is identical to the third person singular pronoun in Aghem; both it and 'body' work for Lamnso'.

(iv) Neither works for Oku wēǹ (with ML tone), where the 'word for 'body' is ēbwún and demonstratives have the vowel /i/ and L tone.

Table 7: Oku demonstratives with vowel /i/ and L tone

1	vìn	2	yìn	7	kìn	8	vìn	19	fìn	6a	mìn
3	vìn	4	ʒìn	9	ʒìn	10	fìn				
5	yìn	6	kìn	13	tìn		(w, y → v, ʒ / __ i)				

Table 8: Comparative data from different Ring languages

Language	cl.1/2 pronouns		'body'	cl.1 demonstratives			class 1 3sg.			sg. logophorics		
	3sg.	3pl.		'n.s.'	'n.h.'	'far'	subj.	obj.	poss.	subj.	obj.	poss.
Aghem	wín	yé	ówé	wín	vɔ́	òvɔ́	ò	wín	wín	é	yé	yé
Babanki	wɛ́n	vəwɛ́ⁿná	ə̀wɛ́n"	ə̀yɛ́n	ʒíá	əʒì	yə̀	wɛ́n	wɛ́n		yi	
Babessi	yǐ	ŋwɛ̂	ŋú/ŋwɛ́ná	ŋwɛ̂	yí:		yí	ŋə́	yí:	yí		
Babungo	ŋwá	vǎŋ	ŋwá̰	ŋwə̀	yɔ́⁻	wí	ŋwá	ŋwá	wí	yì	yì	(wì)
Bafmeng	vɛ́ŋ	yə̀nə̂	ēwìŋ	vìŋ	vě'	vî	évá	vɛ̀ŋ	vɛ̀ŋ	èzə́	(vɛ̄ŋ)	(vɛ̄ŋ)
Bum	wūn	yənV'	ūwún	wùnā'	wɛ̄'	wɔ̀kɔ́	ù					
Isu	'wé	yú~wú	úwéé	'wɔ́	'wíy	'wíy		'wé	'wé	íyé	íyé	íyé
Kom	ŋwēn	ə̀ŋə̄ná	ə̄wúín	wɛ̄n	vī'	vî̄	wù	ŋwēn	ŋwēn	yī	yī	vì
Lamnso'	wùn'	áwùnē'	wùń	vən	vəy	vəsə̄	wù	wùn	və̀'	wùn		
Mbizinaku	wēìn	āŋéìn	ə̄wóìn	vàìn	vɔ̄'				wēìn			
Oku	wēn	yēnè	ēbwún	vìn	vì	vìì	èb	wēn	wēn	ʒī	ʒī	
Weh	'wì	yî	úwì̵'	wén	wɛ́ì	wɛ́ì	tə́'	'wì	'wì	í		vī
Zoa	'wì	yʲi	úfù'			wî	má	wóŋ				

6 Third person pronouns in Grassfields Bantu

Could this mean that the demonstrative became a pronoun in one language which had the appropriate vowel and tone, and then spread to the other languages? All of this could have diffused areally (cf. the discussion of Noni in (5) below).

Let us assume the historical derivation Dem > Pron for the present discussion. Why were the new pronouns innovated? The following observations may serve as hints:

(i) Dem > Pron first affects Obj (object, oblique and independent pronouns), then possessive or subject in the following stages:

Stage 1: Obj : Lamnso'

Stage 2: Obj + Poss : Aghem, Babanki, Bafmeng, Kom, Oku

Stage 3: Obj + Subj : Babungo

Stage 4: Obj + Poss + Subj : no Ring language yet attested

(ii) It is the demonstrative 'this' that is involved—vs. 'that' (near hearer) or 'that' (remote); cf §7.

(iii) The same languages develop logophoric marking—starting first with subject position:

Stage 1: Subj : Bafmeng

Stage 2: Subj + Obj : Babungo

Stage 3: Subj + Obj + Poss : Aghem, Kom, Oku

The hypothesis that we can therefore advance is that both innovations have to do with marking co- vs. non-co-referential pronouns. As is well-known, 'this' is often an introducer of a new referent (non-coferential): *I ran into this guy and he said...* (vs. 'that': *I don't like that guy!*). In addition, non-subject (Obj) pronouns are more likely to be "new" than subjects (hence non-coreferential?). It therefore should be the case that the demonstrative would become a pronoun first in non-subject positions. Contrasting with this, logophoric pronouns are coreferential, systematically opposed to coreferential third persons, and are best suited for subject position (= most "given", referring back to the speaker).

However, at least two systems do not fit the pattern. The first, seen in Table 9, is the curious "reverse" case of Lamnso' third person singular subject: *wù* (anaphoric) vs. *wùn* (logophoric).

Table 9: Lamnso' personal pronouns including logophoric

	1sg	2sg	3sg	Log	1pl	2pl	3pl
subject	ḿ, mo-	á´, wō-	wù	wùn	vèr´	vèn´	vé-, á
object	mō´	wò	wūn‘		vēr´	vēn´	áwūnē´
cl. 1 poss.	wōm´	wò	vɔ̄		wōr´	wōn´	wōv´
cl. 2. poss.	vém	vé‘	vɔ́		vér	vén	vév
	-ém	-é‘	-ɔ́		-ér	-én	-év (e → o / w __)

About these, Grebe (1982: Appendix II) says the following:

> /wùn/ is used in speech quotation referring to original speaker.... (Appendix II, p.23)

> /vé-/ is used in contexts where the subject pronoun receives a suffix to mark tense or mood, e.g. /vé-é/ 'they-past-tense'. /á/ is used in all other contexts if the referent is impersonal, as well as for personal referents if the pronoun occurs in a relative or various other subordinate clauses. A third form, /áwūnē/ 'they' is always personal and occurs only in independent clauses (Appendix II, p.7)

Even more curious is Noni, a Beboid (Bantoid) language spoken near Lamnso' and Oku (Hyman 1981: 15, 20), where the logophoric pronouns resemble the demonstrative forms in the Ring languages:

Table 10: Noni personal pronouns including logophoric

	1sg	2sg	3sg$_j$	3sg$_i$	Log	1pl	2pl	3pl	Log
subj/obj	mē	wɔ̀	wvù	—	wēn	bèsèn	bèn	bɔ́	bɔ̀wēn
cl. 1 poss.	wèm	wɔ̀	wè	—	wēn	wèsèn	wènè	(wù)bɔ́	bɔ̀wēn
cl. 2 poss.	bēm̀	bōẁ	bêw	bêŋ	bɔ́-wēn-ɛ́	bɔ̀sésèn	bɔ̀nên	bɔ̀bɔ́ɔ́lɛ́	bɔ́-bɔ̀wēn-ɛ́
cl. 7 poss.	kēm̀	kōẁ	kêw	kêŋ	ke-wēn-ɛ́	kèsésèn	kènên	kēbɔ́ɔ́lɛ́	kē-bɔ̀wēn-ɛ́

As I have elsewhere speculated (Hyman 1981: 15-16), Noni apparently borrowed wēn, but got it "wrong", allowing it in subject position (as elsewhere only in Babungo) and developing a plural form bɔ̀-wēn, which I have not found in Ring:

(5) a. sg.:
    wvù dòó lē   wvù béɛ̀   gɛ̀n fɔ̀wǎy   'he$_i$ says that he$_j$/she$_j$ went to market' (today)
    wvù dòó lē   wēn béɛ̀   gɛ̀n fɔ̀wǎy   'he$_i$ says that he$_i$ (LOG.) went to market'
    s/he say that PRON PAST.FOC go to.market

b. pl.:
    bɔ́ dóó lē bɔ́ béɛ̀   gɛ̀n fɔ̀wǎy   'they$_i$ say that they$_j$ went to market' (today)
    bɔ́ dóó lē bɔ̀wēn béɛ̀   gɛ̀n fɔ̀wǎy   'they$_i$ say that they$_i$ (LOG.) went to market'
    they say that PRON PAST.FOC go to.market

Noni does not provide an exact form wēn 'this' > PRON, but related Naki comes closer (Good 2010):

Table 11: Noni and Naki proximate demonstratives 'this'

	Noni	Naki		Noni	Naki		Noni	Naki
1	wvùñ	wə̀n	6	ɛ̄yān	nə̀n	10	yīn	yə̀n
2	bān	bə̀n	6a	mān	mə̀n	13	jīn	—
3	wvūn	wə̌n	7	kīn	kə̀n	14	bvūn	wə̌n
4	yīn	—	8	bīn	byə̀n	19	fīn	fyə̀n
5	jīn	—	9	yìñ	yə̀n	18	mvūn	mə̀n

Finally, note that Weh has generalized the associative to all possessives except first and second person singular, e.g. ndɔ́ŋ/tə̀ndɔ́ŋ 'horn(s)' 9/13:

Table 12: Weh possessive pronouns and generalized associative

'my'	'your sg.'	'his/her'	'our'	'your pl.'	'their'
ndɔ́ŋ zú⁺ŋ́	ndɔ́ŋ zɯ	ndɔ̀ŋ à wé	ndɔ̀ŋ à sà	ndɔ̀ŋ à ɣà	ndɔ̀ŋ à ɣɯ́
ndɔ́ŋ tú⁺ŋ́	ndɔ́ŋ tɯ̀	ndɔ̀ŋ tɔ́⁺wé	ndɔ̀ŋ tɔ́ sà	ndɔ̀ŋ tɔ́ ɣà	ndɔ̀ŋ tɔ́⁺ɣɯ́

5 Momo Grassfields Bantu

This section will be shorter, as less material has been available to me on Momo languages than on Ring. The important observation to make is that new third person personal pronouns have been introduced (mostly different in form from the Ring pronouns), including reflexives. There is considerable variation. We start with Ngamambo, whose independent possessive pronouns are shown in Table 13.

Table 13: Ngamambo independent possessive pronouns

cl.	'mine'	'yours sg.'	'his/hers'	'ours'	'yours pl'	'theirs'
1	ɨ̀-wūm	ɨ̀-wē `	wū mʌ́t	ɨ̀-wā	ɨ̀-wɔ́n	wū mə̀- mʌ́t
2=8	m̀-búm	m̀-bê	m̀bɔ́ mʌ́t	m̀-bá	m̀-bɔ́n	m̀bɔ́ mə̄- mʌ̌t
3	ɨ̀-wúm	ɨ̀-wê	wú mʌ́t	ɨ̀-wá	ɨ̀-wɔ́n	wú mə̄- mʌ̌t
6=7	ʌ̀-zúm	ʌ̀-bê	zʌ́ mʌ́t	ʌ̀-zá	ʌ̀-zɔ́n	zʌ́ mə̄- mʌ̌t
9	ɨ̀-zúm	ɨ̀-zē `	zɔ̄ mʌ́t	ɨ̀-zā	ɨ̀-zɔ̄n	zɔ̄ mə̀- mʌ́t
10=13	ɨ̀-túm	ɨ̀-tê	lɔ́ mʌ́t	ɨ̀-tá	ɨ̀-tɔ́n	lɔ́ mə̄- mʌ̌t
19	ɨ̀-fúm	ɨ̀-fê	fɔ́ mʌ́t	ɨ̀-fá	ɨ̀-fɔ́n	fɔ́ mə̄- mʌ̌t
6a	m̀-búm	m̀-bē `	m̀bɔ̄ mʌ́t	m̀-bā	m̀-bɔ̄n	m̀bɔ̄ mə̀- mʌ́t
	/-úm/	/-ê/		/-á/	/-ɔ́n/	

Note the third person pronominal root /mʌ́t/ (< ?), whose plural form mə̀-mʌ́t has a class 2 prefix (*bə̀-).

As seen in Table 14, the above possessive pronouns occur after a noun (the noun glosses are given in Table 15).

Table 14: Ngamambo possessive pronouns that follow the noun

cl.	'my'	'your sg'	'his/her'	'our'	'your pl'	'their'
1	kánʌ́ ꜛwúm	kánʌ́ ꜛwē `	kánʌ́ mʌ̌t	kánʌ́ ꜛwā	kánʌ́ ꜛwɔ́n	kánʌ́ mə̀mʌ̌t
3	ɨ̌kón wúm	ɨ̌kón wē `	ɨ̌kón mʌ̌t	ɨ̌kón wá	ɨ̌kón wɔ́n	ɨ̌kón mə̀mʌ̌t
7	ʌ̄tsám ʌ́ zúm	ʌ̄tsám ʌ́ zē `	ʌ̄tsám ʌ́ mʌ̌t	ʌ̄tsám ʌ́ zā	ʌ̄tsám ʌ́ zɔ́n	ʌ̄tsám ʌ́ mə̀mʌ̌t
9	gwí ꜛzúm	gwí ꜛzē `	gwí mʌ̌t	gwí ꜛzā	gwí ꜛzɔ́n	gwí mə̀mʌ̌t
10	gwí túm	gwí tē `	gwí lɔ́ mʌ̌t	gwí tā	gwí tɔ́n	gwí lɔ̄ mə̀mʌ̌t
19	fə́kámə́ fúm	fə́kámə́ fē `	fə́kámə́ fɔ́ mʌ̌t	fə́kámə́ fá	fə́kámə́ fɔ́n	fə́kámə́ fɔ̄ mə̀mʌ̌t

Shorter preposed variants exist in first and second person, but not third person, and are shown in Table 15.

6 Third person pronouns in Grassfields Bantu

Table 15: Ngamambo shorter possessive pronouns for 1sg & 2sg that precede the noun

cl.	noun		'my'	'your sg'	'our'	'your pl'
1	kánʎ	'monkey'	mā́ kánʎ	ē kánʎ	ā kánʎ	wā́ kánʎ
3	īkón	'hill'	mɔ́ kón	ē kón	á kón	wɔ́ kón
7	ʎtsám	'home'	mʎ tsám	ē tsám	á tsám	zɔ́ tsám
9	gwí	'goat'	mā́ gwí	ē gwí	ā gwí	wā́ gwí
10	gwí	'goats'	túm gwí	tē gwí	tá gwí	tɔ́n gwí
19	fɔ́kámɔ́	'crab'	fúm fɔ́kámɔ́	fēʻ fɔ́kámɔ́	fá fɔ́kámɔ́	fɔ́n fɔ́kámɔ́

Turning to another Momo language, Ngie has a full set of sg logophoric possessive pronouns, which Watters (1980) shows preposed to the noun in Table 16. Class 4 iɲí is not completely certain.

Table 16: Ngie logophoric possessive pronouns

	[-LOG]	[+LOG]		[-LOG]	[+LOG]		[-LOG]	[+LOG]
1	ùŋgwēn	ùŋgwī́	5	ùŋgwēn	ìnjí	9	ùŋgwēn	ìnjī́
2	ùŋgwēn	ùmbí	6	ùŋgwēn	ìnjí	10	ùŋgwēn	ìtí
3	ùŋgwēn	ùŋgwí	7	ùŋgwēn	ìnjí	13	ùŋgwēn	ùfí
4	ùŋgwēn	iɲí ?	8	ùŋgwēn	ùmbí	19	ùŋgwēn	ìtí

Table 17 presents a comparison of four Momo pronoun systems: Ngie (Elimelech 1980; Watters 1980), Ngwo (Voorhoeve 1980), Mundani (Parker 1986; 1989), Metta (Spreda 1991; 2000; Mihas 2009). Different third person forms are innovated (wɛn, mɔ́t, ta/to), again affecting non-subject pronouns first, sometimes only the singular (e.g. Moghamo mɔ́t 'his/her' vs. -ɔ́p 'their'). In Table 18 I present the class 1/2 demonstratives in six Momo languages. (The Moghamo and Oshie data are due to Stallcup 1980; in addition, the 'near hearer' forms may also/instead mean 'the one in question, the one referred to'.)

It appears that the new forms do not closely resemble the current demonstratives (although n-final forms do occur), nor does the word 'body' look promising as a source, except that it ends in -t, like mɔ́t (PGB *-nód, PB *-yʊ́tʊ). While the original pronominal forms show up again as logophoric -í, -é in Table 17, there also are new reflexive pronouns of the shape ma and mɔ. This latter development

Table 17: Momo pronoun systems: Ngie, Ngwo, Mundani, and Metta

Ngie	1sg	2sg	3sg	log	refl	1pl	2pl	3pl	log	refl
subj	mə̄	ŋgwə̄	wə	yī		m̀ba	m̀bèna	m̀bī	m̀bì	
obj	ŋwū	yə‘	ùŋwēn	yī	mā	(ŋ)gwā	(ŋ̀)gwēn	ūŋwɛn	ŋgwī	ùmă°
cl. 1 poss	ùŋwū	ùŋgwê	ùŋgwēn	ùŋgwi	umā	ùŋgwā	ù-ŋgwēn	uŋ̀gwi	uŋ̀gwi	ùmă
cl. 2 poss	ùmbîŋ	ùmbiè	ùŋwēn	ùmbíέ	ūmā	ù-mbā	ù-mbēn	um̀bí	um̀bí	ùmă

Ngwo	1sg	2sg	3sg	log	refl	1pl	2pl	3pl	log	refl
subj	m̀mè	ŋgwɔ̄	ŋgɔ́	m̀bè		m̀byὲ	m̀bɔ̀n	áŋɔ́ɔ́	m̀bɔ̀ɔ̀	
obj	āŋgú	awē‘		āŋgwé	ámɔ́	āŋgwé	āŋgón	áŋɔ́ɔ́	āŋgɔ́ɔ́	àmɔ°
cl. 1 poss.	ŋgwā	ŋgwē‘	ŋgɔ́	ŋgwē	mɔ́	ŋgwē	ŋgwɔ̄n	áŋɔ́	ŋgwɔ̀ɔ̀	àmɔ̀
cl. 2 poss.	mbá	mbyê	ŋgɔ́	mbé	mɔ́	mbyέ	mbɔ́n	áŋɔ́	mbɔ́ɔ́	âmɔ

Mundani	1sg	2sg	3sg	log	refl	1pl	2pl	3pl	log	refl
subj	mâ	a	ta, a, e	yé		bâ	bɨ̂	bɔ̂, bé, é		
obj	m	wē‘	tò, we	vi	vi	wá	wɨ́	wɔ́b, be		
cl. 1 poss	wɔ́	wê	è-tò	vi	vi	wá	wɨ́	wɔ́b		
cl. 2 poss	bɔ́	bê	é-tò	bi ?	bi ?	bá	bɨ̀	bɔ́b		

Metta	1sg	2sg	3sg	log	refl	1pl	2pl	3pl	log	refl
subj	mə	əwɔ̀	wɨ́			mbă (tɨ̀)	mbə̄	mbɨ̄		
emphatic	mɔ́	əwɔ̀	mɔ́t			mbă	mbə̀nə	mɨ̀mɔ́t		
object	əmɨ́	əwê	əmɔ́t		əwí	əwá	əwə́n	mɨ̀mɔ́t		əwə́n
cl. 1 poss	iwúm	iwê	-mɔ́t			iwɔ́	iwə́n	iwɔ́p		
cl. 2 poss	ìmbúm	ìmbê	-mɔ́t			ìmbə	ìmbə́n	ímbɔ́p		

Moghamo	1sg	2sg	3sg	log	refl	1pl	2pl	3pl	log	refl
cl. 1 poss	iwúm	iwê	'mɔ́t			iwá	iwə́n	iwɔ́p		
cl. 2 poss	ìmbúm	ìmbê	mɔ́t			ìmbá	ìmbən	ìmbɔ́p		

Table 18: Class 1/2 demonstratives in six Momo languages

	'near speaker'		'near hearer'		'remote'		'body'
Ngamambo	ɨwɔ́ɔ̀	m̀bɔ́ɔ̀	ɨwē	m̀bé	ɨywīì	m̀bîì	iɲɔ́t
Ngie	ù-ŋwû	u-mbɨ̂ŋ	ù-wə	u-biɛ	ù-wî	u-mbî	iɲó
Mundani	wáā	báā	wū	bū	wiá	biá	əɲót
Metta	wɔ̂	mbɔ̂	wē	mbé	wîn	mbîn	əɲót
Moghamo	wɔ̂n	m̀bɔ̂n			wîn	mbîn	iɲɔ́t
Oshie	wâŋ	bâŋ			wî	bî	ɛɲét

is quite rare in West Africa, where nouns such as 'body' or 'head' are used as a reflexive (but cf. PB *-méné (~ *-jéné) 'self, same'). Thus:

> The reflexive pronoun in Kenyang is actually a phrase comprised of the word for 'body' (m-mwɛt) and a possessive. (Ramirez 1998: 22)

However, note that the similar Momo root -mə́t is non-reflexive and non-logophoric. To conclude this section, anaphoric, logophoric and reflexive 3pl are exemplified in Ngie (Watters 1980: 48); cf. Voorhoeve (1980: 174) for Ngwo:

(6) a. m̄bī   ɛ̀γɑ̀ì kwī m̄bī   ɛ̀kɔ̀mɔ̀ ŋ̄wɛn
       they[A] said that they[A] hit   them[A]
       'they$_1$ said that they$_2$ hit them$_3$'

   b. m̄bī   ɛ̀γɑ̀ì kwī m̄bī   ɛ̀kɔ̀mɔ̀ ŋgwī
       they[A] said that they[A] hit   them[L]
       'they$_1$ said that they$_2$ hit them$_1$'

   c. m̄bī   ɛ̀γɑ̀ì kwī m̄bī   ɛ̀kɔ̀mɔ̀ ùmà°
       they[A] said that they[A] hit   them[R]
       'they$_1$ said that they$_2$ hit themselves$_2$'

   d. m̄bī   ɛ̀γɑ̀ì kwī m̀bì   ɛ̂kɔ̀mɔ̀ ŋ̄wɛn
       they[A] said that they[L] hit   them[A]
       'they$_1$ said that they$_1$ hit them$_2$'

   e. m̄bī   ɛ̀γɑ̀ì kwī m̀bì   ɛ̀kɔ̀mɔ̀ ŋgwī
       they[A] said that they[L] hit   them[L]
       'they$_1$ said that they$_1$ hit themselves$_1$'

Note in (6e) that the logophoric takes precedence over the reflexive form!

6 Beyond Grassfields Bantu

Perhaps if we take a look outside the Grassfields Bantu proper, there will be more hints as to where the WGB third person pronouns came from. Table 19 compares pronouns and demonstrative forms from Wider Bantu and Narrow Bantu zone A: Basaá (Hyman 2003), Tunen (Mous 2003), Akɔɔse (Hedinger 1980), Mankon (Leroy 2007), Ejagham (Watters 1981), Tikar (Stanley 1991), Bafia (Guarisma 2000). It is striking that Tunen, Mankon, Akɔɔse and Kenyang all have a final -t or second syllable [r] (< *d) plus mid unrounded vowel, which is reminiscent of

Table 19: Pronouns and demonstratives from Wider Bantu and Narrow Bantu

	Basaá pron	Tunen pron	Mankon ind.pron	Akɔɔse ref.	Kenyang 'def.art.'	Ejagham ind.pron	Tikar pron	Akɔɔse 'this'	Bafia ref.
1sg	mè	mìàŋó	/mè/			m̀mè	mùn		
2sg	wè	àŋó	/yɔ̀/	[r] = /d/		wâ	wù		
1pl	bě́s	bʷə̀sú	/bʉy´/			êd	bwi?		
2pl	bee	bʷə̀nú	/bə̀n´/			ên	byin		
cl. 1	ɲɛ́	wɛ́y	zɪ́ɑ́, wɛ́rɔ́	àwèré	rɛ	yê	nun	ànén	ànéèn
cl. 2	bɔ́	bʷə̀bú	bó, bɛ́rɔ́	á⁺béré	bérɛ	ábɔ̀	bon	ábén	béèn
cl. 3	wɔ́	múit	wɛ́rɔ́	m⁺méré	rɛ	m̀mɔ́nè̀	son	m̀mén	wîin
cl. 4	ŋwɔ́	mít		m⁺méré			yon	m̀mén	méèn
cl. 5	jɔ́	nɛ́t	nɛ́rɔ́	á⁺déré	nérɛ	ńjɔ́nè̀	yon	ádén	dîin
cl. 6	mɔ́	mát	mɛ́rɔ́	m⁺méré	mérɛ	m̀mánè̀	nun	m̀mén	méèn
cl. 7	yɔ́	yét	zɛ́rɔ́	é⁺céré	rɛ			écén	kîin
cl. 8	gwɔ́	bét	tsɛ́rɔ́	á⁺béré	bérɛ	m̀bɔ́nè̀		ábén	bîin
cl. 9	yɔ́	mɛ́t	zɛ́rɔ́	ècèré	rɛ	ɲ́ɲɔ́nè̀		ènén	ì-néèn
cl. 10	yɔ́	mít	tsɛ́rɔ́	é⁺céré	rɛ			écén	yîin
cl. 13	cɔ́	túét		á⁺déré	kérɛ			ádén	tîin
cl. 14		búét		á⁺béré		m̀bɔ́nè̀		ábén	
cl. 19	hyɔ́	hít	fɛ́rɔ́	á⁺béré	sérɛ	m̀fɔ́nè̀		ábén	fîin

the Momo pronoun *mɔ́t*. Additional Tunen forms from Mous (2003: 301) reveal an [n], including *wə̂n* 'that one' (cl.1) which looks more like the Ring pronoun seen in §4. Also to be considered is Tunen *měl* 'body', where the final [l] likely reconstructs as **d*, hence strikingly similar again to Momo *mɔ́t*.

When comparing all of these forms to Proto-Bantu we see just how widespread **d* and **n* are in these forms. Thus, Guthrie offers the Common Bantu forms **-nʊ́*, **nó* 'this', **dá*, **dé*, *-dɪ́á* 'that' and Meeussen (1967) has **-nóò* 'this', *-ó* 'that (not here)', **-dɪ́á* 'that' (remote). There are, however, other forms (see Weier 1985). The PB independent and possessive pronouns reconstructed by Kamba Muzenga (2003: 215) are given in Table 20. As seen, these are of considerably lesser help in explaining the third person pronominal forms in WGB. For proposed reconstructions of Proto-Bantoid 1st and 2nd person pronouns, see Babaev 2008: 161.

7 Summary and conclusion

In the previous sections we have seen that EGB languages have kept their pronouns largely intact, descending directly from pronouns reconstructed for Proto-Bantu and likely Proto-Bantu-EGB. On the other hand, WGB languages have changed their pronoun systems in several ways:

6 Third person pronouns in Grassfields Bantu

Table 20: Proto-Bantu independent and possessive pronouns (Kamba Muzenga 2003: 115)

	independent pronouns		possessive pronouns	
	sg	pl	sg	pl
1st person	*a-a-mi-e	*a-i-cu-e	*-a-ngu-Ø	*-i-tu-Ø
		*a-i-cʊ-e	*-a-nga-Ø	*-i-ʊ-Ø
2nd person	*a-u-bɪ-e	*a-i-ɲu-e	*-a-ku-o	*-i-nu-Ø
		*a-i-ɲʊ-e		*-i-nʊ-Ø
3rd person	*a-i-ju-e	*a-a-ba-o	*-i-ndi-e	*-a-ba-o
	*a-i-jʊ-e		*-ɪ-ndi-e	
			*-a-ka-e	
			*-a-ku-e	

(i) New third person anaphoric pronouns have been innovated from two different shapes which appear to reconstruct as *-én in Ring vs. *-ád in Momo.

(ii) Where kept, the original third person pronouns have become restricted as logophorics.

(iii) A subset of Momo languages have also introduced reflexive third person pronouns.

(iv) In some languages the new pronouns resemble the demonstrative 'this', in others the noun 'body'. This is hardly surprising as demonstratives are often used as pronouns in African languages (cf. Creissels 1991: 215-220):

> *Mundani:* "Demonstratives Used as Emphatic Pronouns. Independent pronouns can be formed from certain dependent demonstrative modifiers.... The independent demonstratives are used in a range of grammatical functions: direct object, complement of the verb 'to be', and as the second element in an associative construction." (Parker 1989: 146)

> *Ejagham:* "...the Eastern Ejagham dialect has different forms for the 3ps pronoun for the various noun classes. These forms are identical to the 'distal' demonstratives used in the dialect." (Watters 1981: 355)

Larry M. Hyman

This fits in exactly with what is known about the diachronic development of new third person pronouns elsewhere in the world:

> Most languages allow their demonstrative pronouns to be used as anaphoric pronouns. (Bhat 2004: 184)

> ... demonstratives are primarily the source of third-person forms. (Siewierska 2004: 249)

The expected derivation of demonstrative > third person pronoun contrasts with observed diachronic sources of first and second person pronouns:

> Whereas the known sources of first- and second-person markers tend to be nominals denoting human relationships [e.g. 'master', 'lord'], those of the third person are typically words such as 'thing', 'human', 'man', 'person' or 'body'. (Siewierska 2004: 248)

Although 'body' is specifically mentioned as a possible nominal source of third person pronouns, it would fit this second pattern if 'body' were the source of the new third person pronouns in WGB.

Although we have focused on two likely sources of the new pronouns in WGB, demonstratives and the noun 'body', Siewierska (2004: 257) mentions a third potential development:

> Another not uncommon way in which new person markers may develop is from conjugated auxiliary verbs in periphrastic constructions. (Siewierska 2004: 257)

Consider in this context the Kom reduplicative present vs. the "locative present" (cf. *wèn* 'this (cl.1)', *yēn* 'these (cl.2)') in (7).

(7) a. *wù ǹ ʒūʒū* 'he is eating'
   yə ń ʒūʒū 'they are eating'
 b. *wù wēn ʒū* 'he's here eating, here he is eating' (cf. *fēǹ* 'here')
   yə yēn ʒū 'they're here eating, here they are eating'
 c. *wù vɨ́ ʒū* 'there he is eating' (*vɨ* ` 'that [near hearer]')

Basic present progressive is expressed by reduplicating the verb in (7a). In (7b) the near-speaker demonstrative root *-ɛn* is used to give a sense of locative proximity of the action. (The initial [f] of the form *fēǹ* 'here' is cognate with the PB locative class 16 prefix *pa-.) (7c) shows that other demonstratives can become involved in this construction. Since *wù* and *yɔ́* are not the independent pronouns in Kom, it is unlikely that (7b) should be interpreted as 'he this-one eats' etc., rather 'he here eats'. If correct, this would mean that in addition to potential multiple sources, multiple functions of the SAME source may give rise to new third person pronouns. In some WGB languages there are other grammatical markers having the shape *Cɛn*, including the above imperfective *wɛ̄n*, *yɛ̄n*, (etc.), invariant perfective *mɛ̄n`*, and an invariant definite marker *tɛ̄n* (cf. Oku *tɛ̄ǹ* 'inanimate third person object pronoun'). While such speculations are non-conclusive, it is hoped that the above survey will aid further research in unraveling the interesting history of third person pronouns in Grassfields Bantu and environs.

Acknowledgements

This is a revised version of a paper originally presented at the Niger-Congo Personal Pronouns Workshop, St. Petersburg, Sept. 13-15, 2010. I would like to thank the editor and an anonymous reviewer for helpful comments on the original manuscript.

References

Babaev, Kirill V. 2008. Reconstructing Benue-Congo person marking 1: Proto-Bantoid. *Journal of West African Linguistics* 35. 131–183.

Bhat, D. N. S. 2004. *Pronouns*. Oxford: Oxford University Press.

Creissels, Denis. 1991. *Description des langues négro-africaines et théorie syntaxique*. Grenoble: Ellug.

Elimelech, Baruch. 1980. *Noun class and concord system [of Ngie]*. Los Angeles. Manuscript.

Good, Jeff. 2010. *Naki noun class system sketch*. Buffalo, NY. Manuscript.

Grebe, Karl. 1982. *Nouns, noun classes, and tone in Lam Nso'*. Yaounde, Cameroon. Unpublished manuscript.

Guarisma, Gladys. 2000. *Complexité morphologique, simplicité syntaxique: Le cas du bafia, langue bantoue périphérique* (SELAF A 50). Paris: Peeters.

Harro, Gretchen & Nancy Haynes. 1991. *Grammar sketch of Yemba*. Yaounde, Cameroon. Unpublished manuscript.

Hedinger, Robert. 1980. The noun classes of Akɔ́ɔ̄sē (Bakossi). In Larry M. Hyman (ed.), *Noun classes in the Grassfields Bantu borderland* (Southern California Occasional Papers in Linguistics 8), 1–26. Los Angeles: Department of Linguistics, University of Southern California.

Hyman, Larry M. 1979. Phonology and noun structure. In Larry M. Hyman (ed.), *Aghem grammatical structure: With special reference to noun classes, tense-aspect and focus marking* (Southern California Occasional Papers in Linguistics 7), 1–72. Los Angeles: University of Southern California Department of Linguistics. http://gsil.sc-ling.org/pubs/SCOPILS_6_7_8_9/Aghem_grammatical_structure.pdf.

Hyman, Larry M. 1980a. Babanki and the Ring group. In Luc Bouquiaux (ed.), *L'expansion bantoue: Actes du colloque international du CNRS, Viviers (France) 4–16 avril 1977. Volume III*, 225–258. Paris: SELAF.

Hyman, Larry M. 1980b. Reflections on the nasal classes in Bantu. In Larry M. Hyman (ed.), *Noun classes in the Grassfields Bantu borderland* (Southern California Occasional Papers in Linguistics 8), 179–210. Los Angeles: Department of Linguistics, University of Southern California. http://gsil.sc-ling.org/pubs/SCOPILS_6_7_8_9/Noun_classes_in_the_grassfields_bantu_borderland.pdf.

Hyman, Larry M. 1981. *Noni grammatical structure: With special reference to verb morphology* (Southern California Occasional Papers in Linguistics 9). Los Angeles: University of Southern California Department of Linguistics. http://gsil.sc-ling.org/pubs/SCOPILS_6_7_8_9/Noni_grammatical_structure.pdf.

Hyman, Larry M. 2003. Basaá. In Derek Nurse & Gérard Philippson (eds.), *The Bantu languages*, 257–282. London: Routledge.

Hyman, Larry M. & Maurice Tadadjeu. 1976. Floating tones in Mbam-Nkam. In Larry M. Hyman (ed.), *Studies in Bantu tonology* (Southern California Occasional Papers in Linguistics 3), 57–111. Department of Linguistics, Univ. of Southern California.

Stallcup, Kenneth L. 1980. La géographie linguistique des Grassfields. In Larry M. Hyman & Jan Voorhoeve (eds.), *L'expansion bantoue: Actes du colloque international du CNRS, Viviers (France) 4–16 avril 1977. Volume I: Les classes nominales dans le bantou des Grassfields*, 43–57. Paris: SELAF.

Jones, Randy. 2001. *Provisional Kom-English lexicon*. Yaoundé, Cameroon: SIL. Unpublished manuscript.

Kamba Muzenga, J. G. 2003. *Substitutifs et possessifs en bantou*. Louvain: Peters.

Leroy, Jacqueline. 2007. *Le mankon: langue bantoue des Grassfields*. Paris: Peeters.

Meeussen, A. E. 1967. Bantu grammatical reconstructions. *Africana Linguistica* 3. 79–121.

Mihas, Elena. 2009. Negation in Metta. *Rice Working Papers in Linguistics* 1. 197–222.

Mous, Maarten. 2003. Nen (A44). In Derek Nurse & Gérard Philippson (eds.), *The Bantu languages*, 283–306. London: Routledge.

Parker, Elizabeth. 1986. Mundani pronouns. In Ursula Wiesemann (ed.), *Pronominal systems*, 131–165. Tübingen: Gunter Narr Verlag.

Parker, Elizabeth. 1989. Le nom et le syntagme nominal en mundani. In Daniel Barreteau & Robert Hedinger (eds.), *Descriptions de langues camerounaises*, 39–127. Paris: ORSTOM.

Piron, Pascale. 1995. Identification lexicostatistique des groupes bantoïdes stables. *JWAL* 25. 3–30.

Pozdniakov, Konstantin. N.d. *Analogical changes in Niger-Congo pronominal systems*. Presentation at Niger-Congo Personal Pronouns Workshop, St. Petersburg, Russia, 13-15 September, 2010.

Ramirez, Cristi. 1998. *The Kenyang noun phrase*. Yaounde, Cameroon. Unpublished manuscript.

Siewierska, Anna. 2004. *Person*. Cambridge: Cambridge University Press.

Spreda, Klaus. 1991. *Linguistic notes on Metta*. Yaounde, Cameroon. Unpublished manuscript.

Spreda, Klaus. 2000. *The noun in Metta*. Yaounde, Cameroon. Unpublished manuscript.

Stanley, Carol. 1991. *Description morpho-syntaxique de la langue tikar*. Yaoundé, Cameroon: SIL.

Voorhoeve, Jan. 1980. Le pronom logophorique et son importance pour la reconstruction du proto-bantou (PB). *Sprache und Geschichte in Afrika* 2. 173–187.

Watters, John R. 1980. *Notes on Ngie*. Manuscript.

Watters, John R. 1981. *A phonology and morphology of Ejagham – with notes on dialect variation*. Los Angeles: University of California at Los Angeles Doctoral dissertation.

Watters, John R. 2003. Grassfields Bantu. In Derek Nurse & Gérard Philippson (eds.), *The Bantu languages*, 225–256. London: Routledge.

Watters, John R. & Jacqueline Leroy. 1989. Southern Bantoid. In John Bendor-Samuel (ed.), *The Niger-Congo languages*, 430–449. Lanham, MD: University Press of America.

Weier, Hans-Ingolf. 1985. *Basisdemonstrativa im Bantu*. Hamburg: Helmut Buske Verlag.

Chapter 7

More reflections on the nasal classes in Bantu

Larry M. Hyman
University of California, Berkeley

> Although long considered to be a Bantu innovation, Miehe (1991) proposed that the nasal consonants present in Bantu noun classes 1, 3, 4, 6, 9 and 10 should be reconstructed in pre-Proto-Bantu, even possibly at the Proto-Niger-Congo stage. Since there has been no comprehensive response to Miehe, the two of us organized a workshop to look at the question in more detail. In this paper I update the problem from Hyman (1980b) and Miehe (1991), expanding the coverage and considering various scenarios that could have led to innovation (or loss). While there have been three hypothetical reconstructions (nasal consonants, nasalized vowels, no nasal consonants), we have not yet arrived at a "solution" that answers the relevant questions discussed in this paper.

The purpose of this paper is to update what we know about the distribution of nasal consonants within certain Bantu noun class prefixes and their cognates outside of Bantu proper. Whereas Narrow Bantu languages have nasal consonants in the noun prefixes in classes 1, 3, 4, 6(a), 9 and 10, found also in certain Wide Bantu/Bantoid languages, these nasals are either missing or only partially present in other Bantoid, Benue-Congo and further outlying subbranches of Niger-Congo. Table 1 presents the reconstructions which have been proposed for Proto-Bantu (Meeussen 1967), Proto-Benue-Congo (de Wolf 1971), Proto-Eastern and Western Grassfields Bantu (Hyman 1980c), and Proto-Gur (Miehe et al. 2007). Where two columns appear, the first represents the shapes of noun prefixes, the second the shapes of concord prefixes on agreeing elements. (For a broader discussion of East Benue-Congo noun class systems and their use of nasal consonants as noun prefixes, see Good, Chapter 2 of this volume, and in particular §1.)

Table 1: Reconstructions of Relevant Niger-Congo Noun Class Prefixes

class	Proto-Bantu		Proto-Benue-Congo		Proto-EGB		Proto-WGB		Proto-Gur
1 (sg.)	*mò-	*jò-	*ù-, *ò-	*gwu-, *à-	*N`-	*ò-	*ò(N)-	*ò-	*ʊ, *a
3 (sg.)	*mò-	*gó-	*ú-	*gu-, *u-	*N`-	*ó-	*ó-	*ó-	*ŋʊ
4 (pl.)	*mì-	*gí-	*í-	*zí- (?), í-	—	—	*í-	*í-	*i
6 (pl.)	*mà-	*gá-	*à	*ga-, *a-	*mə̀-	mə́-	*á-	*gá-	*ŋa
9 (sg.)	*N`-	*jì-	*è-, *ì-	*zì-	*N`-	*ì-	*ì(N)-	*ì-	
10 (pl.)	*N`-	*jí-	*í-	*zí- (?), í-	*N`-	*í-	*í(N)-	*Cí-	*ni
6a (-)	*mà-	*gá-	*mà-, *nà-	*ma-, *na-	*mə̀-	*mə́-	*mə-	*mə́-	*ma
6b (pl)	*mò-	*mò-	(?*mʊ-)						*mʊ
7 (sg.)	*kì-	*kí-	*ki-, *ke-	*ki-	à-	*í-	kí-	*kí-	—

As seen, only classes 6a and 6b reveal nasal prefixes through all of the above groups. In the last row I have shown the shapes of class 7 prefixes to illustrate one of the noun classes that is oral throughout Niger-Congo.[1]

Such forms as in Table 1 immediately raise two questions: (i) Where do the nasals come from? Are they innovated in Bantu according to the Crabb-Greenberg hypothesis (Crabb 1965; Greenberg 1963) or should they be reconstructed at the level of Proto-Niger-Congo (Miehe 1991)? (ii) Whichever position one takes, how does one derive the above and other distributions of nasal vs. oral noun class markers? If innovated, why should this occur only on noun markers in Bantu? If lost, why should this occur so generally outside of Bantu—and perhaps more mysteriously, only on concord markers within Narrow Bantu?

It is generally assumed that cognate noun class markers can be reconstructed at the Proto-Niger-Congo (PNC) level. Thus consider the resemblance in forms in Table 2, modified from the German Wikipedia entry "Kordofanische Sprachen", following Schadeberg (1981); Schadeberg (2011). While some of these resemblances are unmistakable, it is sometimes difficult to identify cognate noun classes between the most distant sub-branches, e.g. North Atlantic (Fula, Sereer) vs. Bantu (Wilson 1989: 96). While Schadeberg (2011) presents Kordofanian classes which are cognate with Bantu classes 1, 3, 4, 6, as in Table 3, there are several Kordo-

---

[1] I have changed Meeussen's and my transcriptions for Proto-Bantu and Proto-Grassfields Bantu, respectively. While Adere (EGB) has a class 7 nominal prefix e-, its prevocalic realization cw- may suggest *kɪ- for Eastern Grassfields Bantu as well. (Voorhoeve 1980).

7 More reflections on the nasal classes in Bantu

fanian pairings that Schadeberg is not able to identify with Bantu genders, e.g. Talodi ts-/ɲ-, ŋ-/s-, g-/n-, ḍ-/r- etc.

Table 2: Comparison of selected noun class marking across NC groups

	Class 1 Man, Woman	Classes 3/4 Tree(s), Wood(s)		Classes 5/6 Head(s), Name(s)		Class 6a Blood, Water
Kordofanian	gu-, w-, b-	gu-, w-, b-	j-, g-	li-, j-	ŋu-, m-	ŋ-
Atlantic	gu-	gu-	ci-	de-	ga-	ma-
Gur	-a	-bu	-ki	-de	-a	-ma
Kwa	o-	o-	i-	li-	a-	n-
Benue-Congo	u-	u-	ti-	li-	a-	ma-
Bantu nouns	mò-	mò-	mì-	ì-	à-	mà-
Bantu agr.	(j)ò-	gó-	gí-	dí-	gá-	má- ~ gá-

Table 3: Cognate noun classes in three branches of Kordofanian (Schadeberg 2011)

class	Heiban	Talodi	Rashad	class	Heiban	Talodi	Rashad
1 (sg.)	gw-	b-	w-	? (sg.)	ŋ-	ŋ-	—
3 (sg.)	gw-	b-	w-	? (pl.)	ɲ-	ɲ-	ɲ-
4 (pl.)	j-	g-	y-	? (pl.)	n-	n-	—
6 (pl. of 5)	ŋw-	m-	ŋ-				

As seen in Table 3, the assumed cognates classes cognate with Bantu 1, 3 and 4 do not exhibit nasal prefixes, while class 6, the plural of class 5, does. However, Kordofanian has other unidentified nasal classes, as seen to the right in Table 3. Where would these nasals have come from?

As mentioned, the position of Greenberg (1963) and Crabb (1965) is that Bantu innovated nasals in the noun prefixes of classes 1, 3, 4, 6, 9 and 10:

> ... Bantu has the prefixes *mu- and *mi- as against Semi-Bantu and West Sudanic *u- and *i-. This is certainly a Bantu innovation." (Greenberg 1963: 35)

It is significant, however, that other than the merger of class 6 *a- (plural of class 5) with liquid class 6a *ma-, no compelling explanation has been provided for how this might have happened. In addition, the actual situation is much more complex (cf. the extensive review in Hyman 1980c and below).

Contrasting with the Greenberg-Crabb hypothesis, Miehe's (1991) position is that the nasal prefixes should be reconstructed at the PNC stage. Two arguments are given: (i) There are reasonable cognate nasal prefixes and frozen relics for several nasal class markers outside of Bantu; (ii) The nasals in classes 1, 3, 4, 6, 9 and 10 are claimed to be gradually lost through erosion and possible re-prefixation.

Given the importance of these nasals in the history of Niger-Congo, it is surprising how little reaction there has been to Miehe's evidence, and the issue has been almost ignored. On the one hand there have been some brief reviews, e.g. Hedinger (1993) and Heath (1994), from which we can assume skepticism, but open-mindedness on the part of the latter:

> ... the heavy preponderance of *N- forms in the survey makes direct comparison with Bantu *mu- and *mi- adventurous. Unraveling cognate relationships among noun class prefixes is treacherous because of mergers and splits among noun classes, and analogical interaction between nominal prefixes and verbal agreement markers, in addition to phonological attrition and (in some languages) contraction or elimination of the prefix system. However, M does succeed in making a strong case for an original wide distribution of nasal prefixes in the semantic domains typical of Bantu classes, 1, 3 and 4 (among others). (Heath 1994: 863)

One can also cite positive mention by Williamson (1989: 40; 1993: 43-44), who however accepts Stewart's (1999b, 1999a; 2002) PNC reconstruction of nasalized V- prefixes instead of VN- (and presumably NV-):

> Accepting Stewart's hypothesis that the prefixes of classes 9 and 10 were originally close nasalized vowels rather than homorganic nasals, it is somewhat easier to explain why these old prefixes surface sometimes as close vowels, sometimes as homorganic nasals, and sometimes as both. (Williamson 1993: 44)

If we include Stewart in the mix, we are left with three hypotheses concerning nasality in the indicated noun classes: proto nasal consonants, proto nasalized vowels, no nasality. In my view we have not yet arrived at a solution that answers all of the relevant questions. Those following the Greenberg-Crabb hypothesis have to address the following questions: (i) Where did the Bantu nasals come from? This is not a problem for Miehe, who assumes they were present in PNC.

7 More reflections on the nasal classes in Bantu

(ii) How do we account for the nasals that Miehe reports outside Bantu? Again, this is not a problem for Miehe, as these represent retentions from PNC. However, even if these questions disappear with Miehe's hypothesis, other questions remain unresolved: (i) Why were the nasals lost in so much of Niger-Congo? While we can attribute this to phonetic erosion or replacement, it would seem odd that only nasal consonants were lost in those Benue-Congo languages which otherwise maintain CV- prefixes. (ii) Why were nasal consonants preserved in Bantu? (iii) Why does Bantu have nasal marking on nominals, but reconstructed non-nasal concord marking? E.g. Luganda class 3 ò-mù-tí gù-nó 'this tree'; class 4 è-mì-tí gì-nó 'these trees'. (iv) Is the nasal/oral distinction found anywhere in Niger-Congo outside Bantu? If not, why not? (v) What is the relation of the two sets of marking, e.g. class 3/4 *mò-/*mì- vs. *gʊ́-/*gí-? Why labial nasals vs. voiced oral velars? Why L tone on noun prefixes vs. H concord tone in most noun classes? Significantly, it is the concord forms which generally correspond to noun marking outside of Bantu.

To explain the nasal vs. oral marking of classes 1, 3, 4, 6, 9 and 10 in Bantu one might adopt one of three strategies: The first would be to reconstruct two sets of PNC allomorphs for these classes. While this could work, it simply delays the ultimate question of why there should be two sets of markers? We would want to know how they arose in pre-PNC, if that's the correct historical stage. To respond to this problem we might instead reconstruct two sets of distinct noun classes, which subsequently merged, as everyone assumes in the case of class 6 *a- (plural of class 5) and liquid/mass class 6a *ma-. There might also have been a plural class *mʊ- that merged with class 4 *mɪ-. In this view, PNC likely had more noun classes than Proto-Bantu (PB).

A quite different proposal would be to reconstruct one set of markers which split into two sets of allomorphs in a way as yet unexplained.[2] In order to consider how a single set of reconstructions might have split into labial nasal vs. velar oral allomorphs, note the partial or complete complementarity between reconstructed V, N, mV and gV markers in Table 4.

Among the gaps seen in Table 4, PB clearly lacks voiced velars on noun prefixes.[3] The concord prefixes, however, fill this gap: *jò- (1), *gʊ́- (3), *gí- (4), *gá- (6), *jì- (9), *jí- (10). Perhaps Gur *ŋV fills in the *gV gap, in which case Proto-Gur may have nasalized PNC *gʊ- and *ga-, which are of course identical to

---

[2] It is generally assumed that the [m] of classes 1, 3, and 4 and the homorganic nasal N- ([n]?) of classes 9 and 10 have similar distributions, although possibly different origins.

[3] I am ignoring cases where certain Bantu languages exploit a concord marker in secondary derivations, e.g. Luganda augmentative class 3 gu-/class 6 ga-: o-gu-tî 'a big tree', pl. a-ga-tî.

Table 4: Reconstructed Noun Class markers arranged by place of articulation

	Labial	Dental-Alveolar	Velar	Vowel/Nasal
PBC	*(pi-) *ba-, *bi-, *bù-	*ti- *li, *lu- *ma- ~ *na- (6a)	*kà-, *ki-, *ku-	*ù- (1), *ì- (9), *ú- (3), *í- (4,10), *a- (6)
PGur	*pʊ, *fʊ *ba, *bi, *bʊ, *wa *ma (6a), *mʊ (pl.)	*sɪ, *tʊ *ɖa, *ɖɪ *nɪ (9), *ni (10), *na	*ka, *kʊ *ŋʊ (3), *ŋa (6)	*ʊ (1), *i (4), *a
PB (nouns)	*pì-, *pà- *bà-, *bì-, *bʊ̀- *mʊ̀- (1,3), *mì- (4), *mà- (6a),	*tʊ̀- *dì-, *dʊ̀-	*kà-, *kɪ-, *kʊ̀-	*ì- (5) *N` - (9,10)

the PB class 3 and 6 concords. A proposal made by the students in my Spring (2013) Bantu and Niger-Congo seminar, inspired by the correlation between [gw, ŋw] and [b, m] in Kordofanian (Table 3), is the historical derivation $^*g^w > \eta^w > m$ (in PB noun prefixes).[4] The major question is where the nasality would have come from? Perhaps there was a nasal that preceded PB noun prefixes, thereby producing a derivation such as: $^*N\text{-}g^w > \eta g^w > \eta^w > m$.

Although this is speculative, and there are other possibilities (e.g. why not *bʊ-, *bɪ-, etc.?), Table 5 shows that there are attested shifts between labials and velars in Niger-Congo languages (Hyman 1980c: 200).

However, we still have the issue of determining where the nasality would have come from. Since Miehe (1991) there have been other developments that potentially interface with the problem at hand. First, Stewart (1999b), 1999a; 2002 proposes PNC nasalized vowels, which Williamson (1989: 40; 1993: 43-44) extends to noun class prefixes (although they are almost totally lacking in present-day languages). Also of potential importance is the role of the PB determiner prefix known as the "augment":

> A correct view of the augment as a correspondence in Bantu may enable us to bridge a gap between Bantu and the other Benue-Congo languages, by showing how the system of prefixes with differential m- ... arose. (Meeussen 1973: 13)

---

[4]Table 3 shows that Kordofanian likes nasals in its noun prefixes, including palatals and velars, which may represent an innovation of the sort considered here. Cf. Williamson's (1989: 40) proposal: $^*g^wu\text{-} > wu\text{-} > m\tilde{u} > mu\text{-}$.

Table 5: Labial-velar correspondences in Nupoid and Grassfields Bantu

	Gwari	Nupe	PNupoid		'child'	cf. PB	
a.	ēɓí	ēgī	*ɓí		'child'	*-bí-al-	'give birth'
	ēɓwá	ēgwā	*ɓɔ́(k)		'hand'	*-bókò	'arm, hand'
b.	Mankon	Bafmeng	PGB				
	àɓô	āγóʿ	*-ɓóʿ		'hand'	*-bókò	'arm, hand'
	nìɓòmɔ́	īγúm̃	*-ɓùm´		'egg'		
	ɓɨ́	γɔ́	*-ɓá		'they'	*bá-	SM, class 2

As seen in Table 6, the augment resembles oral noun prefixes with H tone as found outside Bantu, but also in the PB concord markers (de Blois 1970):[5]

Table 6: The augment in PB and two daughter languages

PB:	*ʊ́-mʊ- (1)	*gʊ́-mʊ- (3)	*gí-mɪ- (4)	*gá-mà- (6(a))	*ɪ́-Ǹ - (9)	*(j)í-Ǹ - (10)
Bukusu:	ó-mu-	kú-mù-	kí-mi-	ká-mà-	é-N-	cí-N-
Haya:	ó-mu-	ó-mu-	é-mi-	á-ma-	é-N-	é-N-

It has therefore been attractive to relate the non-Bantu oral prefixes to the augment. The significance of this move is seen from Grégoire & Janssens' (1999) demonstration that the augment+noun prefix sequence can simplify in one of two ways: (i) loss of the augment: V-CV- > CV-; (ii) loss of the noun class prefix: V-CV > V-. Starting with a PB reconstruction such as class 3 *gʊ́-mʊ̀-, loss of the augment would leave mʊ̀- as the noun prefix, while loss of the prefix would yield gʊ́- in concords (and in noun prefixes and suffixes outside of Bantu). This still does not explain why the two noun class markers should be different from each other.[6]

---

[5] In Table 6 Bukusu devoices *g > k by the Luyia Law (Hinnebusch et al. 1981), while Haya deletes the augment consonant, as in most Bantu. While the classes 1 and 9 augments are reconstructed as *L, I know of no Bantu language where they are distinguished tonally from other noun class augments.

[6] Williamson (1993) relates the class 9/10 split to the augment: Ǹ- (or a nasal vowel?) is the class 9/10 prefix, with class 10 often enhanced by an augment, e.g. Kikongo m-bwa 'dog', pl. zi-m-bwa.

Note that de Wolf (1971) reconstructs the above noun class prefixes in PBC with the shape V-, not CV-. However, Hyman (1980c), Miehe (1991) and especially Grégoire & Janssens (1999) show different ways to derive a V- prefix (variant VN-). In the following potential changes, note the potential differences in tonal outcome (although high tone prefixes, especially V-, can independently become L as a kind of reduction process):

(1) a. CV prefix without augment
   i. the consonant drops: *CV̀- > V̀-, e.g. class 7 *kì- > ì-; class 12 *kà- > à-
   ii. the NV metathesizes: *mV̀- > V̀m- > V̀N-

b. CV prefix with vocalic augment
   i. the prefix drops: *V́-CV̀- > V́-, e.g. class 7 *í-kì- > í-; class 12 *á-kà- > á-
   ii. the prefix vowel drops: *V́-mV̀- > V́-N- (>V́-), e.g. class 3 *ó-mò- > óN-; class 4 *í-mì- > *íN-

With this in mind, note the different realization of classes 1, 3, 4, 6 vs. 6a and plural "18a" in Tuki (Hyman 1980a; cf. Musada (1995)), which derives *VN*- from /V-mV-/:

(2) a. class 1: òŋ-gìnī 'guest, stranger' (but cf. *mo-to* 'person', *mw-ànā* 'child')
   class 3: òŋ-gòlō 'foot' òm-bàβē 'wing' ò-tēmā 'heart'
   class 4: ìŋ-gòlō 'feet' ìm-bàβē 'wings' ì-tēmā 'hearts'
   class 6: àŋ-bāné 'breasts' àŋ-bīlé 'palmtree' à-tānē 'stones' (àŋ- > à-)

b. class 6a: mà-tīá 'water' mà-wūtē 'fat'
   class 18a: mù-nū 'brain' mù-nɔ́ɔ̀ní 'birds' (cf. PNC "6b", PGur 22 **mʊ*)

In (2b), the two *mV*- classes (6a, 18a) perhaps lacked an augment by virtue of their semantics. Tuki has other *CV*- prefixes, *bà*- (2), *bì*- (8), *nò*- (11), *wù*- (14) without augment, which may have fallen out. Dugast (1971: 65) reports comparable data concerning collectives in Tunen (cf. Mous 2003: 302–303), e.g. *ò-n-dɔ̀mb* 'sheep' (class 3), pl. *è-n-dɔ̀mb* (class 4), *mà-n-dɔ̀mb* 'types of sheep' (class 6).

Signalons enfin que nous rencontrerons un collectif dont le préfixe paraît présenter un prépréfixe (ama- > am-, əm-). (Dugast 1971: 65)

7 More reflections on the nasal classes in Bantu

The history of noun class marking and ultimately nasality may thus implicate the presence of an augment—or different augments, as the case may be. The differential behavior of 1, 3, 4, 6, 9, 10 marking may also be attributed to a reconstructed (or evolved) *V vs. *CV shape. One attractive idea (for which, unfortunately, there is no evidence), is that there was a morpheme whose final [m] syllabifies with V-initial prefixes, but otherwise drops out before a consonant-initial prefix:

(3) a. *Vm-V- > V-mV- > mV- (1, 3, 4, 6)
    b. *Vm-CV- > V-CV- > CV- (2, 7, 8 etc.)

The loss of the initial *j or *g may also account for the merger of classes 4 (pl.) and 9 (sg.) in a number of Bantu languages (Tables 7 & 8).

Table 7: Merger of classes 9 and 4 in Haya (Byarushengo 1977: 8)

	Haya	noun	subject	numeral	object	connective
	class 9	Ǹ-	è-	è-	-gi-	ya-
	class 4	mì-	è-	è-	-gi-	ya-
cf.	class 8	bì-	bí-	bí-	-bi-	bya-

Table 8: Merger of classes 9 and 4 in Tunen (Dugast 1971, Mous 2003: 300-2)

	Tunen	noun	subject	numeral	ProPref	cl.6 collective
	class 9	mè-, èN-	yè-	é-	yè	
	class 4	mè-, èN-	yé-	í-	yí	mà-Ñ-
cf.	class 8	bè-	bé-	bé-	-bí-	

Another factor that should be considered is the sporadic evidence of relic noun class suffixation in Bantu, which is more widespread elsewhere in Niger-Congo. It is likely that such suffixes never contained a nasal in classes 1, 3, 4, 6, 9 and 10. Again, the nasal classes may have had -V (vs. -CV) suffixes, as in Tiv (Voorhoeve & de Wolf 1969: 52, based on Arnott).

If classes 1, 3, 4, 6, 9 and 10 had a -V suffix, then when suffix vowels dropped, the whole suffix was lost. The alternative is that these classes had earlier wV, yV and ɣV markers, where the glide first drops out, then the vowel. Note also that class 14 and 15 *Cu- prefixes drop out entirely (class 3 leaves relics). There

Table 9: Tiv Noun Classes

class	noun affixes	adjective	subject (pr.cont.)	subject (past)	'my'
1	∅	ù-	ŋgù	a	w-àḿ
2	ù-, mbà- -v	mbà- -v́	mbá↓	ve	á↓ -v́
3	(ú-)	ú-	ŋgú↓	u	w-áḿ
4, 5, 10	í-	í-	ŋgí↓	i	y-áḿ
6	á-	á-	ŋgá↓	a	áḿ
6a	ḿ- -ḿ	mà- -ḿ	má↓	ma	á↓ -ḿ
7	í- -ý	kì- -ý	kí↓	ki	y- á↓ -ý
8	í- -v́	mbì- -v́	mbí↓	mbi	á↓ -v́
9	ì-	ì-	ŋgì	ì	y-àḿ
14	-v́	mbù- -v́	mbú↓	mbu	á↓ -v́
15	-ý	kù- -ý	kú↓	ku	á↓ -ý

is a similar distribution of suffixes in Noni (Hyman 1980c: 188). Understanding the nasals thus necessarily means understanding that the forms from different parts of a paradigm may originally have been different, may come to be different, and may influence the future of a system, e.g. whether nasals are spreading vs. retracting.

Finally, it should be noted that having a nasal (N) vs. oral (O) concord is not an all or nothing thing (Hyman 1980c: 194-5). One of the aforementioned noun classes can have nasal concord, another oral. Thus note the following out of 52 Bantu languages (mostly Northwest, Table 10).

Table 10: Distribution of nasal concord by Noun Class

class 3	class 4	class 6(a)	total	observations
N	N	N	20	11/20 are in zone C
O	N	N	18	12/18 are in zones A-B
O	O	N	14	7/20 are in zones D-F

The class 3, 4, and 6(a) distributions N-O-N, N-N-O, O-N-O and O-O-N are all unattested. We thus can draw the following implicational scale: class 3 N ⊃ class 4 N ⊃ class 6 N.

7 More reflections on the nasal classes in Bantu

Occasionally non-Bantu languages have a nasal in their pronoun system which resembles Bantu. Thus the Fula [North Atlantic] third person singular human subject and object pronoun *mo* (Arnott 1970) and the Wawa [Bantoid] third person singular human pronoun *mū* (Martin 2012: 169) ought to be cognate with the Proto-Bantu class 1 object marker *-mu-. Similarly re class 1 *mù* and class 3 *mū* pronouns in Esimbi [Bantoid]. As seen in Table 11, from Stallcup (S) (1980: 142) and Koenig et al. (2013: 8–9, 27), the other pronouns resemble the corresponding noun class prefixes. For some reason the two sources give different oral vs. nasal reflexes on the noun prefixes of classes 2, 6a, 14, and 18a (Table 11).

Table 11: Esimbi Noun Class prefixes and pronouns

class	noun (S)	noun (K et al)	Pronoun	/I, U, A/ =archiphonemes
1	(w)Ǔ-	((w)U)-	mù[a]	Koenig et al. exx. have L or M tone
2	bÀ-	mA-	bú	why L tone?
3	Ú	U-	mū	
5	Í			
6	Á	A-	zú	
6a	bÀ-, m-	mA-	bù	note L tone; *m-* is used before /b/
7	kI-	kI-	kī	
8	bI-	mI-	bī	
9	Ì-	I-	zù	exx. from Koenig et al. have L tone
10	Í-	I-	zú	exx. from Koenig et al. have non-L tone
12	kA-	kU-, kA-	kū	
13	tA-	tU-, tA-	tí	
14	bÚ-	mU-	bú	
18a	bÙ-	mU-	bù	note L tone
19	sÍ-	sI-	sī	

[a]Cf. the object marker -ŋw-. In symbols /I, U, A/ stand for archiphonemes whose vowel height depends on the following stem.

The fact that one dialect denasalizes class 6 and 18a prefixes and the other nasalizes class 2 and 8 prefixes is something which repeats itself elsewhere in Bantoid, e.g. Ekoid (Watters 1980: 133), Kenyang (Voorhoeve 1980), and Mbe (Bamgbose 1965)—and even Narrow Bantu, e.g. zone C denasalization of *mV- > bV-. Any proposed scenario such as *gw > m must be grounded in what we know about the natural history of nasality.

In conclusion, Miehe's (1991) demonstration of widespread nasals still leaves a lot to interpret: Who had what when? How did everyone get what they have today? What does this say about the evolution of noun class systems: mergers, splits, loss? (cf. Good 2012). There is still a lot of work to do before we can arrive at a definitive solution to the issues that I have outlined above.

Acknowledgements

I would like to thank Gudrun Miehe, my co-organizer in Paris of the workshop "Nasal Noun Class Prefixes in Bantu: Innovated or Inherited?", at the 5th International Conference on Bantu Languages, June 12, 2013, at which this paper was first presented, and the other presenters: Jeff Good, Jesse Lovegren, Konstantin Pozdniakov, Valentin Vydrin, and John Watters. I also thank the doctoral students in my Spring (2013) Seminar on Bantu and Niger-Congo who were full of ideas and enthusiasm: Matt Faytak, Florian Lionnet, Jack Merrill, Zachary O'Hagan, Nik Rolle.

References

Arnott, D. W. 1970. *The nominal and verbal systems of Fula*. Oxford: Clarendon Press.

Bamgbose, Ayo. 1965. Nominal classes in mbe. *Afrika und Übersee* 49. 32–53.

Byarushengo, Ernest Rugwa. 1977. Preliminaries. In Alessandro Duranti Ernest R. Byarushengo & Larry M. Hyman (eds.), *Haya grammatical structure* (Southern California Occasional Papers in Linguistics 6), 1–15. Los Angeles: Department of Linguistics, University of Southern California. http://gsil.sc-ling.org/pubs/SCOPILS_6_7_8_9/Haya_grammatical_structure.pdf.

Crabb, David W. 1965. *Ekoid Bantu languages of Ogoja, Eastern Nigeria* (West African Languages Monographs 4). Cambridge: Cambridge University Press.

de Blois, Kees F. 1970. The augment in the Bantu languages. *Africana Linguistica* 4. 85–165.

de Wolf, Paul P. 1971. *The noun class system of Proto-Benue-Congo*. The Hague: Mouton.

Dugast, Idelette. 1971. *Grammaire du tunɛn*. Paris: Klincksieck.

Good, Jeff. 2012. How to become a "Kwa" noun. *Morphology* 22. 294–335.

Greenberg, Joseph H. 1963. The languages of Africa. *IJAL* Part II, No. 1(29).

Grégoire, Claire & Baudouin Janssens. 1999. L'augment en bantou du nord-ouest. In Jean-Marie Hombert & Larry M. Hyman (eds.), *Bantu historical linguistics: Theoretical and empirical perspectives.* 413–429. Stanford: CSLI. http://gsil.sc-ling.org/pubs/SCOPILS_1_3_4/studies_in_bantu_tonology.pdf.

Heath, Jeffrey. 1994. Review of miehe (1991). *Language* 70. 862–3.

Hedinger, Robert. 1993. Review of Miehe 1991. *Afrika und Übersee* 76. 145–147.

Hinnebusch, Thomas H., Derek Nurse & Martin Mould. 1981. *Studies in the classification of Eastern Bantu languages.* Hamburg: Helmut Buske Verlag.

Hyman, Larry M. 1980a. Esquisse des classes nominales en tuki. In Larry M. Hyman (ed.), *Noun classes in the Grassfields Bantu borderland* (Southern California Occasional Papers in Linguistics 8), 27–36. Los Angeles: Department of Linguistics, University of Southern California.

Stallcup, Kenneth L. 1980. Noun classes in Esimbi. In Larry M. Hyman (ed.), *Noun classes in the Grassfields Bantu borderland* (Southern California Occasional Papers in Linguistics 8), 139–153. Los Angeles: Department of Linguistics, University of Southern California.

Hyman, Larry M. 1980b. Reflections on the nasal classes in Bantu. In Larry M. Hyman (ed.), *Noun classes in the Grassfields Bantu borderland* (Southern California Occasional Papers in Linguistics 8), 179–210. Los Angeles: Department of Linguistics, University of Southern California. http://gsil.sc-ling.org/pubs/SCOPILS_6_7_8_9/Noun_classes_in_the_grassfields_bantu_borderland.pdf.

Hyman, Larry M. 1980c. Reflections on the nasal classes in Bantu. In Larry M. Hyman (ed.), *Noun classes in the Grassfields Bantu borderland* (Southern California Occasional Papers in Linguistics 8), 179–210. Los Angeles: Department of Linguistics, University of Southern California.

Koenig, Brad, Arnie Coleman & Karen Coleman. 2013. *Grammar sketch of Esimbi.* Ms.

Martin, Marieke. 2012. *A grammar of Wawa.* University of Kent Doctoral dissertation.

Meeussen, A. E. 1967. Bantu grammatical reconstructions. *Africana Linguistica* 3. 79–121.

Meeussen, A. E. 1973. Test cases for method. *African Language Studies: Papers on Comparative Bantu* 14. 6–18.

Miehe, Gudrun. 1991. *Die Präfixnasale im Benue-Congo und im Kwa: Versuch einer Widerlegung der Hypothese von der Nasalinnovation des Bantu.* Berlin: Reimer.

Mous, Maarten. 2003. Nen (A44). In Derek Nurse & Gérard Philippson (eds.), *The Bantu languages*, 283–306. London: Routledge.

Musada, Augustin. 1995. *Eléments de description du tuki (langue bantoue du Cameroun A61)*. Université Libre de Bruxelles Mémoire de Licence.

Schadeberg, Thilo. 1981. The classification of the Kadugli language group. In Thilo C. Schadeberg & M. Lionel Bender (eds.), *Nilo-Saharan*, 291–305. Dordrecht: Foris Publications.

Schadeberg, Thilo C. 2011. *The unique nature of the Niger-Congo noun class system, and a comparison of event participant marking in Bantu and Ebang (Kordofanian)*. Paper presented at the Fourth International Conference on Bantu Languages, Berlin.

Stewart, John M. 1999a. An explanation of Bantu vowel height harmony in terms of a pre-Bantu nasalized vowel lowering. *Journal of African Languages and Linguistics* 21. 161–178.

Stewart, John M. 1999b. Nasal vowel creation without nasal consonant deletion, and the eventual loss of nasal vowels thus created: The pre-Bantu case. In Jean-Marie Hombert & Larry M. Hyman (eds.), *Bantu historical linguistics: Theoretical and empirical perspectives*, 207–233. Stanford: CSLI.

Stewart, John M. 2002. The potential of Proto-Potou-Akanic-Bantu as a pilot Proto-Niger-Congo, and the reconstructions updated. *Journal of African Languages and Linguistics* 23. 197–224.

Voorhoeve, Jan. 1980. Kenyang. In Larry M. Hyman & Jan Voorhoeve (eds.), *Les classes nominales dans le bantou des grassfields*, 275–285. Paris: SELAF.

Voorhoeve, Jan & Paul P. de Wolf (eds.). 1969. *Benue-Congo noun class systems*. Leiden: Afrika Studiecentrum.

Watters, John R. 1980. The Ejagham noun class system: Ekoid Bantu revisited. In Larry M. Hyman (ed.), *Noun classes in the Grassfields Bantu borderland* (Southern California Occasional Papers in Linguistics 8), 99–137. Los Angeles: Department of Linguistics, University of Southern California.

Williamson, Kay. 1993. The noun prefixes of Benue-Congo. *Journal of African Languages & Linguistics* 14. 29–45.

Wilson, W. A. A. 1989. Atlantic. In John Bendor-Samuel (ed.), *The Niger-Congo languages*, 81–104. Lanham, MD: University Press of America.

Name index

Adwiraah, Eleonore, 115, 125
Akumbu, Pius Wuchu, 182
Anderson, Stephen C., 82, 86, 87
Anonymous, 115, 126
Armstrong, Robert G., 7, 118, 164
Arnott, D. W., 177, 233

Babaev, Kirill V., 216
Bamgbose, Ayo, 234
Bastin, Yvonne, 15
Bearth, Thomas, 43
Bendor-Samuel, John, 72, 74
Bennett, Patrick R., 1, 2
Bertho, J., 62
Bhat, D. N. S., 218
Bila, Emmanuel Neba, 182, 191–193
Blench, Roger M., 1, 2, 4, 6–8, 18, 20, 28, 36, 59–61, 77, 82, 89, 94, 108–111, 113, 115, 119, 121, 125, 129, 132, 141, 142, 148, 152, 154, 155, 158, 160, 164, 166, 174, 179, 180
Boettger, E., 65
Boettger, V., 65
Bond, Oliver, 43
Bostoen, Koen, 178, 193
Boum, Marie Anne, 37
Bouquiaux, Luc, 109, 114, 120, 121
Boyd, 4
Bryan, Margaret A., 14, 62, 109
Byarushengo, Ernest Rugwa, 231

Campbell, Lyle, 10
Childs, G. Tucker, 35
Clements, George N., 34
Conant, Francis Paine, 72, 89
Connell, Bruce, 31, 33, 178
Cook, Thomas L., 36
Crabb, David W., 15, 224, 225
Creissels, Denis, 37, 217
Crozier, David, 59, 63, 78, 80–82, 108, 109, 125, 142, 152, 154

Davey, Niffer, 89–91
De Blois, Kees F., 37, 229
De Wolf, Paul P., 2, 10, 12, 21, 27–35, 39–41, 44–47, 50, 51, 100, 110, 164, 223, 230, 231
Demuth, Katherine, 36, 41
Dettweiler, Sonia G., 65, 74, 78, 94
Dettweiler, Stephen H., 65, 72–74, 78, 94
Di Carlo, Pierpaolo, 31
Di Luzio, Aldo, 82, 86
Dihoff, Ivan, 115, 131
Dimmendaal, Gerrit J., 35, 36, 40, 41, 51
Doneux, Jean L., 177
Dryer, Matthew S., 39
Dugast, Idelette, 230, 231
Dunn, Ernest F., 33
Dusu, B., 120

Ehret, Christopher, 8

Name index

Elimelech, Baruch, 213

Faraclas, Nicholas G., 33, 36
Fennig, Charles D., 4, 5
Follingstad, Carl, 125
Follingstad, Joy A., 115, 125, 128, 129

Gerhardt, Ludwig, 2, 33, 47, 59, 62, 94, 109, 110, 125, 134, 141, 142, 191
Good, Jeff, 21, 31, 32, 34, 41, 211, 234
Goroh, Martin K., 134
Grebe, Karl, 210
Green, M. M., 32
Greenberg, Joseph H., 1, 2, 14, 18, 34, 35, 59, 62, 109, 142, 164, 224, 225
Guarisma, Gladys, 193, 215
Gunn, Harold D., 72, 89, 108
Guthrie, Malcolm, 14, 15, 33, 42
Gya, Daniel, 115

Hackett, Chris, 89–91
Hagen, Eva, 115, 125, 133
Hall, Robert A., 10
Hansford, Keir L., 142
Harro, Gretchen, 202
Haynes, Nancy, 202
Heath, Jeffrey, 226
Hedinger, Robert, 215, 226
Heine, Bernd, 4, 15
Henrici, Alick, 4, 15
Henson, Bonnie, 178
Hinnebusch, Thomas H., 229
Hoffmann, Carl, 35–37, 70, 72, 74, 78, 80, 116, 141
Hombert, Jean-Marie, 39
Horton, A. E., 42

Hyman, Larry M., 15, 18, 20, 29, 31, 33, 34, 36, 37, 40, 43–46, 71, 173–178, 183, 193, 202–204, 210, 215, 223, 226, 228, 230, 232
Hyuwa, Daniel D., 115

Idiata, Daniel Franck, 173
Idiatov, Dmitry, 42
Igwe, Rev. G. E., 32
Imoh, Philip Manda, 96

Janssens, Baudouin, 229, 230
Jisa, Harriet, 182
Jockers, Heinz, 110, 115, 131
Johnston, Harry H., 1, 14
Jones, Randy, 204
Jungraithmayr, Herrmann, 29, 33, 34

Kamba Muzenga, J. G., 202, 216, 217
Kanu, Sullay Mohamed, 177
Katamba, Francis X., 29, 37
Kaufman, Terrence, 51
Kiessling, Roland, 182, 191
Koelle, Sigismund W., 62, 109, 125
Koenig, Brad, 233
Kuhn, Hanna, 120

Leroy, Jacqueline, 174, 178, 200, 202, 215
Longtau, Selbut R., 118, 161, 163
Loos, Eugene, 113
Lovegren, Jesse, 21, 30, 33, 39, 47, 48

MacDonell, James, 94
Mackay, H. D., 118, 164
Maddieson, Ian, 109, 117
Magaji, Daniel J., 71
Maho, Jouni Filip, 27, 28, 30, 33, 34, 123

Name index

Martin, Marieke, 233
Mba, Gabriel, 173, 178, 191
McGill, Stuart, 60, 61, 63, 78–80, 100
Mchombo, Sam A., 177
McKinney, Carol, 115, 125
McKinney, Norris, 125
Meek, Charles K., 62, 108
Meeussen, A. E., 15, 18, 40, 44, 173, 176, 216, 223, 228
Miehe, Gudrun, 31, 109, 176, 223, 224, 226, 228, 230, 234
Mihas, Elena, 213
Mort, Katharine, 89, 92
Moser, Rex, 118, 119
Mous, Maarten, 215, 216, 230, 231
Muller, Jean-Claude, 109
Musada, Augustin, 230

Ndawouo, Martine, 191
Nettle, Daniel, 117, 152
Newman, Paul, 189
Ngangoum Bernard, R. P., 191
Ngantcho Lebika, Francine, 178
Ngue Um, Emmanuel, 178
Nguendjio, Emile-Gille, 190
Ngum, Comfort Che, 188, 189
Nichols, Johanna, 191
Nurse, Derek, 17
Nzang-Bie, Yolande, 178, 193

Orwig, Carol, 178

Parker, Elizabeth, 213, 217
Paterson, Rebecca, 63, 72, 75, 76
Piron, Pascale, 174, 200
Poser, William J., 10
Pozdniakov, Konstantin, 199
Price, Norman, 116, 141

Ramirez, Cristi, 215

Regnier, Clark D. A., 75
Rialland, Annie, 34
Rikoto, Bulu Doro, 73
Rowlands, E. C., 59, 62, 75, 89, 111
Rueck, Michael J., 116, 137

Schadeberg, Thilo, 224
Schadeberg, Thilo C., 30, 38, 173, 176, 177, 224, 225
Schaub, Willi, 192
Seitz, Gitte, 114, 118, 119
Shimizu, Kiyoshi, 2, 82, 86, 89, 109, 110, 118, 119, 121, 152, 164
Sibomana, Leo, 117, 118, 161
Siewierska, Anna, 218
Simons, Gary F., 4, 5
Smith, Philip, 94
Smith, Rebecca Dow, 63
Spreda, Klaus, 213
Stallcup, Kenneth L., 21, 174, 175, 194, 200, 201, 213, 233
Stanley, Carol, 215
Sterk, Jan P., 1, 2
Stewart, John M, 228
Stofberg, Yvonne, 117, 155, 156
Storch, Anne, 33

Tadadjeu, Maurice, 202
Tamanji, Pius, 178, 191
Temple, Olive, 74, 75, 108
Thomas, John Paul, 33
Thomason, Sarah G., 51
Thwing, Rhonda Ann, 36, 190
Trager, George L., 10

Van de Velde, Mark L. O., 30, 39
Voeltz, Erhard, 177, 194
Voorhoeve, Jan, 15, 21, 31, 33, 174, 205, 213, 215, 224, 231, 234

Name index

Watters, John R., 15, 17, 18, 20, 21, 33, 37, 39, 48, 174, 182, 200, 213, 215, 217, 234
Weier, Hans-Ingolf, 216
Welmers, William E., 30, 35
Westermann, Diedrich, 1, 14, 62, 109
Williamson, Kay, 1, 2, 4, 7, 15, 18, 28–30, 33, 35, 37, 40, 47, 60, 109, 118, 152, 164, 176, 226, 229
Wilson, Janet E., 141
Wilson, W. A. A., 177, 224
Winston, F. D. D., 14
Wolff, Hans, 114
Wood, Esther Jane, 186, 187

Yoder, Zachariah, 89

Language index

Abadi, 78
Abar, 48, 49
Acipa, 78, 89
Acipawa, 78
Acrɔ, 114
Acrɔ-Obiro, 118
Adamawa, iv
Adere, 175, 200, 203, 224^1
Afo, 164
Agadi, 78
Agaushi, 78
Aghem, 36, 36^{12}, 38, 174, 200, 203, 204, 207–209
Agwara, 66, 78, 103
Ahwai, 137
Ake, 109, 117, 155, 157–160
Akɔɔse, 215, 216
Alumic, 112, 148
Alumu, 148
Alumu-Təsu, 117, 147
Alumu-əsu, 148
Amic, 83
Amo, 86
Angan, 133
Anib, 116, 142
Ashe, 115, 134
Atakar, 115, 128
Atlantic, iv, 8, 176, 225
Auna, 78
Ayu, 107, 116, 142

Baangi, 66, 103

Baba I, 180
Babadjou, 203
Babanki, 174, 184, 187, 189, 200, 203, 204, 207–209
Babanki (Kejom), 180, 182
Babessi, 174, 200, 208
Babete, 203
Babungo, 174, 180, 192, 200, 207–210
Bafia, 181, 193, 215, 216
Bafmeng, 174, 200, 207–209, 229
Bafut, 175, 178, 181, 182, 184, 189, 191, 192, 200
Bagam, 203
Bakoko, 181
Baleng, 203
Bali, 175, 200, 203
Balong, 181
Baloum, 203
Bamendjou, 203
Bamenyan, 203
Bamileke, 33, 175, 182, 190, 200
Bamun, 175, 200, 203
Bandjoun, 203
Bane, 21
Bangang, 203
Bangangte, 33, 202, 203
Bangawa, 78
Bangou, 203
Bangwa, 181, 190, 203
Bantoid, 2–4, 4^2, 5, 6, 8–11, 14–22, 28, 39, 60^1, 92, 107, 112, 174,

Language index

174^2, 179, 189, 191–194, 223, 233
Bantoid-Cross, 2, 4, 5, 8, 17
Bantu, v, 1, 2, 4, 6, 8–10, 12–22, 27, 29, 30, 30^4, 30^5, 31–33, 33^9, 34, 35, 36^{12}, 37, 38, 38^{15}, 39, 40, 42, 43, 43^{20}, 44, 44^{22}, 45, 45^{23}, 60, 62, 63, 65, 68, 77, 80, 82, 92, 100, 108, 110, 123, 127, 129, 130, 137, 143, 159, 164, 166, 173^1, 174, 176, 176^3, 176^4, 178, 178^6, 179, 187^9, 190–194, 200, 223–227, 227^3, 228, 229, 229^5, 231–234
Bantu zone A, 178
Bapi, 203
Bariba, 62
Basa, 60, 62, 64, 67, 95–98, 100, 103
Basa Kontagora, 67, 103
Basa language cluster, 96
Basa-Benue, 67, 96–98, 103
Basa-Gumna, 67, 96, 103
Basa-Gurara, 67, 96, 103
Basa-Gurmana, 96
Basa-Kamuku, 97
Basa-Kontagora, 96
Basa-Kwali, 96
Basa-Kwomu, 96
Basa-Makurdi, 67, 96, 103
Basaa, 181, 194
Basaá, 215, 216
Bashar, 118
Basherawa, 110
Bati, 203
Batie, 203
Batoufam, 203
Baushi, 67, 94, 94^7, 95, 103

Beboid, 4, 19, 182, 210
Begbere, 134
Benue, 110, 225
Benue-Congo, iv, v, 1, 2, 4^2, 5–8, 14, 18, 27, 28^1, 32, 32^6, 33–35, 37, 38, 43, 60^1, 77, 100, 110, 112, 118, 122, 164, 191, 194, 223, 227, 228
Benue-Cross, 1, 109
Berom, 107, 108, 111, 114, 120–124
Beromic, 2, 112, 120, 121
Bin, 83
Bina, 83
Bishi, 83
Bo-Rukul, 112, 117, 152
Bobe, 14
Boze, 82, 86, 103
    see also εBoze
Bu-Niŋkada, 116, 142
Buji, 82, 83
Bukusu, 229, 229^5
Bum, 174, 200, 207, 208
Busa, 69
Butu-Ningi, 83

C'lela, 36, 36^{12}, 37, 39
Cahwai, 83
Cara, 109, 114, 120, 121
Ce, 116, 142, 144
Central Berom, 121
    see also Berom
Central Nigerian, 2, 5
Chadic, 111, 121, 148, 152, 160, 189
Chichewa, 177
Cicipu, 63, 64, 66, 78, 80, 100, 103
Cinda, 67, 89, 92, 103
Cinda cluster, 90
CiShingini, 66, 103

Language index

Cishingini, 80, 82
cLela, 66, 70, 72, 73, 75, 77
cLela Ribah, 102
cLela Zuru, 102
Cokobo, 83
Common Bantoid, 174
    see also Bantoid
Common Bantu, 15, 216
    see also Bantu
Cori, 115, 131
Cross River, 2, 3, 5, 8, 15, 19, 20, 27, 36, 43, 60^1, 107, 112
Cumbri, 77
Cèn, 129
cəHungwəryə, 90
C'lela, 13

Dakarkari, 36, 62, 72
Dakoid, 4, 4^2, 110, 112
Damakawa, 66, 72, 102
Dogon, iv
Doka, 114, 118
Dschang, 202, 203
Du, 121
Duguza, 83
Duka, 62, 74
Dukanci, 74
Dukawa, 74
Dungu, 83

East, 103, 112
    see also East Kainji; East Plateau
East and West Kainji, 62
East Benue-Congo, v, 1, 2, 7, 8, 27, 28, 28^1, 29, 30, 30^5, 31–33, 33^8, 33^9, 35, 35^{11}, 36, 37, 37^{14}, 38, 38^{16}, 39, 40, 40^{17}, 41, 42^{19}, 43, 44, 44^{22}, 47, 48, 50, 51, 60, 60^1, 107, 109, 111
East Kainji, 59, 60, 63, 64, 82, 83, 101, 119, 158
East Plateau, 152
Eastern Benue-Congo, 1
Eastern Berom, 122
Eastern Ejagham, 217
Eastern Grassfields, 21, 200
    see also Eastern Grassfields Bantu; EGB
Eastern Grassfields Bantu, 175, 199–201, 224^1
    see also Eastern Grassfields; EGB
Eastern Kwa, 1, 60^1
Eastern South-Central Niger-Congo, 2
εBoze, 83, 84, 84^6, 86
Eda, 114, 118
Ẹda, 118, 119
Edo, 32, 33^7
Ẹdo, 164
Edoid, 60^1
Edra, 114, 118
Ẹdra, 118
Efik, 36
EGB, 174, 175, 178, 182, 200–203, 205, 207, 216, 224^1
    see also Eastern Grassfields (Bantu)
Eggon, 107, 110, 117, 155, 157
Eggonic, 112, 117, 154, 155, 157
Ẹhwa, 114, 118
Ejagham, 17, 20, 48, 182, 215–217
Ẹjẹgha, 114, 118
Ekoid, 4, 11, 14–17, 20, 234
Eleme, 33, 43

Language index

Eloyi, 112, 118, 164
Esimbi, 233
ət-Jiir, *see* Jiir
ət-Kag, *see* Kag
ət-ma-Koor, *see* Koor
ət-Us, *see* Us
ət-Zuksun, *see* Zuksun
Evadi, 78

Fakai, 63, 75
Fakawa, 75
Fer, 75, 102
Fe'fe', 175, 191, 200, 202, 203
Fomopea, 203
Fondanti, 203
Foron, 121
Fotouni, 203
French, 10[4], 108
Fula, 177, 224, 233
Fungwa, 67, 94, 94[7], 95, 103
Fyem, 117, 152
Fəràn, 115, 129

Gamo-Ningi, 83
Gana, 83
Ganda, 37
Ganàng, 115, 129
Gbari, 71
Gbiri, 103
Gbiri-Niragu, 83
Ghomala, 175, 200
Gokana, 33
Grassfields, 4, 9, 16, 19–21, 46, 123
    see also Grassfields Bantu
Grassfields Bantu, 33, 33[9], 36, 37[14], 174, 175, 178, 194, 200, 215, 219
    see also Grassfields
Gunu, 178, 178[5], 181, 185

Gur, iv, 4[2], 62, 194, 225, 227
Gurmana, 62, 67, 94, 94[7], 95, 103
Gwamhyə, 102
Gwamhyə, 66
Gwantu cluster, 142
Gwara, 115, 134
Gwari, 229
Gworok, 115, 128
Gyem, 83
Gyong, 115, 133, 134
Gyongic, 115, 125

Ham, 109
Hasha, 117, 147, 148
Hausa, 60, 74, 75, 82, 84, 88, 118
Haya, 229, 229[5], 231
Heiban, 225
Horom, 117, 152, 153
Horom-Fyem, 112
Hun, 66, 102
Hun-Saare, 60, 62, 72, 74
Hungwəryə, 67, 103
Hungwəryə, 90, 92
Hungwəryə, 89, 90, 100
Huntu, 155
Hyam, 109, 131, 132, 157
Hyam cluster, 115
Hyamic, 115, 125, 131–133
Hɨpɨn, 95
Hɨpɨna, 103

Ibeto, 78
iBunu, 82, 83
Icèn, 115
Idoma, 164
Idomoid, 164
Idon, 114, 118
Idũ, 115, 134
Igbo, 32, 33[7], 164

Language index

Igboid, 8
iGusu, 83
Iguta, 83
Ijoid, iv
Iku-Gora-Ankwe, 114, 118
iLoro, 83
Indo-European, iv, 10
Inkwai, 90
iPanawa, 83
Isu, 174, 180, 200, 208
Iten, 114, 120, 121
iZele, 83
Izere, 109, 111, 115, 125, 129, 129^6, 130, 164
Izere of Fobur, 129, 130
Izeric, 115, 125, 129
ì-Zora, *see* Zora

Janji, 83
Jarawan, 4, 4^1
Jarawan Bantu, 191
Jere, 83
Jiir, 75, 102
Jijili, 117
Jili, 117, 157
Jilic, 112, 117, 154, 155
Jju, 115, 128, 128^4
Jos Group, 83
Jukunoid, 2, 3, 5, 8, 15, 19, 20, 27, 60, 60^1, 62, 107, 109, 110, 112

Kacicere, 115, 128
Kadara, 118
Kaduna, 83
Kafancan, 115, 128
Kag, 72, 75, 102
Kagare, 103
Kagoma, 115, 133

Kainji, 2–5, 8–13, 15, 19, 20, 36, 59, 60, 60^1, 61–65, 70, 73, 77, 94, 97, 99–102, 107, 109–112, 151, 166
Kaivi, 83
Kakihum, 78
Kako, 181
Kamanton, 115, 133
Kambari, 62–64, 66, 77, 78, 80, 89, 94, 97, 103
Kambari cluster, 101
Kambari I, 78
Kambari I and II, 77
Kambari II, 78
Kamberi, 77
Kamuku, 62, 64, 67, 78, 89, 94^7, 97, 103
Kamuku cluster, 94
Kaniji, 86
Kaninkwom, 142
Kanufi, 142
Karisen, 78
Kataf, 128
Katanza, 142
Kelawa, 75
Kelinchi, 75
Kemezung, 180
Kenyang, 180, 215, 216, 234
Kere, 83
Khana, 33
Kikongo, 229^6
Kimba, 78
Kinuku, 83
   see also Nu
Kom, 174, 180, 200, 204, 207–209, 218, 219
Komo, 33
Kono, 83

245

Language index

Koor, 102
Kordofanian, iv, 224, 225, 228, 228[4]
Koro, 115, 125, 132, 134, 137, 154, 155, 166
Koro Ija, 155
Koro of Lafia, 109, 155
Koro Zuba, 155
Koro-Ija, 155
Koro-Zuba, 155
Koromba, 96
Kru, iv
Kudu-Camo, 83
Kuki, 67, 90, 103
Kulu, 109, 113, 114, 118–120
Kumbashi, 78
Kurama, 83
Kurmi, 83
Kuturmi, 118
Kwa, iv, 110, 225
Kwa-Benue-Congo, 34
Kwang, 160, 161
Kwang cluster, 160
Kwang-Ya-Bijim-Legeri, 118
Kwanka-Boi-Bijim-Legeri, 142
Kwasio (A81), 178
Kɔrɔmba, 67, 96, 103
Kər, 75, 102

Lame cluster, 83
Lamnso', 180, 193, 207
Lamnso', 174, 180, 200, 207–210
Laru, 62, 66, 69, 102
Lela, 62, 72
Lemoro, 83
Lere cluster, 83
Limbum, 175, 180, 182, 189, 200, 203
Lopa, 62, 69
Lower Cross River, 31
Luganda, 227, 227[3]

Luyia, 229[5]
Lwena, 42

Ma'in, 72
ma-Koor, 75
Mabo-Barkul, 152
Macro-Sudan, 18
Macro-Sudan Belt, 34
Mada, 111, 116, 142, 145, 147
Makici, 90
Mala-Ruma, 83
Mambiloid, 4, 4[2], 19, 36, 110, 112
Mamfe, 16
Mande, iv, 69
Mankon, 175, 178, 181, 200, 202, 203, 215, 216, 229
maor, 75
Map, 82, 83, 86
    see also Ut-Ma'in
Mba, 66, 102
Mbam-Nkam, 15, 174
Mbe, 11, 180, 234
Mbizinaku, 207, 208
Mbui, 203
Medumba, 175, 200
Menchum, 37[14]
Menemo, 175, 200
Meta, 180, 188, 190
    see also also also Metta
Metta, 175, 200, 213, 214
    see also Meta
Migili, 109
Mijili, 155
Moghamo, 175, 194, 200, 213, 214
Mokpe, 178, 181
Momo, 21, 174, 175, 182, 188, 194, 200, 202, 203, 205, 207, 212, 213, 215–217

Language index

Momo Grassfields, 200
Moro, 103
Mpompon, 178, 181
Mundani, 175, 180, 200, 214, 217
Mungbam, 30[5], 33[9], 39, 48
Mɨɨ, 95
Mɨɨn, 103

Naki, 39, 211
Nandu, 125, 137
Nandu-Tari, 137
Narrow Bantu, 176, 179, 199, 215, 223, 224, 234
Narrow Grassfields Bantu, 174
Ndemli, 174, 200
Ndun, 125, 137, 138, 140, 141, 166
Ndun-Nyeng-Shakara, 116
Ndun-Shakara, 125
Ndunic, 109, 112, 125, 137, 138
Ndəkə, 95, 103
Ngamambo, 175, 200, 212, 214
Ngas, 160
Ngemba, 175, 182, 189, 192, 200
Ngembu, 175, 200
Ngie, 175, 200, 213–215
Ngiemboon, 181
Ngmgbang, 82, 83
Ngombale, 181
Ngwe, 181, 203
Ngwo, 175, 200, 205, 213–215
Ngwoi, 90
Ngwunci, 78
Niger-Congo, iii–v, 5, 6, 8, 9, 11, 17, 18, 20, 28, 28[1], 29, 30, 32–34, 34[10], 35, 36, 40[17], 42[19], 43, 51, 60, 62, 65, 73, 80, 94, 100, 116, 123, 127, 129, 130, 140, 143, 144, 164, 166, 174, 176, 190, 194, 223, 224, 226–228, 231, 234
Nigerian Semi-Bantu, 62
Nindem, 116, 142
Ningi cluster, 83
Ningon, 137
Ningye, 142
Ningye-Ninka, 116
Ninka, 142
Ninkyob, 116, 142
Ninzam, 142
Ninzic, 109, 112, 121, 141, 144, 148, 157
Ninzo, 116, 141–143, 149
Njen, 175, 200
Nko, 142
Nomaante, 181
non-Bantu East Benue-Congo, 31
Noni, 29, 33[9], 39, 45, 46, 180, 182, 189, 193, 209–211, 232
North, 175, 200
    see also Eastern Grassfields Bantu
North Atlantic, 224, 233
    see also Northern, Proto-East-Kainji
    see also East Kainji
North-central cluster, 83
North-West, 112
    see also Plateau
    see also Proto-East-Kainji
Northwest, 64, 66
    see also Central Proto-Kainji
Northwest Kainji, 72, 74, 77, 90
Northwest Plateau, 118, 119
Nu, 83
Nuba, 176[4]
Numana-Nunku-Gwantu-Numbu,

Language index

116
Nun, 175, 200
Nungu, 110, 116, 142
Nupe, 71, 164, 229
    see also PNupoid
NW Bantu, 174, 178, 192
    see also North West Bantu
Nyang, 4, 16
Nyankpa-Barde, 115, 134
Nyeng, 125

Obiro, 114
Ogoi, 33
Ogoni, 33
Oku, 174, 200, 204, 205, 207–210, 219
Oshie, 175, 200, 213, 214

Pai, 118, 142
PB, 184, 185, 191, 193, 194, 213, 215, 216, 227–229
    see also Proto-Bantu
PBC, 228, 230
    see also Proto-Benue-Congo
Pe, 118, 142, 160
PGB, 202, 203, 205, 213, 229
    see also Proto-Grassfields (Bantu)
PGur, 228, 230
    see also Proto-Gur
Piti, 83
Plateau, 2, 5, 8–11, 15, 19, 20, 60, 60^1, 62, 86, 107–113, 119, 123, 148, 152, 157–159, 164–166
Platoid, 2–4
PNC, 224, 226–228, 230
    see also Proto-Niger-Congo
PNupoid, 229

    see also Nupe
Pongu, 94
Proto-Ake, 157
Proto-Atlantic, 177
Proto-Bantoid, 9, 16–19, 21, 175, 189, 191, 193, 194, 216
Proto-Bantoid-Cross, 9, 17
Proto-Bantu, 8–11, 14–21, 28, 29, 31, 33, 33^9, 34, 42, 47, 62, 80, 173–175, 177, 194, 202, 216, 223, 224, 224^1, 227, 233
    see also PB
Proto-Bantu-EGB, 216
    see also Proto-Bantu; Proto-EGB
Proto-Basa, 96, 99
Proto-Benue-Congo, 2, 10, 27, 28^1, 29, 31–33, 33^9, 34–36, 38–42, 42^{19}, 44, 44^{21}, 45–50, 100, 110, 223, 224
Proto-Burgundian, 10^4
Proto-East Benue-Congo, 101
Proto-Eastern and Western Grassfields Bantu, 223
    see also Proto-EGB; Proto-WGB
Proto-EBC, 9–13, 16–20
    see also Proto East-Benue Congo
Proto-EGB, 224
    see also Proto-Eastern Grassfields Bantu
Proto-Ekoid, 21
Proto-Francian, 10^4
Proto-French, 10^4
Proto-Gallo-Romaic, 10^4
Proto-Grassfields, 19, 189
    see also Proto-Grassfields

Language index

Bantu; PGB
Proto-Grassfields Bantu, 175, 201–203, 224[1]
　　see also Proto-Grassfields; PGB
Proto-Gur, 223, 224, 227
　　see also PGur
Proto-Ibero-Romaic, 10[4]
Proto-Italian, 10[4]
Proto-Kainji, 10, 11, 13, 62, 64, 65, 100, 101
Proto-Kamuku, 90
Proto-Koro, 134
Proto-Ndunic, 141
Proto-Niger-Congo, iii–v, 17, 20, 176, 177, 224
　　see also PNC
Proto-Norman-Picard, 10[4]
Proto-Northwest Kainji, 72
Proto-Plateau, 11–13, 108–110, 165, 166
Proto-Provencal, 10[4]
Proto-Romaic, 10[4]
Proto-Romance, 10
Proto-Shiroro, 95
Proto-Tarokoid, 160
Proto-WGB, 224
　　see also Proto-Western Grassfields Bantu

Rashad, 225
Regi, 67, 90, 103
Rerang, 69
Reshe, 60, 64, 65, 65[3], 66, 68, 69, 71, 74, 100–102
Rigwe, 115, 125–127
Rim, 121
Rin, 67, 94, 94[7], 95, 103
Ring, 21, 174, 180, 182, 189, 192, 200, 202, 203, 205, 207, 209, 210, 212, 216, 217
Ring Grassfields, 200
Riyom, 121
Rogo-Shyabe, 67, 90, 103
Ron, 152
Rop, 64, 66, 69, 102
Ror, 75, 102
Rub, 95
Rubu, 103
Rukuba, 142
Ryom, 121
Rĩ, 94

Salka, 78, 80
Sambe, 107, 117, 147–149, 151, 152
Samburu, 95, 103
Sanga, 83
Semi-Bantu, 14, 62, 225
Semitic, iv
Sereer, 224
Sesotho, 36[12]
Sha, 148
Shakara, 125, 137
Shall, 120, 121
Shall-Zwall, 114, 121, 142
Shama, 66, 103
Shama Sambuga, 90
Shamang, 115, 131
Shang, 115, 132
Shau, 83
Shen, 60, 64, 66, 69, 102
Sheni, 83, 103
Sheni cluster, 83
Shingu, 181, 191
Shiroro, 64, 67, 94, 103
Sholyo, 115, 128
Shuba, 64, 66, 69–71, 74, 100, 102

Language index

Shuwa–Zamani, 83
Si, 83
South Plateau, 154, 155
Southeastern Plateau, 152
Southern, 112
    see also Eggonic; Jilic
Southern Zaria, 115, 125
sSaare, 66, 102
Sur, 118, 160
Surubu, 83
Səgəmuk, 67, 103

Takaya, 83
Talodi, 225
Tapshin, 118
Tari, 116, 125, 137
Tarok, 2, 109–111, 118, 160, 161, 163
Tarokoid, 62, 110, 112, 160
Temne, 177
Teriya, 121
tHun, 66, 70, 73–75, 77, 90, 102
Tikar, 4, 19, 180, 215, 216
tiMap, 86
Tinɔr, 115, 132
Tiv, 21, 231
Tivoid, 4, 16
Toro, 117, 147, 148
Tsam, 83
Tsamic, 83
Tsivaɗi, 66, 103
Tsureshe, 65
Tsɨkimba, 66, 103
Tuki, 181, 230
Tumi, 83
Tunen, 181, 215, 216, 230, 231
Tunzu, 83
Turkwam, 147
Tyap, 115, 125, 128, 128^4, 129, 164

Tyapic, 115, 125, 128
Təsu, 148, 149

Ucinda, 89
Ujijili, 155
Umbundu, 38^{15}
Ungwai, 90
Upper Cross, 51^{25}
Upper Niger, 64, 66, 69
Us, 75, 102
Ut-Ma'in, 63, 72, 75–77
ut-Ma'in, 77
    see also Ma'in

Volta, 62
Volta-Niger, 164
Vom, 121
Vono, 83
Vori, 83
Vute, 4^2, 36, 180, 189, 190
Vwang, 121

Waci, 134, 137
Waci-Myamya, 115
Wara, 78
Wawa, 233
Weh, 174, 200, 207, 208, 211
West Benue-Congo, 1, 5, 7, 8, 32, 32^7, 164
West Kainji, 59, 60, 62, 82, 97
West Sudanic, 225
West-Central, 112
    see also West-Central Plateau
West-Central Plateau, 125
Western Acipa, 78
Western Grassfields, 21
    see also Western Grassfields Bantu; WGB

Western Grassfields Bantu, 46, 175, 199–201
Western Kainji, 60
Western vs. Eastern Grassfields Bantu, 174
Western Momo, 174
WGB, 174, 175, 182, 194, 200, 201, 205, 215, 216, 218, 219
    see also Western Grassfields (Bantu)
Wide Bantu/Bantoid, 223
Wide Grassfields, 4[3]
Wider Bantu, 215
Wurə, 66, 102
Wurə-Gwamhyə-Mba, 72
Wãyã, 95, 103
Wəgə, 67, 103

Yamba, 181
Yambassa, 14
Yangkam, 107, 160
Yasgua, 109
Yashi, 147
Yaŋkam, 110, 118
Yemba, 175, 181, 200, 202
Yergam, 110
Yeskwa, 109, 110
Yoruba, 32, 32[7], 164
Yoruboid, 60[1]
Yurok, 186

Zhire, 115
Zhire-Shang, 131
Ziriya, 82, 83
Zoa, 208
zone A Bantu, 191
    see also Bantu Zone A
Zora, 82, 83, 86, 88
Zubazuba, 67, 90, 103

Zuksun, 75, 102
Zusu, 75
Zwall, 120, 121